# Social Work Law in Scotland

Second edition

**Janet Fabb** BA, DIPSW, CQSW
Senior Lecturer in Social Work, University of Paisley

**Thomas G Guthrie** LLB (HONS)
Lecturer in Law, University of Glasgow



Tottel publishing

**Published by**
**Tottel Publishing Ltd**
**Maxwelton House**
**41–43 Boltro Road**
**Haywards Heath**
**West Sussex**
**RH16 1BJ**

**Tottel Publishing Ltd**
**9–10 St. Andrew Square**
**Edinburgh**
**EH2 2AF**

ISBN 978 1 84592 412 6

First published entitled *Social Work and the Law in Scotland* by LexisNexis Butterworths 1992
Second edition entitled *Social Work Law in Scotland* 1997
Second edition reprinted by Tottel Publishing Ltd 2006
Reprinted 2008



**British Library Cataloguing-in-Publication Data**
A catalogue record for this book is available from the British Library

Typeset by Phoenix Photosetting, Chatham, Kent
Printed and bound in Great Britain by
CPI Antony Rowe, Eastbourne, East Sussex

# Preface

Our first edition was titled *Social Work and the Law in Scotland* which seemed to us to express adequately the relationship between the two disciplines and professions. Clearly, that relationship has changed in the years since publication. Whether that change is for good or ill could be the subject of another book, but in retitling this edition we have sought to reflect the decreasing distance between social work and law as well as the recognition that with the burgeoning interest in this subject, social work law as a discipline in its own right has begun to be acknowledged. Why have we needed a second edition so soon or at all? Our social context has been characterised by rapid change and the relationships which individuals have with society and with each other has consequently also mirrored those changes. Our laws are one of the ways in which we express those changes and so we have seen the appearance of major new pieces of legislation like the Children (Scotland) Act 1995, many other significant new pieces of legislation, and a plethora of case law and statutory instruments with the force of law.

In the preface to the first edition we set out our intention of providing a single text which would serve as the beginning of a process of learning about and/or reviewing social work law in Scotland. Our rationale was then and continues to be to include a broad selection of topics which comprise the core of the subject and to offer direction to pursue topics in depth elsewhere. Since then the interest in social work law has mushroomed, as has the availability of excellent texts and learning packages which examine and explore the details which cannot be covered in a book of this sort. Our primary aim is to enable the reader to gain an understanding of the legal framework within which social work is practised in Scotland, and to facilitate the acquisition or review of specific legal knowledge necessary to make sense of most day-to-day social work practice.

A secondary aim is to provide one basic text which covers the most commonly encountered areas of law for social workers in Scotland in a way which will serve as a ready reference. Often there is confusion about what is law, what is policy, what are procedures, and what is the status of each, and so another aim is to clarify the law and its status and thus distinguish the law from policy and procedures.

Social work students and social workers need to know the law as it relates to their practice, but increasingly there are others who have an interest in this selection of topics: solicitors, sheriffs, children's panel members, safeguarders, curators, guardians, reporters, doctors, health visitors, community psychiatric nurses, occupational therapists, teachers, parents, young adults, children and others. Social work is touching more lives and an informed contact is always preferable. We have attempted to avoid being prescriptive since this seems to us to invite reductionist thinking, could well be wrong, and does little to value the experience of the reader. Sometimes, however, the material is best served by some limited prescription and we hope it will be accepted in the spirit in which it is written. We have sought to offer suggestions which highlight the unique and specific opportunities, constraints, and responsibilities for social workers in this context rather than an exhaustive programme for all social work involvement.

The first edition of this book was based very closely on a course for qualifying social workers which had evolved over a number of years; we were the staff primarily responsible for the curriculum development and teaching. Since then, we have become located in different universities and broadened considerably the scope of our research and teaching experience. One of us brings a social work background and one a legal background to the work and in some sense the text exhibits graphically the tensions experienced between these two professions.

After completion of the text it was announced that the Sex Offenders Act 1997 would come into force on 1 September 1997. This requires certain sex offenders, mainly those serving a sentence or on supervision following release from custody on or after this date, to notify the police of their home address. There is also to be a review of arrangements for the supervision of sex offenders in the community.

Our thanks are due to the many readers of the first edition who gave us feedback about that book, to the current social work practitioners who have contributed enormously and directed us to what was relevant from the point of view of current practice and to our current students and graduates who have worked with us in the development of the material. Particular thanks are due to our colleagues, and especially to June Hyslop, for their comments and contributions. The responsibility for any errors and infelicities in expression remains, of course, ours.

Finally, and most importantly, thanks are due to Edward, Frances, Nigel and Veronica for their support and understanding.

We have attempted to state the law and practice issues as at August 1997.

Where we refer to particular sections of Acts of Parliament we have referred only to the section of the original or principal Act. Readers should be aware that in many cases the provisions of the original Act will have been subsequently amended; for the sake of simplicity we have not referred to the amending legislation.

Janet Fabb
Tom Guthrie
*Glasgow*
*August 1997*

# Contents

*Preface* *v*
*Table of statutes* *xiii*
*Table of orders, rules and regulations* *xviii*
*Table of cases* *xx*
*Further reading* *xxiv*
*Abbreviations* *xxx*

**1 The Scottish legal context of social work 1**
1 Introduction 1
2 The functions of law in society 4
3 Law and social problems 5
4 Formal sources of law 5
5 Rights, powers and duties 7
6 Legal personnel 8
7 Civil court system and procedures 13
8 Criminal court system and procedures 15
9 Evidence 25
10 European courts 32
11 Children's hearings 33
12 Administrative tribunals 33
13 Judicial review 34
14 Legal aid 35
15 The Social Work (Scotland) Act 1968 36
16 The Children (Scotland) Act 1995 39

**2 General law relevant to social work 41**
1 Introduction 41
2 Housing 42
3 Debt recovery 55
4 Discrimination 59
5 Disability discrimination 65
6 Access to information 70
7 Education 76

**3 Children and their families 78**
1 The responsibilities, rights and powers of parents and children 78
2 Marriage, separation and divorce 86
3 Adoption 92
4 Matrimonial Homes (Family Protection) (Scotland) Act 1981 102

**4 Local authority services to children 108**
1 Introduction 108
2 Services for children in need 110
3 Children 'looked after' by the local authority 123
4 Foster placements 132
5 Secure accommodation 138
6 Parental responsibilities orders 141
7 Aftercare 145
8 Challenging decisions 145

**5 Children in need of supervision or emergency protection 147**
1 Introduction 147
2 Overriding principles governing decisions by the court or hearing 148
3 Children in need of compulsory measures of supervision 150
4 Referrals from the court system 174
5 Court orders sending children to local authority accommodation 175
6 Emergency protection of children 176
7 Exclusion orders 183
8 Short-term refuges 185
Appendix 186

**6 Special needs 189**
1 Introduction 189
2 Community care 189
3 Assessments 191
4 General provisions on disability 199
5 Mental illness and handicap: compulsory admission to hospital 202
6 Mental illness and handicap: guardianship 212
7 Mental disability 214
8 Mental illness and disability: other local authority functions and duties 222
9 Old age 222

7 **Offenders 227**
1 Law and crime 227
2 Social work functions 229
3 Sentencing: objectives and criteria 236
4 Non-custodial disposals 237
5 Diversion from prosecution 253
6 Compensation for criminal injuries 255
7 Custodial disposals 255
8 Release from prison and detention 259
9 Mental health and criminal law 267
10 Rehabilitation of offenders 271
11 Crimes and offences 272

8 **Professional responsibility and accountability 277**
1 Introduction 277
2 The legal framework 278
3 Liability in child care and child protection 281
4 Liability in other cases 283
5 Judicial review: examples 285
6 Confidentiality and disclosure 289
7 Duties to warn 290
8 Employers' liability for and to social workers 296
9 Conclusion 297

*Index 299*

# Table of statutes


PAGE

Access to Health Records Act 1990 . . . . . . . . . . . 75
Access to Medical Reports Act 1988 . . . . . . . . . . . 75
Access to Personal Files Act 1987 . . . . . . . . 70–72, 131
Adoption (Scotland) Act 1978 . . . . . . . . . . . . 40, 92
s 1(2) . . . . . . . . . . . . . 102
6 . . . . . . . . . . . . . . . 93
6A . . . . . . . . . . . . . . 93
11 . . . . . . . . . . . . . . 99
12 . . . . . . . . . . . . . . 95
(9) . . . . . . . . . . . . . 100
13 . . . . . . . . . . . . . . 95
14 . . . . . . . . . . . . . . 93
15 . . . . . . . . . . . . . . 94
16(2), (4) . . . . . . . . . 96
18 . . . . . . . . . . . . . . 97
19 . . . . . . . . . . . . . . 98
22 . . . . . . . . . . . . . . 99
22A . . . . . . . . . . . . . 97
27 . . . . . . . . . . . . . . 98
51A . . . . . . . . . . . . . 101
Age of Legal Capacity (Scotland) Act 1991: 79, 80, 81, 131, 132, 153
s 2 . . . . . . . . . . . . . . . 79
(1)(a) . . . . . . . . . . . 131
Carers (Recognition and Services) Act 1995 . . . . . . 193
Child Abduction and Custody Act 1985 . . . . . . . . . . 144
Child Support Act 1991 . . . . 90
Children Act 1948
s 1 . . . . . . . . . . . . . . . 116
Children Act 1989: 39, 109, 110, 112, 116, 119
s 17(11) . . . . . . . . . . . 111
Sch 2, para 5 . . . . . . . . 183

Children and Young Persons Act 1933
Sch 1 . . . . . . . . . . . . . 137
Children and Young Persons (Scotland) Act 1937
s 12 . . . . . . . . . . . . . . 187
(1) . . . . . . . . . . . . . 156
15 . . . . . . . . . . . . 187, 188
22 . . . . . . . . . . . . 187, 188
33 . . . . . . . . . . . . 187, 188
Children (Scotland) Act 1995 . 5, 6, 35, 36, 39, 40, 62, 78, 81, 82, 85, 93, 108, 109, 111, 113, 114, 116, 117, 120, 121, 124, 145, 147, 148, 151, 154, 160, 162, 168, 172, 173, 176, 183, 185, 188, 201
Pt I (ss 1–15) . . . . . . . . 40
s 1 . . . . . . . . . . . . . . . 81
2 . . . . . . . . . . . . . . . 83
(7) . . . . . . . . . . . . . 119
5 . . . . . . . . . . . 84, 122, 128
6 . . . . . . . . . . . . . . . 82
7 . . . . . . . . . . . . . . . 84
11 . . . . . . . 80, 84, 100, 120, 128, 149, 155, 175
(5) . . . . . . . . . . . . . 120
(7) . . . . . . . . . . . . . 85
(11) . . . . . . . . . . . . 86
12 . . . . . . . . . . . . . 86, 89
Pt II (ss 16–93) . . . . . . . 33, 40
s 16(1) . . . . . . . . . . . . 148
(2) . . . . . . . . . . . . . 149
(3) . . . . . . . . . . . . . 150
(4) . . . . . . . . . . . . . 149
17 . . . . . . . . . . . . . 59, 124
(1)(c) . . . . . . . . . . . 129
(6) . . . . . . . . . . . . . 123

PAGE

Children (Scotland) Act 1995 – *contd*
s 19 . . . 108
20 . . . 108
21 . . . 114
22 . . . 108, 110, 116, 183, 193
(2) . . . 62, 111, 115
(3)(b) . . . 122
23 . . . 112, 193
24 . . . 113
(1)(b) . . . 113
25 . . . 116, 118, 138
26 . . . 118
27 . . . 117
29 . . . 145
30 . . . 145
38(1)(a) . . . 185
43 . . . 162
45 . . . 160
(2) . . . 161
(4), (5) . . . 140
(7) . . . 140
46 . . . 162
51 . . . 172
(5)(c) . . . 172
(11) . . . 174
52(2) . . . 154
53(1) . . . 151
(b) . . . 121
54 . . . 86, 175
55 . . . 152
56 . . . 159
(4)(b) . . . 159
57 . . . 176, 177
(1) . . . 176
(2) . . . 177
(4) . . . 178
(6) . . . 179
58 . . . 179
59 . . . 180
(2) . . . 180
60(1) . . . 179
(3) . . . 180
(4) . . . 180
(5) . . . 180
(7) . . . 181
(8) . . . 181
(10) . . . 181
(12) . . . 181
(13) . . . 181
61 . . . 182
(5) . . . 122
64 . . . 162

PAGE

Children (Scotland) Act 1995 – *contd*
s 65 . . . 164
(2) . . . 181
(4) . . . 161
66 . . . 166
(2) . . . 166
(6) . . . 138
67 . . . 166
(1) . . . 140
(3) . . . 138
68(3)(b) . . . 167
(11) . . . 138
69(1)–(10) . . . 165
(11) . . . 138, 165
70 . . . 168
(7) . . . 168
(10) . . . 139
71 . . . 170
73 . . . 171
(4)(c) . . . 97, 142
(5) . . . 99
(8) . . . 97
(a) . . . 142
(9) . . . 97
(12) . . . 171
(13), (14) . . . 97, 142
76 . . . 183
(2), (3) . . . 184
(9) . . . 184
(11) . . . 184
77 . . . 183, 185
78 . . . 183, 185
79 . . . 183
(1) . . . 185
80 . . . 183
85 . . . 173
86 . . . 142
87(2) . . . 144
(3) . . . 144
(7) . . . 143
89(a) . . . 144
90 . . . 80, 153
93(1) . . . 109
(2)(a), (b) . . . 109
(4)(a) . . . 110
Pt III (ss 94–98) . . . 40
s 95 . . . 93
96 . . . 93
Pt IV (ss 99–105) . . . 40
Sch 2 . . . 40
Chronically Sick and Disabled Persons Act 1970: 111, 197–199, 215

PAGE

Chronically Sick and Disabled Persons Act 1970 – *contd*
s 1 . . . . . . . . . . . . . . . 199
2 . . . . . . . . . . . 193, 198, 199
(1) . . . . . . . . . . . . 114
Civic Government (Scotland) Act 1982
s 52 . . . . . . . . . . . . . . 188
Community Care (Direct Payments) Act 1996 . . . . . 196
Consumer Credit Act 1974 . . 75
Crime and Punishment (Scotland) Act 1997 . . . 24, 232, 266
s 2 . . . . . . . . . . . . . . 266
5 . . . . . . . . . . . . . . 266
6 . . . . . . . . . . . . . . 271
7 . . . . . . . . . . . . . . 271
11 . . . . . . . . . . . . . 267
13 . . . . . . . . . . . . . 16, 17
25 . . . . . . . . . . . . . 24
29 . . . . . . . . . . . . . 31
38 . . . . . . . . . . . . . 267
Pt V (ss 49–54) . . . . . . . 266
Criminal Justice Act 1993 . . . 262
Criminal Justice (Scotland) Act 1980 . . . . . . . . . . . 252
Criminal Justice (Scotland) Act 1995
s 306(1)(b) . . . . . . . . . 228
Criminal Law (Consolidation) (Scotland) Act 1995 . . . 158
Pt I (ss 1–17) . . . . . . . . 186
Criminal Procedure (Scotland) Act 1995
s 7 . . . . . . . . . . . . . . 16
42(7) . . . . . . . . . . . . 236
(8) . . . . . . . . . . 232, 236
43 . . . . . . . . . . . . . 176
44 . . . . . . . . . . . . 257, 265
(1) . . . . . . . . . . . . 175
(3) . . . . . . . . . . 120, 175
48 . . . . . . . . . . . . . 175
49 . . . . . . . . . . . . . 175
51 . . . . . . . . . . . . . 175
(1)(a) . . . . . . . . . . . 141
58(10) . . . . . . . . . . . 267
59A . . . . . . . . . . . . . 271
76 . . . . . . . . . . . . . 24
102 . . . . . . . . . . . . . 24
118(7) . . . . . . . . . . . 237
190(7) . . . . . . . . . . . 237
Pt XA (ss 194A–194L) . . . 24
s 196 . . . . . . . . . . . . 237

PAGE

Criminal Procedure (Scotland) Act 1995 – *contd*
s 201 . . . . . . . . . . . . 232
203 . . . . . . . . . . . . . 233
205 . . . . . . . . . . . . . 141
208 . . . . . . . . . . . 141, 257
214(4) . . . . . . . . . . . 240
219(1)(b) . . . . . . . . . . 240
225(2) . . . . . . . . . . . 16
228 . . . . . . . . . . . . . 247
(1) . . . . . . . . . . . . 244
(b) . . . . . . . . 232, 245
229(4)(a) . . . . . . . . . . 245
235 . . . . . . . . . . . . . 242
(1) . . . . . . . . . . . . 242
(4) . . . . . . . . . . . . 242
236 . . . . . . . . . . . . . 242
237 . . . . . . . . . . . . . 242
238(1) . . . . . . . . . . . 250
(2)(c) . . . . . . . . . . 233
271 . . . . . . . . . . . . . 32
302 . . . . . . . . . . . . . 253
303 . . . . . . . . . . . . . 253
Sch 1 . . . . . 137, 156–158, 160, 167, 168, 186, 188
Sch 7 . . . . . . . . . . . . 242
para 5(1) . . . . . . . . . 244
Curators Act 1585 . . . . . . . 217
Data Protection Act 1984 . . . 70–72
Debtors (Scotland) Act 1987 . 57
s 16 . . . . . . . . . . . . . 57
24 . . . . . . . . . . . . . 57
Disability Discrimination Act 1995 . . . . . . . . 65–68, 199
s 1 . . . . . . . . . . . . . . 65
6(3) . . . . . . . . . . . . . 67
19(1) . . . . . . . . . . . . 67
20(3), (4) . . . . . . . . . . 68
Sch 1 . . . . . . . . . . . . 65
Disabled Persons (Employment) Act 1944 . . . . . . . . . 199
Disabled Persons (Services, Consultation and Representation) Act 1986 . . . 39, 192, 194, 197, 198, 215
s 13(8) . . . . . . . . . . . . 201
Divorce (Scotland) Act 1976 . 87
Education (Scotland) Act 1980: 200, 215
Education (Scotland) Act 1981: 200
Equal Pay Act 1970 . . . . . . 60
Family Law (Scotland) Act 1985: 88, 89
s 1 . . . . . . . . . . . . . . 81

| | PAGE |
|---|---|
| Foster Children (Scotland) Act 1984 | 136 |
| s 7 | 137 |
| Health and Safety at Work etc Act 1974 | 297 |
| Housing (Homeless Persons) Act 1977 | 46 |
| Housing (Scotland) Act 1987: | 47, 49, 116 |
| Pt II (ss 24–43) | 46 |
| s 47 | 44 |
| 135–137 | 48 |
| Sch 10 | 43 |
| Housing (Scotland) Act 1988 | |
| s 19 | 45 |
| 36, 37 | 45 |
| Interpretation Act 1978 | |
| Sch 1 | 121 |
| Law Reform (Parent and Child) (Scotland) Act 1986 | 121 |
| s 3 | 120 |
| Local Government etc (Scotland) Act 1994 | 147 |
| s 45 | 37 |
| 180 | 37 |
| Sch 14 | 37 |
| Matrimonial Homes (Family Protection) (Scotland) Act 1981 | 48, 90, 102, 103, 104, 106, 107, 183, 185 |
| s 1 | 103 |
| 3 | 103 |
| 4 | 103 |
| 13 | 105 |
| 14(2) | 106 |
| 15 | 106 |
| 18 | 107 |
| Matrimonial Proceedings (Children) Act 1958 | |
| s 11 | 89 |
| Mental Health (Patients in the Community) Act 1995 | 210 |
| Mental Health (Scotland) Act 1984 | 13, 35, 110, 192, 202, 205, 209, 212, 215, 220, 222, 267–269 |
| s 1(2) | 202 |
| 7 | 192 |
| 8 | 192, 202, 209 |
| 11 | 192, 202 |

| | PAGE |
|---|---|
| Mental Health (Scotland) Act 1984 – *contd* | |
| s 17–21 | 203 |
| 22(4) | 206 |
| 24 | 203, 205 |
| 25 | 208 |
| 26 | 206 |
| 30 | 206 |
| 35A–35K | 210 |
| 36 | 212 |
| 37–40 | 213 |
| 47 | 213 |
| 50, 51 | 214 |
| 62A | 271 |
| 94 | 219 |
| 97, 98 | 208 |
| 103 | 208 |
| Misuse of Drugs Act 1971 | 159 |
| National Assistance Act 1948 | |
| s 47 | 224 |
| 48(2) | 225 |
| National Health Service and Community Care Act 1990: | 38, 189, 215 |
| Official Secrets Act 1989 | 258 |
| Police (Scotland) Act 1967 | |
| s 41 | 272 |
| Prisoners and Criminal Proceedings (Scotland) Act 1993 | 259, 262 |
| s 3 | 262 |
| Public Order Act 1986 | 60 |
| Race Relations Act 1965 | 59 |
| Race Relations Act 1968 | 59 |
| Race Relations Act 1976 | 60, 62 |
| s 5(2)(d) | 61 |
| 71 | 64 |
| Rehabilitation of Offenders Act 1974 | 271 |
| Rent (Scotland) Act 1984 | |
| s 22 | 45 |
| 23 | 45 |
| 112 | 44 |
| Road Traffic Offenders Act 1988 | 254 |
| Sex Discrimination Act 1975 | 60 |
| s 7(2)(e) | 61 |
| Sexual Offences (Scotland) Act 1976 | |
| ss 2A–2C | 158 |
| Sheriff Courts (Scotland) Act 1907 | |
| s 36B(3) | 56 |

PAGE

Sheriff Courts (Scotland) Act 1907 – *contd*
s 37, 38 . . . . . . . . . . . 44
Social Work (Scotland) Act 1968 . . . . . . 3, 7, 33, 36–38, 39, 71, 143, 144, 150, 155, 162, 164, 170, 173, 192, 198, 200, 215, 223
s 5 . . . . . . . . . . . . . . . 195
Pt II (ss 12–29) . . . . . . . 192
s 12 . . . . . . . . . 37, 44, 59, 145, 146, 192, 200
(6) . . . . . . . . . . . . . 38

PAGE

Sheriff Courts (Scotland) Act 1907 – *contd*
s 12A . . . . . . 38, 191, 192, 198
12B . . . . . . . . . . . . . 196
12C . . . . . . . . . . . . . 196
14 . . . . . . . . . . . . . 38, 200
15 . . . . . . . . . . . . . . 116
27 . . . . . . . . . . . . . . 38
(1) . . . . . . . . . . . . . 232
Pt III (ss 30–58) . . . . . . . 33
s 31 . . . . . . . . . . . . . . 33
Pt IV (ss 59–68) . . . . . . . 39
s 94(1) . . . . . . . 38, 200, 223

# Table of orders, rules and regulations


PAGE

Access to Personal Files (Housing) (Scotland) Regulations 1992, SI 1992/1852 . . . . 71
Access to Personal Files (Social Work) (Scotland) Regulations 1989, SI 1989/251 . . 72
Act of Adjournal (Criminal Procedure Rules) 1996, SI 1996/513
  r 22.1 . . . . . . . . . . . . 31
    22.2 . . . . . . . . . . . . 31
Act of Sederunt (Child Care and Maintenance Rules) 1997, SI 1997/291
  ch 2, Pt V . . . . . . . . . . 143
  ch 3 . . . . . . . . . . . . . 149
    Pt V . . . . . . . . . . . . 183
    Pt VII . . . . . . . . . . . 166
  r 3.5 . . . . . . . . . . . . . 149
Adoption Agencies (Scotland) Regulations 1996, SI 1996/3266
  reg 7 . . . . . . . . . . . . . 92
    10(1) . . . . . . . . . . . 94
    11 . . . . . . . . . . . . . 92
      (2) . . . . . . . . . . . 93
    14 . . . . . . . . . . . . . 96
    15 . . . . . . . . . . . . . 96
    16 . . . . . . . . . . . . . 96
    17(2), (3) . . . . . . . . . 96
    18 . . . . . . . . . . . . . 97
    19 . . . . . . . . . . . . . 98
    21 . . . . . . . . . . . . . 98
Adoption Allowance (Scotland) Regulations 1996, SI 1996/3257 . . . . . . . . . . . 101
Arrangements to Look After Children (Scotland) Regulations 1996, SI 1996/3262 . . . . . . . . . . 124, 129

PAGE

Arrangements to Look After Children (Scotland) Regulations 1996, SI 1996/3262 – *contd*
  reg 3 . . . . . . . . . . . . . 125
    4 . . . . . . . . . . . . . 125
    5 . . . . . . . . . . . 126, 135
    6 . . . . . . . . . . . . . 126
    9 . . . . . . . . . . . . . 130
    11 . . . . . . . . . . . . . 131
    13 . . . . . . . . . . . . . 128
      (2) . . . . . . . . . . . 128
    16(2) . . . . . . . . . 116, 118
    17 . . . . . . . . . . . . . 129
    18 . . . . . . . . . . . . . 130
    19(1) . . . . . . . . . 130, 286
  Sch 1 . . . . . . . . . . 125, 126
Children's Hearings (Scotland) Rules 1996, SI 1996/3261: 6, 160
  r 4 . . . . . . . . . . . . . . 162
    5(1), (3) . . . . . . . . . 163
    6 . . . . . . . . . . . . . 165
    12 . . . . . . . . . . . . . 162
    20 . . . . . . . . . . . . . 164
      (2) . . . . . . . . . . . 161
      (3) . . . . . . . . . . . 163
      (4) . . . . . . . . . . . 163
      (6) . . . . . . . . 136, 168, 169
Community Care (Direct Payments) (Scotland) Regulations 1997, SI 1997/693
  reg 2(2) . . . . . . . . . . . 196
    3 . . . . . . . . . . . . . 196
    4 . . . . . . . . . . . . . 196
Disability Discrimination (Employment) Regulations 1996, SI 1996/1456 . . . . 66
Disability Discrimination (Meaning of Disability) Regulations 1996, SI 1996/1455: 65

PAGE

Disability Discrimination (Services and Premises) Regulations 1996, SI 1996/1836: 68
Emergency Child Protection Measures (Scotland) Regulations 1996, SI 1996/3258
reg 3 . . . . . . . . . . . . . 182
4 . . . . . . . . . . . . . 182
8 . . . . . . . . . . . . . 182
Foster Children (Private Fostering) (Scotland) Regulations 1985, SI 1985/1798 . . . . 136
Fostering of Children (Scotland) Regulations 1996, SI 1996/3263 . . . . . . . . . . . 134
reg 6 . . . . . . . . . . . . . 133
8 . . . . . . . . . . . . . 134
(1) . . . . . . . . . . . 134
12 . . . . . . . . . . . . . 134
(4) . . . . . . . . . . . 134
13 . . . . . . . . . . . . . 135
14 . . . . . . . . . . . . . 135
15 . . . . . . . . . . . 136, 168
Sch 1 . . . . . . . . . . . . 133
Sch 2 . . . . . . . . . . . . 134
Sch 3 . . . . . . . . . . . . 135
Parental Responsibilities and Parental Rights Agreements (Scotland) Regulations 1996, SI 1996/2549 . . . . 84
Prisons and Young Offenders Institutions (Scotland) Rules 1994, SI 1994/1931 . . . . 258

PAGE

Refuges for Children (Scotland) Regulations 1996, SI 1996/3259 . . . . . . . . . . . 186
School Pupil Records (Scotland) Regulations 1990, SI 1990/1551 . . . . . . . . . . . 76
Secure Accommodation (Scotland) Regulations 1996, SI 1996/3255
reg 4 . . . . . . . . . . . . . 138
5 . . . . . . . . . . . . . 138
6 . . . . . . . . . . . . . 139
(1) . . . . . . . . . . . 139
7 . . . . . . . . . . . . . 139
(1) . . . . . . . . . . . 139
8 . . . . . . . . . . . . . 139
9(1)(b) . . . . . . . . . 139
(2)(a), (e) . . . . . . . 140
10 . . . . . . . . . . . . 169
11 . . . . . . . . . . . . 170
12 . . . . . . . . . . . . 170
13–15 . . . . . . . . . . 141
Secure Tenants (Right to Repair) (Scotland) Regulations 1994, SI 1994/1046 . 44
Social Security (Claims and Payments) Regulations 1987, SI 1987/1968
reg 33 . . . . . . . . . . . . 219

# Table of cases

PAGE

A v G 1996 SCLR 787 . . . . . 26
A v G 1996 SLT (Sh Ct) 123 . . . . . 170
A v Kennedy 1993 SLT 1188 . . . . . 157
AB and CB v E 1987 SCLR 419 . . . . . 209
Advocate (HM) v Hood 1987 SCCR 63 . . . . . 250
Attorney-General, ex rel Tilley v London Borough of Wandsworth [1981] 1 All ER 1162 . . . . . 117
B v Harris 1990 SLT 208 . . . . . 157, 272
B v Kennedy 1987 SLT 765 . . . . . 167
B, Petitioner 1992 SCCR 596 . . . . . 257
Barrett v Enfield London Borough Council [1997] 3 All ER 171 . . . . . 282
Britton v Britton's Curator Bonis 1992 SCLR 947 . . . . . 217
Byrd v Wither 1991 SLT 206 . . . . . 157, 272
Cameron v Normand 1992 SCCR 866 . . . . . 273
Caparo Industries plc v Dickman [1990] 1 All ER 568 . . . . . 279
Central Regional Council v B 1985 SLT 413 . . . . . 143
Chapman, Petitioners 1993 SCLR 236 . . . . . 217
City of Edinburgh Council v M 1996 SCLR 779 . . . . . 120
Clarke and Powell v Eley (IMI) Kynoch Ltd [1982] IRLR 482 . . . . . 61
Clunis v Camden and Islington Health Authority (1996) Times, 27 December . . . . . 283
Council of Civil Service Unions v Minister for the Civil Service [1985] AC 374 . . . . . 288
D v Kelly 1995 SLT 1220 . . . . . 155
D v Kennedy 1988 SLT 55 . . . . . 158
D v NSPCC [1978] AC 171 . . . . . 26
D v Strathclyde Regional Council 1991 SCLR 185 . . . . . 170
Davers v Butler 1994 SCLR 717 . . . . . 26
Dewar v Dewar 1995 SLT 467 . . . . . 86
Dorset Yacht Co Ltd v Home Office [1970] AC 1004 . . . . . 283
F v Kennedy (No 2) 1993 SLT 1284 . . . . . 28, 29
F v Management Committee and Managers, Ravenscraig Hospital 1989 SLT 49 . . . . . 207
F v Wirral Metropolitan Borough Council and Liverpool City Council [1991] Fam 69 . . . . . 122
Ferguson v P 1989 SCLR 525 . . . . . 167
Ferguson v S 1992 SCLR 866 . . . . . 158
Finlayson, Applicant 1989 SCLR 601 . . . . . 80, 156
Gillick v West Norfolk and Wisbech Area Health Authority [1985] 3 All ER 402 . . . . . 83

PAGE
H v Lees, D v Orr 1994 SLT 908 . . . . . 156
H v McGregor 1973 SLT 110 . . . . . 172
H v Norfolk County Council (10 May 1996, unreported) CA . . . . . 282
H v Sweeney 1983 SLT 48 . . . . . 11
Hamilton v Scott 1987 SCCR 188 . . . . . 239
Hardie v Hardie 1993 SCLR 60 . . . . . 89
Harris v F 1991 SLT 242 . . . . . 167
Houston, Applicant 1996 SCLR 943 . . . . . 80
Hughes' Tutrix v Glasgow District Council 1982 SLT (Sh Ct) 70 . . . . . 43
Humberside County Council v B [1993] 1 FLR 257 . . . . . 177
Humphries, Petitioner 1982 SLT 481 . . . . . 167
JL v Kennedy (6 March 1995, unreported) IH . . . . . 26, 173
K v Craig 1997 SLT 748 . . . . . 211
K v Kennedy 1993 SLT 1281 . . . . . 29
K v Murphy 1997 SLT 248 . . . . . 210
Kelly v Monklands District Council 1986 SLT 169 . . . . . 34, 50, 53
Kennedy v A 1986 SLT 358 . . . . . 163
Kennedy v A 1993 SLT 1134 . . . . . 157
Kennedy v B 1992 SCLR 55 . . . . . 167
Kennedy v M 1989 SLT 687 . . . . . 167
Kennedy v M 1995 SCLR 88 . . . . . 173
Kennedy v R's Curator ad litem 1993 SLT 295 . . . . . 158
Kennedy v S 1986 SLT 679 . . . . . 156
Khaliq v HM Advocate 1984 SLT 137 . . . . . 228
Kirkham v Chief Constable of the Greater Manchester Police [1990] 3 All ER 246 . . . . . 283
L v L 1996 SCLR 11 . . . . . 29
L, Petitioner 1996 SCLR 538 . . . . . 217, 221
L, Petitioners (No 1) 1993 SLT 1310 . . . . . 173
L, Petitioners (No 2) 1993 SLT 1342 . . . . . 173
Law Hospital NHS Trust v Lord Advocate 1996 SC 301 . . . . . 221
London Borough of Lewisham v Lewisham Juvenile Court Justices [1979] 2 All ER 297 . . . . . 121
M (a minor) v Newham London Borough Council. *See* X (minors) v Bedfordshire County Council
M v Dumfries and Galloway Regional Council 1991 SCLR 481 . . . . 120, 177
M v Kennedy 1991 SCLR 898 . . . . . 164
M v Kennedy 1993 SCLR 69 . . . . . 27, 29
M v Kennedy 1995 SCLR 15 . . . . . 173
M v Kennedy 1996 SLT 434 . . . . . 168
M v McGregor 1982 SLT 41 . . . . . 155
M and M v Glasgow Corporation 1976 SLT (Sh Ct) 45 . . . . . 285
McArdle v City of Glasgow District Council 1989 SCLR 19 . . . . . 42
McCafferty v McCafferty 1986 SLT 650 . . . . . 104
McCallum, Applicant 1990 SLT (Sh Ct) 90 . . . . . 57
McD v Orr 1994 SCCR 645 . . . . . 156
MacDougall v Dochree 1992 SCCR 531 . . . . . 273
McGregor v H 1983 SLT 626 . . . . . 157
McGregor v K 1982 SLT 293 . . . . . 156
McGregor v L 1981 SLT 194 . . . . . 155
McMichael v United Kingdom [1995] 20 EHRR 205 . . . . . 33, 163
Matt v Burrell Inc (1995) 892 SW 2d 796 . . . . . 291
Merrin v S 1987 SLT 193 . . . . . 158

PAGE

O v Rae 1993 SLT 570 . . . . . . 164
P v Kennedy 1995 SCLR 1 . . . . . . 167
P v Tayside Regional Council 1989 SCLR 165 . . . . . . 26, 285
Peebles v MacPhail 1990 SLT 245 . . . . . . 157
Quinn v Lees 1994 SCCR 159 . . . . . . 272
Quinn v Monklands District Council 1995 SCLR 393 . . . . . . 43
R v Avon County Council, ex parte Crabtree (22 March 1994, unreported) QB . . . . . . 286
R v Avon County Council, ex parte Hills (1995) 27 HLR 411 . . . . . . 117
R v Avon County Council, ex parte M [1994] 2 FCR 259 . . . . . . 146, 289
R v Bedfordshire County Council, ex parte C [1987] 1 FLR 239 . . . . . . 288
R v Birmingham City Council, ex parte A (10 February 1997, unreported) QB . . . . . . 280
R v Devon County Council, ex parte L [1991] 2 FLR 541 . . . . . . 294
R v Gloucestershire County Council, ex parte Barry [1996] 4 All ER 421, [1997] 2 All ER 1 . . . . . . 197
R v Gloucestershire County Council, ex parte Mahfood (1995) 30 BMLR 20 . . . . . . 197
R v Gloucestershire County Council, ex parte RADAR (21 December 1995, unreported) QB . . . . . . 194, 195
R v Harrow London Borough Council, ex parte D [1990] 3 All ER 12: 287, 288
R v Hay 1993 SCLR 112 . . . . . . 206, 207
R v Hereford and Worcester Councy Council, ex parte D [1992] 1 FLR 448: 286
R v Hertfordshire County Council, ex parte B [1987] 1 FLR 239 . . . . . . 288
R v Kingston-upon-Thames Royal Borough Council, ex parte T [1994] 1 FLR 798 . . . . . . 112, 146
R v Lewisham London Borough Council, ex parte P [1991] 3 All ER 529 . 285
R v London Borough of Bexley, ex parte B (31 July 1995, unreported) QB 114
R v London Borough of Ealing, ex parte Leaman (1984) Times, 10 February: 288
R v London Borough of Islington, ex parte Rixon (1996) Times, 17 April: 146, 195
R v London Borough of Wandsworth, ex parte P [1989] 1 FLR 387 . . . . 286
R v Norfolk County Council, ex parte M [1989] 2 All ER 359 . . . . . . 287
R v North Yorkshire County Council, ex parte Hargreaves (1995) 26 BMLR 121 . . . . . . 146, 195
R v Northavon District Council, ex parte Smith [1994] 2 AC 402 . . . 116, 117
R v Tower Hamlets London Borough Council, ex parte B (13 January 1997, unreported) . . . . . . 117
R, Petitioner 1993 SLT 910 . . . . . . 165
Raffaeli v Heatly 1949 SC 101 . . . . . . 273
Renfrew District Council v Gray 1987 SLT (Sh Ct) 70 . . . . . . 43
Rice v Connolly [1966] 2 QB 414 . . . . . . 295
S v County of San Diego (1993) 16 Cal App 4th 887 . . . . . . 286
S v HM Advocate 1989 SLT 469 . . . . . . 87
S v Kennedy 1996 SCLR 34 . . . . . . 157, 167
Sanderson v McManus 1997 SLT 629 . . . . . . 29
Sloan v B 1991 SLT 530 . . . . . . 168
Stallard v HM Advocate 1989 SCCR 248 . . . . . . 275
Stephens v Avery [1988] 2 All ER 477 . . . . . . 289
Stewart v Lockhart 1991 SLT 835 . . . . . . 273
Stewart v Thain 1981 SLT (Notes) 2 . . . . . . 157
Swift v Westham Central Mission (6 June 1984, unreported) QB . . . . . . 284
T (a minor) v Surrey County Council [1994] 4 All ER 577 . . . . . . 284
T (Accommodation by Local Authority), Re [1995] 1 FLR 159 . . . . 118, 146

PAGE

T, Petitioner 1996 SCLR 897 . . . . . . . . . . 94
Tagro v Cafane [1991] 2 All ER 235 . . . . . . . . . . 45
Tarasoff v Regents of the University of California (1976) 17 Cal 3d 425: 290–294
V v F 1991 SCLR 225 . . . . . . . . . . 80
Vicar of Writtle v Essex County Council (1979) 77 LGR 656 . . . . . . . . 284
Young v Heatly 1959 JC 66 . . . . . . . . . . 273
W (a minor) (medical treatment), Re [1992] 4 All ER 627 . . . . . . . . . . 80
W v Egdell [1989] 1 All ER 1089 . . . . . . . . . . 293
W v Egdell [1990] 1 All ER 835 . . . . . . . . . . 292, 293
W v Essex County Council (1997) Times, 16 July . . . . . . . . . . 285, 298
Walker v Northumberland County Council [1995] 1 All ER 737 . . . . . . 297
Wilson v Nithsdale District Council 1992 SLT 1131 . . . . . . . . . . 53
Wincentzen v Monklands District Council 1988 SLT 259 . . . . . . . . . . 49
Woods v Normand 1992 SCCR 805 . . . . . . . . . . 274
Wyness v Lockhart 1992 SCCR 808 . . . . . . . . . . 274
X (minors) v Bedfordshire County Council, M (a minor) v Newham London Borough Council [1994] 4 All ER 602 . . . . . . . . . . 283, 287, 298
X (minors) v Bedfordshire County Council, M (a minor) v Newham London Borough Council [1995] 2 AC 633 . . . . . . . . . . 281, 287
X v Y [1988] 2 All ER 648 . . . . . . . . . . 292

# Further reading

## CHAPTER 1

C Ball: *Law for Social Workers* (3rd edn, 1996, Ashgate)

S Braye and M Preston-Shoot: *Practising Social Work Law* (1992, Macmillan)

CCETSW: *Law for Social Workers in Scotland* (1996, CCETSW)

D Field and F Raitt: *Evidence* (2nd edn, 1996, Greens)

S Warner and G McIvor: *Pre-Trial Services in Scotland: An Evaluation of Two Experimental Bail Information and Accommodation Schemes* (1994, Scottish Office Central Research Unit)

A B Wilkinson: *The Scottish Law of Evidence* (1986, Butterworths/ Law Society of Scotland)

## CHAPTER 2

S Banks: *Ethics and Values in Social Work* (1995, Macmillan)

C Barnes: *Disabled People in Britain and Discrimination* (1994, Hurst)

CCETSW: *Rules and Regulations for the Diploma in Social Work* (1995)

CPAG: *Rights Guide to Non-Means Tested Benefits* (published annually)

CPAG: *National Welfare Benefits Handbook* (published annually)

P Carlen and A Worrall (eds): *Gender, Crime and Justice* (1987, Open University Press)

V Craig and K Miller: *Employment Law in Scotland* (1991, T & T Clark), ch 7

L Dominelli: *Anti-racist Social Work* (2nd edn, 1997, BASW/Macmillan)

C Gooding: *Disabling Laws, Enabling Acts* (1994, Pluto Press)

C M G Himsworth: *Housing Law in Scotland* (4th edn, 1994, Butterworths/The Planning Exchange)

R Hugman and D Smith (eds): *Ethical Issues in Social Work* (1985, Routledge)

A McAllister: *Scottish Law of Leases* (2nd edn, 1995, Butterworths)

I Macdonald and N Blake: *Immigration Law and Practice* (4th edn, 1995, Butterworths)

M Payne: *What is Professional Social Work?* (1996, Venture)

P Pearce, P Parsloe, H Francis, A Macara and D Watson: *Personal Data Protection in Health and Social Services* (1988, Croom Helm)

R Plant: *Social and Moral Theory in Casework* (1970, Routledge and Kegan Paul)

P Robson and M Poustie: *Homeless People and the Law* (3rd edn, 1996, Butterworths/The Planning Exchange)

Scottish Consumer Council: *What's on my Record? A Practical Guide to your Rights of Access to Personal Information* (1994)

Scottish Office Central Research Unit: *The Code of Guidance on Homelessness* (1994)

D Shemmings: *Client Access to Records: Participation in Social Work* (1991, Avebury)

G and J Stewart: *Social Work and Housing* (1993, Macmillan)

T Thomas: *Privacy and Social Services* (1995, Arena)

## CHAPTERS 3–5

R M Adler: *Taking Juvenile Justice Seriously* (1995, Scottish Academic Press)

S Asquith: *Children and Justice* (1993, Edinburgh University Press)

A Cleland and E Sutherland: *Scots Law and Children's Rights* (1996, Greens)

Lord Clyde: *The Report of the Inquiry into the Removal of Children from Orkney in February 1991* (1992, HMSO)

Department of Health: *Child Protection: Messages from Research* (1995, HMSO)

M D A Freeman: *Children, Their Families and the Law* (1992, BASW/Macmillan)

M Hayes and C Williams: *Family Law: Principles, Policy and Practice* (1995, Butterworths)

B Kearney: *Children's Hearings and the Sheriff Court* (1987, Butterworths/Law Society of Scotland)

A Kelly: *Introduction to the Scottish Children's Panel* (1996, Waterside Press)

M King and C Piper: *How the Law thinks about Children* (2nd edn, 1995, Arena)

P McNeill: *Adoption of Children in Scotland* (2nd edn, 1986, Greens)

A Maluccio and others: *Permanency Planning for Children* (1986, Tavistock)

F M Martin and K Murray (eds): *The Scottish Juvenile Justice System* (1982, Scottish Academic Press)

P Newall: *The UN Convention and Children's Rights in the UK* (1991, National Children's Bureau)

K McK Norrie: *Children (Scotland) Act 1995* (1996, Greens)

Renton and Brown: *Criminal Procedure* (6th edn, 1996, Greens)

G Schofield and J Thoburn: *Child Protection: The Voice of the Child in Decision-making* (1996, Institute for Public Policy Research)

Scottish Child and Family Alliance: *In the Child's Best Interests* (1991)

Scottish Office: *Review of Child Care Law in Scotland* (1990, HMSO)

Scottish Office: *Scotland's Children* (1993, HMSO)

Scottish Office: *The Children (Scotland) Act 1995 Regulations and Guidance: Volume 1, Support and Protection for Children and their Families* (1997, The Stationery Office)

Scottish Office: *The Children (Scotland) Act 1995 Regulations and Guidance: Volume 2, Children Looked After by Local Authorities* (1997, The Stationery Office)

Scottish Office: *The Children (Scotland) Act 1995 Regulations and Guidance: Volume 3, Adoption and Parental Responsibilities Orders* (1997, The Stationery Office)

Scottish Office and BAAF: *The Children (Scotland) Act 1995 – A Training Programme* (1996)

Social Work Services Group: *Effective Intervention: Child Abuse* (1989, HMSO)

J M Thomson: *Family Law in Scotland* (3rd edn, 1996, Butterworths/Law Society of Scotland)

J Wallerstein and S Blakeslee: *Second Chances* (1989)

## CHAPTER 6

D Anderson: *Social Work and Mental Handicap* (1982, Macmillan)

G Ashton and A Ward: *Mental Handicap and the Law* (1992, Sweet & Maxwell)

J Blackie and H Patrick: *Mental Health: A Guide to the Law in Scotland* (1990, Butterworths/Scottish Legal Education Trust)

J Cooper and S Vernon: *Disability and the Law* (1996, Jessica Kingsley)

J Dalrymple and B Burke: *Anti-Oppressive Practice – Social Work and the Law* (1995, Open University Press)

R Griffiths: *Community Care – An Agenda for Action* (1988)

J Lewis and H Glennister: *Implementing the New Community Care* (1996, OUP)

C McKay and H Patrick: *The Care Maze* (1995, ENABLE and SAMH)

M Mandelstam and B Schwer: *Community Care Practice and the Law* (1995, Jessica Kingsley)

M Marshall and M Dixon: *Social Work with Older People* (3rd edn, 1996, Macmillan)

A Norman: *Rights and Risk* (1980, National Corporation for the Care of Old People)

M Oliver: *Social Work and Disabled People* (1983, Macmillan)

M Oliver and others: *The Politics of Disablement* (1991, Open University Press)

M Payne: *Social Work and Community Care* (1995, Macmillan)

A Petch and others: *Delivering Community Care* (1996, HMSO)

H Richards and C McGregor: *Guardianship in Scotland* (1992, HMSO)

M Sheppard: *Care Management and the New Social Work* (1995,Whiting and Birch)

A Ward: *Scots Law of the Mentally Handicapped* (1984, Scottish Society for the Mentally Handicapped)

A Ward: *The Power to Act* (1990, Scottish Society for the Mentally Handicapped)

## CHAPTER 7

S Asquith (ed): *Children and Young People in Conflict with the Law* (1996, Jessica Kingsley)

S Asquith and E Samuel (eds): *Criminal Justice and Related Services for Young Adult* Offenders (1994, HMSO)

H Blagg and D Smith: *Crime, Penal Policy and Social Work* (1989, Longman)

A Bowes and D Sim: *Demands and Constraints – Ethnic Minorities and Social Services in Scotland* (1991, Scottish Council for Voluntary Organisations)

D Denney: *Racism and Anti-Racism in Probation* (1992, Routledge)

M Drakeford and M Vanstone (eds): *Beyond Offending Behaviour* (1996, Arena)

C Fishwick: *Court Work* (2nd edn, 1989, Pepar)

G H Gordon: *The Criminal Law of Scotland* (2nd edn, 1978, Greens/SULI)

R Harris: *Crime, Criminal Justice and the Probation Service* (1992, Routledge)

B Kelly: *Children Inside – Rhetoric and Practice in a Locked Institution for Children* (1992, Routledge)

G McIvor (ed): *Working with Offenders* (1996, Jessica Kingsley)

M W Matlin: *The Psychology of Women* (3rd edn, 1996, Harcourt Brace)

T May: *Probation: Politics, Policy and Practice* (1991, Open University Press)

T May and A Vass (eds): *Working with Offenders* (1996, Sage)

G Moore: *The Practice of Social Inquiry* (1984, Aberdeen University Press)

G Moore and C Wood: *Social Work and Criminal Law in Scotland* (2nd edn, 1992, Mercat Press)

C G B Nicholson: *Sentencing: The Law and Practice in Scotland* (2nd edn, 1992, Greens)

K Pease and W McWilliams: *Community Service by Order* (1980, Scottish Academic Press)

J Pointing (ed): *Alternatives to Custody* (1986, Blackwell)

P Raynor: *Social Work, Justice and Control* (1985, Blackwell)

P Raynor, D Smith and M Vanstone (eds): *Effective Probation Practice* (1994, BASW/Macmillan)

J Rodger: *Family Life and Social Control* (1996, Macmillan)

Scottish Office: *National Objectives and Standards for Social Work Services in the Criminal Justice System* (1996)

D Smith: *Criminology for Social Work* (1995, BASW/Macmillan)

A L Stewart: *The Scottish Criminal Courts in Action* (2nd edn, 1997, Butterworths)

H Walker and B Beaumont (eds): *Working with Offenders* (1981, Macmillan)

## CHAPTER 8

D Besharov: *The Vulnerable Social Worker* (1985, National Association of Social Workers)

M Houston-Vega and others: *Prudent Practice* (1997, National Association of Social Workers)

National Institute for Social Work: *Social Workers: Their Role and Tasks* (1982)

F Reamer: *Social Work Malpractice and Liability* (1994)

# Abbreviations

CASE REPORTS

| | |
|---|---|
| AC | Appeal Cases |
| All ER | All England Law Reports |
| BMLR | Butterworths Medico-Legal Reports |
| EHRR | European Human Rights Reports |
| Fam | Family Law Division |
| FCR | Family Court Reporter |
| FLR | Family Law Reports |
| HLR | Housing Law Reports |
| IRLR | Industrial Relations Law Reports |
| JC | Justiciary Cases |
| LGR | Local Government Reports |
| QB | Queen's Bench Division |
| SC | Session Cases |
| SCCR | Scottish Criminal Case Reports |
| SCLR | Scottish Civil Law Reports |
| SLT | Scots Law Times |
| SLT (Sh Ct) | Scots Law Times (Sheriff Court) |

STATUTES

| | |
|---|---|
| the 1968 Act | the Social Work (Scotland) Act 1968 |
| the 1970 Act | the Chronically Sick and Disabled Persons Act 1970 |
| the 1978 Act | the Adoption (Scotland) Act 1978 |
| the 1981 Act | the Matrimonial Homes (Family Protection) (Scotland) Act 1981 |
| the 1984 Act | the Mental Health (Scotland) Act 1984 |
| the 1985 Act | the Family Law (Scotland) Act 1985 |
| the 1986 Act | the Disabled Persons (Services, Consultation and Representation) Act 1986 |
| the 1987 Act | the Housing (Scotland) Act 1987 |
| the 1991 Act | the Age of Legal Capacity (Scotland) Act 1991 |

| | |
|---|---|
| the 1995 Act | the Children (Scotland) Act 1995 |
| the Act | the Disability Discrimination Act 1995 |

## STATUTORY INSTRUMENTS

| | |
|---|---|
| Adoption Regs | Adoption Agencies (Scotland) Regulations 1996, 1996/3266 |
| Arrangements Regulations | Arrangements to Look After Children (Scotland) Regulations Regulations 1996, SI 1996/3262 |
| Fostering Regulations | Fostering of Children (Scotland) Regulations 1996, Regulations SI 1996/3263 |
| Hearings Rules | Children's Hearings (Scotland) Rules 1996, SI 1996/3261 |

## OTHER

| | |
|---|---|
| BASW | British Association of Social Workers |
| CA | Court of Appeal |
| CCETSW | Central Council for Education and Training in Social Work |
| CICA | Criminal Injuries Compensation Authority |
| CPAG | Child Poverty Action Group |
| CPO | Child Protection Order |
| CSO | Community Service Order |
| DMO | Designated Medical Officer |
| Guidance | The Children (Scotland) Act 1995 Regulations and Guidance (three volumes) |
| HC | House of Commons Papers |
| HL | House of Lords |
| IH | Inner House |
| JSWFL | Journal of Social Welfare and Family Law |
| MHO | Mental Health Officer |
| NAPO | National Association of Probation Officers |
| OH | Outer House |
| OUP | Oxford University Press |
| RMO | Responsible Medical Officer |
| SACRO | Scottish Association for the Care and Resettlement of Offenders |
| SCOLAG | Scottish Legal Action Group |
| SLPQ | Scottish Law and Practice Quarterly |
| SMO | Special Medical Officer |
| SWSG | Social Work Services Group |
| SWSI | Social Work Services Inspectorate |

# 1. The Scottish legal context of social work

## 1. INTRODUCTION

Most social work in Scotland is practised within the context of local authority departments, many of which bear the name social work or social service department. This text will concentrate on this framework and for simplicity's sake refer to these settings as social work departments, except where special reference is made to the voluntary or private sector. There is a legal dimension to all of the work undertaken by social workers employed by the local authority.

Social workers are **obliged** to perform some functions and **permitted** to perform others by the laws passed by Parliament and arising out of court cases. They also have specified **powers** and **duties** which are defined by the law and derive much of their authority from the law. People who come into contact with social workers employed by the local authority have specified **rights** and **responsibilities** which are based in law. The contact between these people and the social worker is therefore driven by the law and without a basic knowledge of that law the social worker cannot function competently and the service user may also forfeit various legal entitlements.

Social workers need to be able to recognise and make use of this legal dimension in social work practice. Social workers occupy a privileged and unique position in relation to people who have legal needs. Here is an opportunity for social workers to assist in enhancing quality of life by sharing their understanding of the law and the legislative framework with service users who may be in crisis and so temporarily unable to make sense of their circumstances, who may be unfamiliar with the legal system, and/or who may be without the necessary social skills to navigate in legal waters.

Further opportunities arise for social workers through direct involvement with offenders and ex-offenders. The retention of the probation service functions under the auspices of social work departments has provided the continuing recognition that social work values, knowledge, and skills are most appropriate in dealing with this service user population.

Social work law has not yet in general proved an attractive area of specialisation for solicitors, and so there is an additional incentive and requirement for social workers to share their awareness and understanding of the legal dimension of their work both with service users and with other professionals. We are not advocating that social workers become second-rate lawyers but that they use their knowledge of law to inform their practice and contribute to the facilitating of shared social work goals. A study of the law relating to social work also contributes to an understanding of the variety of acceptable roles which are appropriate for social workers. In view of society's ambiguous relationship with social workers, these roles are often contradictory and ambivalent. They include investigator, assessor, supervisor, witness, conciliator, reporter, facilitator, liaison, advisor, guide, support, broker, enabler, teacher, mediator and advocate.[1] Social workers may be in a position to help to identify and enforce the rights of vulnerable service users and/or they may be in the position of enforcing service users' compliance with the law. These roles will be explored in more depth subsequently.

The importance of a thorough grounding in the law relevant to social work practice cannot be sufficiently emphasised. When the Central Council for Education and Training in Social Work (CCETSW) statement *Requirements and Regulations for the Diploma in Social Work* (Paper 30) was published in September 1989, there was a stated recognition that 'Parliament lays down the legal framework and delineates the powers of statutory, voluntary and private agencies within which social workers practise'[2] and that qualifying social workers need to demonstrate 'detailed knowledge of legal requirements relevant to the particular area of practice'.[3] This meant that newly qualified social workers may well have chosen working with people who are elderly as a particular area of practice and so could have qualified having demonstrated general knowledge about 'law, statutory duties, powers and legal principles'[4] and detailed knowledge of the law in relation to people who are elderly, but may never have been introduced, for example, to detailed knowledge of child care law.

The revised edition of CCETSW's Paper 30, *Assuring Quality in the Diploma in Social Work – 1: Rules and Requirements for the DipSW*

1 These last four interventive roles are discussed in B Compton and B Galaway *Social Work Processes* (5th edn, 1994), p 126.

2 *Requirements and Regulations for the Diploma in Social Work* (Paper 30) (1989) (*Paper 30*), p 4.

3 *Paper 30*, p 15.

4 *Paper 30*, p 14.

(1995), has given added emphasis to the claim that social workers must know and understand the law in practice by stating that 'it is essential that students learn about and understand the legislative framework ... of the country of the United Kingdom in which they train'[1] and particularly in reference to 'Children, Community Care, Criminal Justice and Mental Health'.[2] There is now a 'practice requirement' that social work students 'work in accordance with statutory and legal requirements'.[3] It is now not acceptable for a qualifying social worker to have detailed legal knowledge and understanding in relation to only one group of service users or way of working. This has very significantly increased the expectation of what is required of new social workers and placed the law curriculum in a much more central position.

Two things should be made clear about the operation of law. The first is that law does not necessarily specify a precise course of action to be followed in given circumstances. In most cases there is room for considerable discretion in applying the law, though once it is applied there may be precise procedures to be followed (a good example of this is the law relating to child protection orders).[4] The way in which discretion is to be exercised in these areas may be the subject of guidance from the Secretary of State or Social Work Services Group or may be the subject of departmental policies. In such areas knowledge of the guidance and policies is essential, but the underlying legal framework must not be ignored.

Secondly, there are many areas of social work which are not covered specifically or in detail by legislation (for example, work with elderly people) and which are simply covered by the general (and very vague) obligation to promote social welfare and assist those in need contained in the Social Work (Scotland) Act 1968 (see part 15 below).

One final general comment needs to be made about the language of the law and the language of social work. The occasional incompatibility of these two is characteristic of the nature and value base of each. Legal language can seem obscure, arcane and even offensive with its insistence on false generics (such as the use of the pronoun 'he' to represent both sexes) while social work language can seem politically correct and driven by the dominant ideology of the day. We have attempted to use language which is representative of

1 *Assuring Quality in the Diploma in Social Work - 1: Rules and Requirements for the DipSW* (1995) (*Assuring Quality*), p 19.
2 *Assuring Quality*, p 20.
3 *Assuring Quality*, p 27.
4 See ch 5, pt 6.

each discipline in an effort to find a language understandable to both.

## 2. THE FUNCTIONS OF LAW IN SOCIETY

Although there has been some dispute about the need for law to regulate society much of that debate is, in fact, about the precise form of law or about its appropriateness as a means of resolving social problems. There is in reality broad agreement about the need for some system of universal rules to regulate the operation of society.[1] Since social workers' interventions are so inextricably entwined with the functions of law, it is imperative that they understand and appreciate these functions.

The principal functions of law are:

### *(a) Social control*

It does this through the enforcement of criminal law and the provision of mechanisms to allow private individuals to resolve their disputes (principally the civil courts). The former of these is often seen, simplistically and erroneously, as the sole or main function of law.

### *(b) Constitution of law-making and law-enforcing bodies*

The law also provides for the make up and procedure of Parliament and the court system. As part of this process individuals may be given certain rights and protections, such as the right of access to legal representation for court appearances.

### *(c) Enabling function*

At a very basic level it is sometimes argued that law, by guaranteeing peace, enables people to carry on with their lives. However, it also makes much more specific provision to allow people to make arrangements which will be legally recognised and enforced, such as adoption and contracts.

1 The Russian anarchist Kropotkin, for example, noted that 'No society is possible without certain principles of morality generally recognised': *Revolutionary Pamphlets* (1970), p 73.

*(d) Promotion of social welfare*

More recently, particularly since the end of the last world war, law has been used as a tool for the promotion of social welfare. Clearly, law cannot do this by itself but rather it provides the framework of organisations, such as local authority social work departments, to do so, gives them powers and duties (as it confers these on the employees of social work departments), and confers rights, such as to social security benefits, on individuals.

## 3. LAW AND SOCIAL PROBLEMS

Social problems are not necessarily amenable to purely legal solutions. However, when the legal solution facilitates the potential resolution of a social problem then the use of such means can be justified and the failure to use such means would be inexcusable.

On a broader level the difficulties of successfully using purely legal means to resolve social problems are illustrated by the failure of anti-discrimination legislation to secure equal pay and employment prospects for women, and the failure, partly as a result of the discretion allowed to local authorities, of the homelessness legislation to cater for those in genuine need of accommodation.[1] In these areas legal intervention has brought about benefits and improvements, but it is not on its own able to provide a complete resolution of the problem to which it is addressed.

## 4. FORMAL SOURCES OF LAW

Formal sources of law are the actual statements of the law, as opposed to textbooks or commentaries on the law. The main formal sources of law as it affects social workers are Acts of Parliament (statutes), such as the Children (Scotland) Act 1995 (see part 16 below); delegated legislation (statutory instruments), such as the regulations governing the fostering of children;[2] and case law, that is the law derived from decisions made by courts.

1 See, for example, the National Audit Office *Homelessness* HC 622 (1989–90); C Gooding *Disabling Laws, Enabling Acts* (1994), ch 6.
2 See ch 4, pt 4.

As we noted in the previous section, one of the functions of law is the promotion of social welfare, and this has necessitated a fairly substantial volume of legislation. The result of this is that most of the law we will be discussing in the remainder of this book is derived from statute. The precise mechanism for the passing of an Act of Parliament need not concern us here, but it is perhaps worth noting that Acts are often preceded by Green or White Papers or other documents produced by the government setting out its intentions as to legislation. These may allow for comment from interested parties on the proposals before they are finalised.

For a variety of reasons, for example because of the need for expert professional advice, statutes often omit detailed regulations. The power to make these is usually delegated to a government minister and in the Scottish context this will be the Secretary of State for Scotland. Examples are the rules regulating the conduct of children's hearings (The Children's Hearings (Scotland) Rules 1996) and those regulating the use of secure accommodation. These rules can be changed fairly rapidly in response to increased awareness of their potential implications. The power to make more detailed rules may be delegated to other bodies. Thus the power to make procedural rules for civil court cases such as adoption cases has been delegated to the Court of Session. Statutes may also provide for the Secretary of State to issue guidance, such as the guidance issued on the Children (Scotland) Act 1995. In practice, this guidance will come from the Social Work Services Group of The Scottish Office Education Department.

One final point of importance on Acts of Parliament is that they do not necessarily or usually become part of the law as soon as they are passed. Instead, an Act will usually provide that it is to be brought into force (that is, become part of the law) by orders made by the appropriate Secretary of State; consequently, different sections of the Act may be brought into force at different times. One example of this is the Children (Scotland) Act 1995. Part of this came into force in November 1995, other provisions came into force in November 1996 and virtually all of the remainder in April 1997.

Case law may offer a definitive interpretation of the provisions of an Act of Parliament, such as, for example, the grounds for compulsory measures of supervision. Finally, regulations and directives made by the European Union or decisions of the European Court of Justice and the European Court of Human Rights can have an important effect on the law in Scotland.

## 5. RIGHTS, POWERS AND DUTIES

As we indicated at the beginning of this chapter, most social workers work for local authorities. It is particularly important for workers in this setting to understand the statutory basis for most of their work. What we mean by this is that local authorities, social work departments and individual workers all owe their existence, their powers and their duties to Acts of Parliament. Were it not for the Local Government (Scotland) Acts local authorities would not exist and would have no powers. Were it not, for example, for the Social Work (Scotland) Act 1968 they would have no duty to provide reports for courts.

The notions of rights, powers and duties merit some further discussion. Duties[1] are obligations imposed on authorities and workers to act. There are different types of duty imposed on social workers. They may be subject to ethical, moral or professional duties, but they, and their employers, also have legal duties. Legal duties are requirements to act (they might be seen as orders to do something). Some of these duties are very general and impose rather vague obligations on local authorities and workers. The classic example of this is section 12 of the 1968 Act, which begins by stating that 'it shall be the duty of every local authority to promote social welfare by making available advice, guidance and assistance on such a scale as may be appropriate for their area'. Other duties are much more specific and will confer rights on specific individuals enabling them to enforce these duties. For example, the local authority has a duty to assess the needs of a disabled person when requested to do so by that person. If the authority failed or refused to carry out an assessment the disabled person could go to court to obtain an order forcing it to do so. The more general duties imposed on local authorities are more difficult to enforce. In many cases the duty will arise only where certain prior conditions have been fulfilled. Not all duties imposed on social workers are imposed by statute or by a statute specific to local authorities, for example duties to exercise reasonable care in the performance of their work. Duties imposed by law can sometimes conflict with other types of duty to a service user and with service users' expectations.[2]

1 Duties are sometimes referred to as responsibilities or obligations.

2 See S Shardlow 'Confidentiality, accountability and the boundaries of client-worker relationships' in Hugman and Smith (eds) *Ethical Issues in Social Work* (1985).

Powers are authorisations to act. They may give the authority or worker the ability or capacity to do something, but do not require that it is done. An example is the power to apply for a child protection order. This discretionary nature of powers means that their use is not determined by the law, but is, rather, informed by the professional judgment of those entitled to exercise them. One consequence of the statutory basis of social work is that local authorities and social workers only have the powers conferred on them by statute or implied by duties imposed on them and any attempt to exercise powers beyond these would be unlawful. The law would describe such an attempt as acting *ultra vires*, that is, beyond the powers conferred by statute.

Legal rights usually refer to entitlements conferred on individuals which they can enforce through the legal system. Some of these rights are general, such as the right to defend yourself against attack; others involve specific claims against individuals or organisations. Examples of this second category are the right to claim damages from someone who has injured you, the right to benefits and the right not to be unfairly dismissed. In many cases the rights exist because of a duty imposed on someone else. Most rights in the context of social work involve service users' rights. Some of these are seen in the duties noted above, such as the right to an assessment, but there are others, for example the right of access to social work records.

As we have seen, use of powers depends on the exercise of judgment by workers. In some cases duties may arise only after the exercise of judgment: for example a duty to provide services to a disabled person arises only after judgments have been made about the needs of that person and what services should be provided to meet these needs. Decisions involving judgment are described in law as discretionary and the discretion enjoyed by workers is not unrestrained: their decisions can be challenged by judicial review (see part 13 below). Workers may also have to take account of guidance issued by the government or by their employers in exercising their discretion.

## 6. LEGAL PERSONNEL

### (1) Solicitors and advocates

The basic division within the legal profession is between solicitors and advocates (the latter are sometimes referred to as counsel).

Solicitors are the most numerous. They have direct contact with their clients and may practice in all areas of the law, as is common in smaller towns, or specialise in a particular area of law. The Law Society of Scotland, the solicitors' professional body, publishes a directory of firms indicating the areas of work which they will undertake. The Law Society also acts as the disciplinary body for solicitors. Often social workers develop a local knowledge of solicitors who have a particular interest in social welfare, family law, and/or criminal law which can prove useful to service users, and the Scottish Child Law Centre has compiled a list of solicitors specialising in family and child care law.

Advocates specialise in court appearance and in giving advice on complex matters of law. Historically, they had an exclusive right to appear in the higher courts (that is the High Court, the Court of Session and the House of Lords) but there are now provisions to allow solicitors to appear in these courts. Advocates have no direct contact or relationship with their ultimate client: the relationship is managed by the client's solicitors. Solicitor-advocates, as the name indicates, are a hybrid of the two and are solicitors who have passed a test of competence and fulfilled certain other requirements to allow them to represent people in the High Court or in the Court of Session.

## (2) Procurators fiscal and the system of public prosecution

Prosecutions for crimes and offences in Scotland have for a long time been undertaken by a public prosecutor. The system is headed by the Lord Advocate, who is a political appointee, and who advises the government on matters of law generally, as well as being the head of the system of prosecution. The Lord Advocate is assisted by the Solicitor General, also a political appointee. Together they are known as 'the Law Officers'. Below these two are a number (currently 14) of Advocates Depute, also referred to as Crown Counsel. Advocates Depute are advocates who are appointed to the position usually for a relatively short period of time. Solicitor-advocates and senior members of the fiscal service may now also be appointed to act as Crown Counsel. In practice, most of the work in the prosecution system is done by procurators fiscal and procurators fiscal depute who are the local representatives of the public prosecution service. These are full-time permanent civil servants and there will be a procurator fiscal in each sheriff court. The administration of the system of prosecution is the responsibility of the Crown Office in Edinburgh which is headed by the Crown Agent, another full-time civil servant.

Where someone has been apprehended on suspicion of having committed a crime, or where a serious crime has been committed, the matter will be reported to the procurator fiscal. The fiscal is, legally, in charge of the investigation of the crime and can direct the police in their conduct of the investigation. In most cases, however, little or no further investigation will be necessary, and the fiscal simply has to decide how to process the report, that is, to decide whether to prosecute or not.

In cases where prosecution will take place in a summary court (for an explanation of this see part 8 below), the decision is entirely one for the fiscal, operating under the guidance of a book of regulations issued by the Lord Advocate. It is the fiscal's decision whether to prosecute or not, and if no prosecution is to take place, whether simply to let the matter drop or to take some form of action which falls broadly into the category of diversion.

In more serious cases, where the crime/offence might be prosecuted before a solemn court (for an explanation of this see part 8 below), the fiscal must seek the advice of Crown Counsel on how to proceed, and in cases which will be prosecuted in the High Court the framing of the indictment against the accused and decisions on procedure are in the hands of Crown Counsel.

In deciding whether to prosecute a fiscal will, according to the 1992/93 Crown Office Annual Report, adopt the following procedure:

'While taking account of all the relevant facts and circumstances of the particular case, the prosecutor will ask a number of questions, including:

- Do the facts disclose a crime?
- Is there sufficient admissible and reliable evidence?
- Was the offence too trivial to justify the expense of a prosecution?
- Are the consequences to the alleged offender of being prosecuted in proportion to the seriousness of the offence?
- Were there mitigating circumstances?
- Would civil proceedings be more appropriate?
- Are there local considerations to be taken into account?
- Is the case old or has there been delay?
- Is the offence alleged to be racially motivated?
- Does the accused have a reasonable excuse?
- What is the accused's attitude to the offence?
- If there is a victim, what is his or her attitude to the offence?
- What are the prospects of securing a conviction?
- Is a suitable alternative to prosecution available?'

Despite the history of public prosecution in Scotland, it is still technically possible for an individual to pursue a private prosecution. Such private prosecutions require the consent of either the Lord Advocate or of the High Court. There have only been two cases this century in which a private prosecution has been allowed to proceed, the more famous being the so-called 'Glasgow rape case' of the early 1980s.[1]

Prosecutions in the sheriff and district courts will be undertaken by the fiscal or a depute. In the High Court the prosecutor will be one of the Law Officers or an Advocate Depute.

In cases where there is sufficient evidence to proceed to prosecution the fiscal may, instead of prosecuting, administer a warning. Before this can be done there must be sufficient evidence to justify proceedings and the case must not be so trivial as to merit no action. Fiscals also have the power in certain types of cases to offer an individual the option of paying a fixed penalty as an alternative to prosecution. Finally, there are a number of diversion schemes in operation where individuals are diverted to social work assistance in place of prosecution. Diversion schemes and procurator fiscal fines are both considered in chapter 7, part 5.

As well as being a prosecutor the fiscal is also responsible for investigating all sudden and suspicious deaths and suicides.

### (3) Judges

District courts are most often presided over by one or more lay magistrates. These are people who have no legal training but have been appointed to act as magistrates. They will be guided as to the law by a legal assessor or by the clerk to the court. The practice as to the number of magistrates sitting to hear a case and the source of legal guidance varies between different areas. There are also, in Glasgow district court, a number of stipendiary magistrates. These magistrates are legally qualified and sit alone to hear cases. They have greater sentencing powers than lay magistrates. Sheriff courts are staffed by sheriffs who are legally qualified, most having been advocates. Finally, there are the judges who preside both in the Court of Session and in the High Court. They are all legally qualified and are variously described as Lords of Session, Lord

1 *H v Sweeney* 1983 SLT 48.

Commissioners of Justiciary and Senators of the College of Justice. How they are described depends on which role they are fulfilling.

### (4) Clerks of court

The most numerous of these are sheriff clerks. They are responsible for the running of sheriff courts, recording of proceedings (though not shorthand note-taking), arranging for reports, arranging (in consultation with the procurator fiscal) the court timetable, maintenance of records, collection of fines, and the organisation and distribution of social enquiry reports. This last task will involve co-operation with the social worker(s) attached to the court, who will make arrangements with the appropriate social work area office for the report to be provided. Each sheriff court will have a sheriff clerk who will be assisted by deputes. The district and High Courts have clerks who broadly perform the same function for them as sheriff clerks do for the sheriff court.

### (5) Sheriff officers and messengers-at-arms

These are officers of court who must fulfil certain requirements and hold a warrant from the sheriff to act. They are not directly employed by the court system but rather are court officers in the sense that they are authorised to do certain things by virtue of their warrant and are accountable to court for their actions. Sheriff officers are used to serve summonses and citations in civil cases, to carry out the enforcement of civil judgments, such as evictions and warrant sales, and to serve witness citations for the defence in criminal cases. Messengers-at-arms perform a similar function in relation to actions in the Court of Session.

### (6) Miscellaneous

As well as those noted above there are a variety of other people involved in the operation of the court system. These include ushers and bar officers who assist in the actual functioning of the courts, directing people to the right court and maintaining order in court.

## 7. CIVIL COURT SYSTEM AND PROCEDURES

The civil court system basically deals with all cases which do not involve the commission of a crime or offence and which are not dealt with by a special body, such as an industrial tribunal. Examples of the sorts of case it deals with are given below. Before going on to look at the various courts in the civil court system some explanation of the distinction between courts of first instance and courts of appeal is necessary. Courts of first instance are the courts where a case appears and is dealt with: in other words, these are the courts at which trials take place and in which civil cases are disposed of. Appeal courts deal only or mainly with appeals from the decisions of courts of first instance.

### (1) Sheriff court

Scotland is divided up into six sheriffdoms, five of which (the exception being Glasgow and Strathkelvin) are then subdivided into sheriff court districts, each of which has a sheriff court building. Each sheriffdom is staffed by a sheriff principal and a number of sheriffs. The precise organisation of the court will depend on the level of business; in rural areas, for example, the court may sit only on one day a week or as necessary to deal with the business.

The sheriff civil court involves a sheriff sitting alone to deal with cases at first instance. It cannot deal with some matters; the main exclusions being legitimacy, setting aside of documents and judicial review (see part 13 below). On the other hand, there are certain matters that can only be dealt with at the sheriff court, for example eviction and actions for sums of money less than £1,500.

The sheriff civil court deals with such matters as adoption, proofs on reference from children's hearings, divorce, applications under the Mental Health (Scotland) Act 1984 and (accounting for most of its business) small debt actions.

Decisions of the sheriff can be appealed to the sheriff principal or direct to the Inner House of the Court of Session.

### (2) Court of Session

The Court of Session sits only in Edinburgh. It is divided into an Outer House, which consists of judges sitting alone to deal with cases at first instance, and an Inner House. The Inner House is divided into two divisions of four judges (though usually only three sit in a case) and deals primarily with appeals from the Outer House and from the sheriff court and sheriff principal. The Inner House is also a court of first instance for a variety of applications under companies legislation and other specialised forms of procedure. Appeals arising from the children's hearing system may end up in the Inner House.

### (3) House of Lords

This operates only as a court of appeal. In cases originating in the sheriff court the appeal must be concerned with a question of law rather than a factual dispute.

### (4) Procedures

#### *(a) Small claims procedure*

This type of procedure was introduced in 1988 and is designed to provide a simple and inexpensive form of action which can be easily used by members of the public. It can be used to recover money up to £750 or for the recovery of property up to that value. Most cases in practice are of the former type and may be actions to recover debts (most commonly) or actions to recover damages.

There is no provision for legal aid in this process (see part 14 below) as the intention is that private individuals will be able to conduct cases themselves. There is, however, provision allowing either party to be represented at any hearing by any other person. Where that person is not a solicitor the sheriff must be satisfied that the person is a 'suitable person'.

#### *(b) Summary cause procedure*

Summary cause procedure, again a simplified form of procedure, is similar to small claims procedure. It is the appropriate means of recovering sums of money between £750 and £1,500; it is also used for actions for eviction.[1]

1 See also ch 2, pt 2.

*(c) Ordinary procedure*

This form of procedure is used in the sheriff court. It is appropriate for claims in excess of £1,500 and for other types of case, including divorces not covered by the 'do-it-yourself' procedure.[1] Procedure in the Court of Session is similar to this. Unlike small claims and summary cause procedure, this type of procedure is based on extensive written pleadings (essentially the claims and counter-claims made by the parties to the court action). This makes it too complex and unsuitable for claims involving small amounts and also means that some delays are built into the process, though changes in the procedure introduced in 1994 should result in less delay.

*(d) Special procedures*

A variety of types of case of interest to social workers have their own special forms of procedure. These include proof of grounds of referral to a children's hearing, appeals from hearing decisions and adoption. The procedures will be explained in more detail when we look at these areas.

### (5) Standard of proof

The standard of proof in civil cases is proof on the balance of probabilities. Generally, then, the person initiating the case must satisfy the court that his/her version of events is more probable than that put forward by the other party. The nature of the evidence used to establish this standard is considered in part 9 below.

## 8. CRIMINAL COURT SYSTEM AND PROCEDURES[2]

Within the criminal court system there is a distinction between solemn and summary courts. The essential distinction between these is that in summary courts the judge(s) takes the decision on guilt or innocence, whereas in solemn courts this is done by a jury of 15. There are also some differences in the procedure followed in

1 See ch 3, pt 2.
2 See ch 7, pts 3, 4, and 7.

the different types of court. These will be considered more fully below.

## (1) District court

District courts are based on local authority districts, and local authorities have certain responsibilities in relation to provision of accommodation and staffing. As noted above, the district court will normally be presided over by a lay magistrate or lay magistrates with legal advice from an assessor or clerk of court.

The sorts of cases the district court can deal with are restricted. It cannot deal with housebreaking cases, serious assaults, forgery, theft and fraud cases where the amount involved is more than £2,500, and cases involving the prosecution of children under 16.

The sentencing powers of the court are limited to a fine of up to level 4 on the standard scale (currently £2,500)[1] and up to 60 days' imprisonment. Where the court is presided over by a stipendiary magistrate it has the same sentencing powers as the sheriff summary court. As always in this chapter, references to sentencing powers are to the maximum sentence that can be imposed in the absence of a specific statutory provision restricting or enhancing the power in respect of particular crimes or offences. Currently the district court deals with about 45% of criminal cases.

## (2) Sheriff summary court

The sheriff summary court is held in the same buildings and staffed by the same personnel as the sheriff civil court.

The sentencing powers of this court are, currently, a fine of £5,000 and 3 months' imprisonment.[2] In cases where the person being sentenced has committed a crime of violence or of dishonesty and has a previous conviction for a crime of violence in the former case or dishonesty in the latter case, the maximum possible period of imprisonment is 6 months.[3] The sheriff summary court deals with just over half of all criminal cases.

1 See the Criminal Procedure (Scotland) Act 1995, ss 7 and 225(2).

2 Increased to 6 months if and when the Crime and Punishment (Scotland) Act 1997, s 13 comes into effect.

3 Increased to 12 months if and when the Crime and Punishment (Scotland) Act 1997, s 13 comes into effect.

### (3) Sheriff solemn court

The sheriff solemn court deals with slightly more serious cases and this is reflected in its sentencing power. The sheriff sitting in this court can impose an unlimited fine and imprison for up to 3 years.[1] In cases where the sheriff considers that these sentencing powers are inadequate the case can be remitted to the High Court for sentence. This happens very rarely in practice. The sheriff solemn court deals with about 2% of criminal cases.

### (4) High Court of Justiciary

Although this has the same personnel as the Court of Session it sits not only in Edinburgh but also at locations throughout Scotland, and is, for example, in almost permanent session in Glasgow. The High Court is the only court which can deal with certain crimes, the most notable being murder and rape. The High Court deals with less than 1% of criminal cases.

### (5) High Court as court of appeal

The High Court has always operated as a court of appeal from summary courts. For this purpose it sits in Edinburgh and is presided over by three judges or, if the appeal is only about sentence, two judges. Since 1926 it has also operated in the same format as the Court of Criminal Appeal to deal with appeals from solemn courts.

### (6) Procedures

#### *(a) Summary procedure*

Summary procedure is initiated by the service of a document known as a 'complaint' on the accused. The complaint will contain brief details of the alleged offence, including the time and date. This narration of events is known as 'the libel'. Attached to the

1 Increased to 5 years if and when the Crime and Punishment (Scotland) Act 1997, s 13 comes into effect.

complaint will be a notice of previous convictions, if relevant, and in the case of statutory offences a notice of penalties setting out the possible penalties on conviction.

On the first appearance of the accused, either from custody or on the date specified for the hearing on the citation accompanying the complaint, the plea will be taken. Proceedings in criminal cases are known as 'diets', and this diet is sometimes referred to as 'the pleading diet'. If the accused pleads guilty the court may proceed to sentence, or may defer sentence (D/S) for reports or for the accused to be of good behaviour. If the accused pleads not guilty a date will be set for trial.

If the accused pleads not guilty there will, in most courts, be an intermediate diet called before the trial diet. The purpose of this diet is to assess the state of preparation on both sides, to establish if the accused intends to maintain the plea of not guilty, and to supervise the extent to which the prosecution and defence have fulfilled their duty to identify and agree uncontroversial evidence. The reason for introducing this intermediate diet was to try to reduce the number of people pleading not guilty at the first diet and changing the plea to guilty at the trial. Procedure at the trial is considered on pages 20–22.

### *(b) Solemn procedure*

The accused's first appearance will be on petition. The petition will specify the preliminary form of the charge against him/her. This first hearing will take the form of a judicial examination in front of the sheriff in the sheriff's chambers. The fiscal may ask questions at this stage and a transcript of the questions and any answers may be read out at any subsequent trial. After examination the accused may be committed for further examination, in which case he/she will appear before the sheriff again, or may be committed for trial (sometimes described as being 'fully committed'), and may be released on bail or kept in custody.

Once the accused has been committed for trial an indictment will be served on him/her (assuming that the case is proceeding). The indictment will contain the final version of the charge against the accused, will specify a date for the trial and will have attached to it, as appropriate, a notice of previous convictions, as well as a list of the prosecution witnesses and of any productions (that is, any physical evidence such as photographs or weapons) the prosecution intend to present at the trial.

If the accused is kept in custody the indictment must be served within 80 days and the trial start within 110 days, in both cases starting with the date of full committal. If the accused is at liberty the trial must start within 12 months of the first appearance on petition. In cases tried at the sheriff court there will a first diet at least ten days before the trial diet. The function of this is similar to that of the intermediate diet in summary proceedings. If the case is to be tried in the High Court there may be a preliminary diet to deal with certain legal issues.

SUMMARY PROCEDURE (Appearance from custody)

Pleading Diet — Guilty — Sentence or D/S
(Duty solicitor available)

Not guilty

Trial date set

May be remanded in custody or liberated pending trial

Application for legal aid

Intermediate diet

Trial diet — Not guilty — Released

Guilty

Sentence or D/S

Where the appearance is not from custody the duty solicitor is not available to assist at the pleading diet.[1]

SOLEMN PROCEDURE

Appearance on petition (ie judicial examination in sheriff court)

continued for further examination

Committal for trial

Bail or custody

Service of indictment (note time limits)

First diet or (optional) preliminary diet

Trial diet (at sheriff or High Court)

*(c) Procedure at trial*

Around 90% of criminal cases do not go to trial. The accused simply pleads guilty and is sentenced. Although the accused has a right to defend him/herself in those cases that go to trial, legal representation can greatly assist the accused's case and make sure it is properly presented.

Procedure at trial is similar in solemn and summary procedure, the chief differences being due to the presence of the jury in solemn procedure. The main stages are:

1 See pt 14 below on legal aid.

(a) Presentation of the prosecution evidence. There are no opening statements in Scottish trials of the sort which might be familiar from American films or television. The prosecution simply call their first witness and the trial proceeds from there. Each witness will be examined by the prosecution (this initial questioning is known as 'the examination-in-chief'); he/she will then be cross-examined by the defence and then, if necessary, be re-examined by the prosecution.

(b) At the end of the prosecution case the defence may move that the charges be dropped on the ground that there is no case to answer, in other words that the prosecution has not produced sufficient evidence to find the accused guilty.

(c) If this motion is rejected the defence will then present their evidence in the same way as the prosecution. There is, of course, no need for the defence to give evidence, or, more particularly, for the accused to give evidence, though failure to give evidence may be commented on by the prosecution and the judge. It is up to the prosecution to prove their case beyond reasonable doubt.

(d) Following the defence case both sides, prosecution first, will make their concluding speeches. In summary cases these are addressed to the judge(s), in solemn cases to the jury.

(e) In solemn cases the judge will then address the jury explaining their function, the standard of proof which the prosecution must meet and any relevant legal points. The judge will usually also highlight some of the significant points of evidence, although the jurors must decide on their own recollection of the evidence. After this the jury will retire to consider its verdict, a process which is widely recognised to be far from scientific.

(f) The judge or jury will then reach a verdict. The verdict may be guilty, not guilty or not proven. This last is a Scottish curiosity and appears to mean 'we rather suspect that you are guilty, but the evidence has not persuaded us beyond a reasonable doubt'. There has been a campaign to abolish this verdict but it appears to have been unsuccessful.[1] The campaign seems in part to be based on the notion that criminal proceedings are concerned with establishing guilt or innocence in some objective sense corresponding to the truth of what actually happened. This, however, is not the case:

1 Objections to the verdict are not new: in 1827 Sir Walter Scott described it as 'that bastard verdict': J G Wilson *Not Proven* (1960), p 7.

> 'It is sometimes maintained that the object of leading evidence in a criminal trial is, or should be, the elucidation of the truth. That statement, however, requires considerable qualification. First, the matter to be elucidated is not the whole truth about all the circumstances of the events narrated in the libel, but only the question of whether the Crown has proved beyond reasonable doubt that the accused committed the crime charged against him. While a verdict of "guilty" answers that question in the affirmative, a verdict of "not guilty" or "not proven" only means that the question has not been so answered: it is not a determination of the accused's innocence. And whatever the verdict, it may not reflect the truth.'[1]

(g) Following a guilty verdict the court will move on to sentence. Sentence may be deferred either for reports or for some other reason, for example, for the accused to show that he/she can be of good behaviour or for repayment of a sum of money dishonestly obtained. In some cases the judge must obtain social enquiry reports before sentencing, for example, when considering a custodial disposal for an offender not previously sentenced to custody or for an offender under 21. Before sentence is passed the accused's solicitor or counsel will normally make a plea in mitigation, the purpose of which is to attempt to influence the sentencer to be lenient.

### *(d) Standard of proof*

As we have noted the standard of proof in criminal cases is proof beyond reasonable doubt. This is more exacting than the standard in civil cases and requires the prosecution to produce evidence which does not leave any reasonable doubt in the mind of the judge (in summary cases) or the jury (in solemn cases) as to the guilt of the accused. This standard of proof is also relevant in hearings before the sheriff to establish a referral to a children's hearing on offence grounds.[2] The nature of the evidence which can be used to establish this standard is considered in part 9 below.

### *(e) Bail*[3]

Bail may be applied for on any appearance in court and refusal of bail can be appealed against except where it takes place in solemn

1 Scottish Law Commission *Evidence: Report on Hearsay in Civil Proceedings* HC 177 1994-95, para 2.14.

2 See ch 5, pt 3(10).

3 Most people who are not kept in custody after a court hearing will not be on bail. They will be released simply on agreeing to attend the next hearing.

proceedings prior to full committal. The only non-bailable offences are murder and treason. However, there are other cases where bail is not available. These are cases where the accused is charged with, or has been convicted of, attempted murder, culpable homicide or rape and has a previous conviction for one of these offences or for murder or manslaughter.

An individual may be released on bail both before conviction and after conviction but before sentence; he/she may also be released pending the outcome of an appeal against a custodial sentence.

In deciding on whether to grant bail the court must consider the public interest and the possibility of intimidation of witnesses. In response to the recognised lack of information about accused persons which militated towards their being remanded in custody, experimental schemes were set up at Glasgow and Edinburgh sheriff courts in 1991. These schemes were run by partnerships between the social work departments and SACRO and targeted procurators fiscal who were opposing the granting of bail. Verified information was provided, and accommodation was found for people of no fixed abode. The schemes proved so successful and cost effective[1] that a significant proportion of people were granted bail who would not otherwise have been bailed and since April 1993 bail information and supervision are amongst the services which attract 100% funding from the Scottish Office.

If bail is granted the person released on bail will be subject to a number of conditions set out in Part III of the Criminal Procedure (Scotland) Act 1995. These are:

(a) a requirement to appear at all court diets;
(b) a requirement not to commit further offences;
(c) a requirement not to interfere with witnesses;
(d) a requirement to be available for the purposes of enabling enquiries or reports to be made to assist the court's disposition of the case. This would include, for example, a social enquiry report requested by a court prior to sentencing.

The court may attach other conditions to the granting of bail as appropriate. Generally speaking, lodging of a sum of money in court by way of guaranteeing future appearances is not required unless there are special circumstances.

It is important to note that breach of any of the bail conditions, except committing another offence while on bail, is itself a criminal offence. So, for example, if a person on bail refused to co-operate

1 See S Warner and G McIvor *Pre-Trial Services in Scotland: An Evaluation of Two Experimental Bail Information and Accommodation Schemes* (1994).

with a social worker in the compilation of a social enquiry report, that would be breaching one of the conditions of bail and committing a further offence. Where an offence is committed while on bail, that breach of bail conditions is to be reflected in the sentence imposed for that offence.

### *(f) Appeals*

Appeals can be made against both conviction and sentence, and the prosecution have a right of appeal against sentence either on a point of law or if the sentence, or a condition attached to it, such as a condition in a probation order, is considered to be too lenient. An offender who wishes to appeal must obtain leave to appeal from the High Court. Offenders can also appeal against sentence or conviction by way of bill of suspension where a miscarriage of justice is claimed. If the appeal is against sentence, the sentence must be shown to be unreasonable. There is a slight disincentive to appealing against sentence, in that the court can increase as well as decrease the sentence on appeal. The Crime and Punishment (Scotland) Act 1997 provides for the setting up of a Scottish Criminal Cases Review Commission, which will have the power to refer cases back to the High Court where this is in the interests of justice, or where there has been a miscarriage of justice.

### *(g) Accelerated diets*

There is provision for accelerated diets to take place. This would happen when an accused who has pled not guilty changes his/her plea to guilty, sometimes after some negotiation of the charges with the prosecution, and wishes the matter dealt with before the date set for the trial diet. In solemn procedure this was known as 'section 102 procedure'.[1]

### *(h) Scottish Criminal Cases Review Commission*

The Crime and Punishment (Scotland) Act 1997, if implemented, provides for the setting up of the Scottish Criminal Cases Review Commission.[2] This body will have the power to review cases and to refer them back to the Court of Criminal Appeal.

1 After s 102 of the Criminal Procedure (Scotland) Act 1975. The current provisions are contained in s 76 of the Criminal Procedure (Scotland) Act 1995.

2 Crime and Punishment (Scotland) Act 1997, s 25 inserting a new Part XA into the Criminal Procedure (Scotland) Act 1995.

## 9. EVIDENCE

In normal circumstances, individuals make use of a wide range of information in order to arrive at conclusions about things. For example, we use physical evidence, things which can be directly perceived, we use information from other people, and we use information about the reported comments of other people. When it comes to taking decisions in court, however, the range of evidence which can be use is restricted. More specifically, if evidence is to be accepted by a court it must be:

(1) relevant;
(2) admissible; and
(3) given by a competent witness.

### (1) Relevant evidence

Relevant evidence is simply evidence which is relevant to proving the matter before the court. Evidence of other matters, such as the past history of the parties or of the accused in a criminal case, are not generally relevant and will not be allowed to be led in evidence. In other words, there must be some logical link between the evidence and the matter before the court.

### (2) Admissible evidence

This is evidence which is not excluded by some rule of law, that is evidence which will be admissible provided it does not run foul of one of the exclusions provided for by the law. Some of these exclusions are:

*(a) Hearsay evidence*

This is considered more fully below.

*(b) Evidence obtained improperly*

One example of this is evidence that the police have obtained illegally in a criminal case, for example by carrying out a search without a necessary warrant or procuring a confession through violence or the threat of violence. The exclusion also applies in civil cases and, of course, in cases involving children. One area where this has been an issue is in cases where the courts have taken the view that social workers and police have not acted properly in obtaining evidence of child abuse. The courts may then take the view that such evidence cannot be relied on (though this may be a question of credibility rather than admissibility) and the referral to a children's hearing based on that evidence is discharged. This is essentially what seems to have happened in the case involving the families in Ayrshire which was decided by the Court of Session in March 1995.[1]

### *(c) Evidence protected by privilege*

In certain circumstances the relationship between two parties may be privileged, with the result that information passing between them is privileged and disclosure of this information cannot be required by the court. The main example of this is the solicitor/client relationship. This, indeed, seems to be the only clearly established case, and it is apparent that privilege does not apply to communications between a social worker and service user. English courts have recognised a 'public interest privilege'. In one case it was held that this allowed the NSPCC to refuse to disclose the identity of someone who had made an allegation of child abuse to the NSPCC.[2] The view of courts in Scotland is that there is no such concept as 'public interest privilege': instead, information will be protected by confidentiality. This was certainly the view expressed in a case where an adoptive parent sought access to social work records concerning the adopted child. It was said that:

> '... [I]f a case arose in Scotland in which a party sought to recover from the RSSPCC [now Children First] the name of an informer, it would only be in exceptional circumstances that such a motion would be granted. This would not be because public interest privilege is extended to the RSSPCC, but because the nature of the work of that body is such that their claim to confidentiality would be awarded a high degree of protection.'[3]

Such information is not, of course, required to be revealed under the Access to Personal Files Act 1987.[4]

1 See *JL v Kennedy* (6 March 1995, unreported) IH.
2 *D v NSPCC* [1978] AC 171.
3 *P v Tayside Regional Council* 1989 SCLR 165 at 168. See also *Davers v Butler* 1994 SCLR 717; *A v G* 1996 SCLR 787.
4 See ch 2, pt 6(3).

*(d) Opinion evidence*

In general, witnesses are not allowed to express opinions in giving evidence. The main exception to this rule is in respect of expert witnesses, who are permitted to make statements of their opinions about facts which they may or may not have observed for themselves. Social workers may be called upon to act as expert witnesses in their areas of competence and expertise.[1] Such expert evidence, it should be noted, does not supersede the court: the court has to take its decision on the basis of the whole evidence presented to it, which frequently involves competing opinions expressed by experts. Of course, it is often not possible to question a non-expert witness without seeking expressions of opinion, for example as to whether a car was being driven fast, or as to whether someone appeared to be upset, and it has been argued that identification evidence is, in fact, opinion evidence.[2] There seems to be no clear rule of law explaining to what extent non-experts can state opinions.

## (3) A competent witness

A witness is competent, that is, legally permitted to give evidence, if the person understands the notion of giving evidence and can clearly understand the requirement to tell the truth. In practice, the assumption is that everyone is a competent witness unless they are excluded by a rule of law. It should be noted that there is no exclusion of children from giving evidence, and the evidence of children as young as 3½ and 4 has been heard in criminal cases. In each case the question which the court has to address is whether the child is competent in the sense noted above. Because each child is different, no general rule can be set down. The competence of the child can be established either by the sheriff or judge asking the child questions in court[3] or, particularly where hearsay evidence is involved (see below), through evidence from others about the child's competence.

1 See ch 7, pt 2(4).
2 See, for example, D Field and F Raitt *Evidence*, (2nd edn, 1996), para 16-04.
3 As in *M v Kennedy* 1993 SCLR 69.

## (4) Hearsay evidence

The hearsay rule is defined in one of the modern Scottish texts on evidence as providing that:

> 'An assertion other than one made by a person while giving oral evidence is inadmissible as evidence of any fact (or opinion) asserted.'[1]

In other words, any statement made by a third party and reported to court by a witness is not admissible as evidence that what is claimed in the statement actually happened. It is only admissible as evidence of the fact that the statement was made. Assume, for example, that X said to Y 'I saw Ramon Mercador killing Trotsky'. If Y was subsequently called as a witness in the trial of Mercador and repeated the statement made by X, that would only be evidence that the statement was made: it would not be evidence, admissible by the court, that Mercador killed Trotsky. There are, however, some exceptions to the general rule where hearsay is admissible evidence of the facts contained in the second hand statement. The main exceptions are:

### *(a) Civil cases*

As a result of the Civil Evidence (Scotland) Act 1988, the hearsay rule was abolished for all civil proceedings in Scotland. This includes all proof hearings on grounds of referral to a children's hearing except where the ground of referral is that the child has committed an offence. The case of *F v Kennedy (No 2)*[2] illustrates the effect of this provision. At a proof hearing a child witness, J, was called to give evidence. In addition, evidence was given of statements which J had made on previous occasions. These statements were not put to J when he was giving evidence and he was not asked about them. They were reported by other witnesses as hearsay evidence. The child's father challenged the decision to admit J's hearsay evidence, arguing that proceeding in this way was at odds with the best evidence rule which would require J to give all of his evidence in court. The challenge was rejected. The Inner House of the Court of Session took the view that 'the fact that the maker of the statement has given oral evidence does not prevent hearsay evidence being given of what he has said upon another occasion.' They then continued: '... there may well be occasions where it will

1 A B Wilkinson *The Scottish Law of Evidence* (1986), p 34.
2 1993 SLT 1284.

be difficult to take the whole of a child's evidence in court. It may therefore be important for the sheriff to be able to rely to some extent at least on hearsay evidence of what the child has said on other occasions.'[1] In one case, hearsay evidence in the form of a statement made to the police was accepted by the sheriff even though the statement was retracted by the witness when she appeared before him.[2]

Before a hearsay statement made by a child can be admitted into evidence, it must be established that at the time of the statement the child would have been a competent witness. One question that might arise is: what happens if the child is competent at the time the statement is made but subsequently becomes incompetent and is so at the time of the court hearing? This question was raised, but not decided, in *M v Kennedy*,[3] where it was suggested that in such a case 'careful attention will have to be given to the leading of evidence about the child's ability to give a trustworthy account at the time when he made the statement and as to the reason or reasons why that test cannot be satisfied when the time comes for the child to give evidence.'[4] In that case an elective mute was held to be a competent witness. More recently, in *L v L*[5] the view was taken that before hearsay evidence of a child's statements could be heard, the child had to be examined by the judge to confirm that he/she was a competent witness. The view was also taken that the date at which competence had to be assessed was the date of the hearing. These views seem slightly at odds with earlier decisions, and with the later view expressed by Lord Hope in the House of Lords when he said that 'it would be sufficient to satisfy the test of competency that the child was a competent witness at the time when the statements were made.'[6] This clearly indicates that examination in court is not always necessary and that the competence of a child witness at the time the statements were made can be established by other evidence.

### *(b) Res gestae*

Where statements are made as part of the events which are claimed to constitute an offence, they will be admissible, even though the

1 1993 SLT 1284 at 1287F-H.
2 *K v Kennedy* 1993 SLT 1281.
3 1993 SCLR 69.
4 Ibid at 78F-G.
5 1996 SCLR 11.
6 *Sanderson v McManus* 1997 SLT 629 at 632K.

identity of the maker of the statement is unknown. One of the standard texts on evidence suggests that two obvious examples of statements forming part of the *res gestae* would be the screams and protests of a rape victim and the use of nicknames in an unguarded moment by members of a team of hooded armed robbers.[1]

*(c) Confessions*

Confessions made by an accused either to the police or to someone else are admissible evidence.

*(d) Previous inconsistent statements*

Where a witness departs from a previous statement, for example if a footballer originally told police that he had been head butted but in the witness box suggests that the head contact was accidental, the previous statement is admissible to attack the credibility of the witness and the evidence being given.

*(e) Statements made by someone who can no longer give evidence*

One example of this is a statement by someone who has died since the statement was made.

*(f) Criminal cases*

Under the Criminal Procedure (Scotland) Act 1995 hearsay evidence can be admitted in criminal trials where someone who would be a competent witness cannot be found, has been authorised not to give evidence on the grounds that to do so might incriminate him/her, or refuses to give evidence.

### (5) Corroboration

Corroboration requires that each fact essential to proving a case is supported by two pieces of evidence. The two pieces of evidence need not be statements by eye witnesses, but may be physical evidence, for example fingerprints, or medical evidence, or circum-

1 Field and Raitt *Evidence* para 8-21.

stantial evidence. The requirement for corroboration no longer applies in civil cases, though the existence of corroboration will strengthen a case. Corroboration is still required in criminal cases (and in referrals based on commission of an offence) and in such cases there are two things which must be established by corroborated evidence: that the crime was committed and that the accused committed it.

### (6) Deciding on the evidence

Once all the relevant admissible evidence has been led, the court has to arrive at a decision on the case. In order to do this it will have to decide whether the evidence led discharges the burden of proof imposed on the parties involved in the case before it. In criminal cases it will have to decide whether the prosecution have proved their case beyond a reasonable doubt; in civil cases whether the pursuer has established his/her case on the balance of probabilities. In arriving at its decision the court will have to weigh up the evidence before it. Doing this involves the court looking at whether the evidence was direct or circumstantial, the sufficiency of any corroboration, the coherence of the evidence and, perhaps most importantly assessing the credibility of the evidence. This last matter is often of crucial importance because there will often be directly contradictory evidence before the court. In such cases the decision as to who is a credible witness will have an important bearing on the outcome of the case.

### (7) Children giving evidence[1]

In criminal cases, there are three procedures designed to make giving evidence less stressful for a child who is called to give evidence and to give the child some degree of protection.[2]

(a) In appropriate cases, the child can be permitted to give evidence via a live video link. A court faced with a request to allow

1 The Crime and Punishment (Scotland) Act 1997, s 29 extends these methods of taking evidence to 'vulnerable people'.

2 The procedural aspects are dealt with in the Act of Adjournal (Criminal Procedure Rules) 1996, SI 1996/513, rr 22.1 and 22.2.

this has to take into account the possible effect on the child if the application is **not** granted and whether the child will be better able to give evidence if the application **is** granted. Relevant considerations include the age and maturity of the child, the nature of the evidence he/she is likely to give, and the relationship, if any, between the child and the accused.[1]

(b) A screen can be placed so as to conceal the accused from the child giving evidence. The same considerations apply to granting an application for this as apply to the permitting of live video evidence.[2]

(c) An application can be made to allow the evidence of the child to be taken on commission, with the proceedings being videotaped.[3]

## 10. EUROPEAN COURTS

### (1) European Court of Justice

The European Court of Justice is the court of the European Union and is responsible for the interpretation of European Union legislation. This interpretation is authoritative and affects the law in member states. The court has made a number of significant decisions regarding equal pay and equal rights at work.

### (2) European Court of Human Rights

The United Kingdom is a signatory to the European Convention on Human Rights and has accepted the jurisdiction of the Court in disputes under the Convention. The procedure for making and deciding on an application is complex and time consuming. Britain has been found guilty of breaches of the Convention on a number of occasions in cases concerning, for example, the censoring of prisoners' mail and the rights of parents of children in care. In early

1 Criminal Procedure (Scotland) Act 1995, s 271.
2 Ibid.
3 Ibid.

1995 in the case of *McMichael v United Kingdom*[1] the UK was held to be in breach of the requirement of the Convention that everyone is entitled to a fair hearing. The fact that the child and his family appearing before a children's hearing were not allowed to see the social background report prepared for the hearing was held to be in breach of this requirement.[2] At the time of writing the government is intending to incorporate the provisions of the Convention into United Kingdom law. This would mean that courts in Scotland would be able to consider its provisions in deciding a case.

## 11. CHILDREN'S HEARINGS

The system of children's hearings was introduced by the Social Work (Scotland) Act 1968 to deal with a whole range of cases relating to children which were formerly dealt with in a variety of different courts. These include offences committed by children, children beyond parental control, children against whom offences may have been committed and children who truant. The relevant provisions (Part III, with the exception of s 31) of the 1968 Act have been repealed and replaced by provisions in Part II of the Children (Scotland) Act 1995. Children's hearings are considered in greater detail in chapter 5, part 3.

## 12. ADMINISTRATIVE TRIBUNALS

Administrative tribunals have been set up to adjudicate in a wide variety of areas affected by state intervention. Examples are social security appeal tribunals, rent assessment committees and industrial tribunals. Procedure and the rules of representation before tribunals are generally much more relaxed than those before courts. This opens up greater possibilities for the representation, for example, of claimants before social security appeals tribunals. This is particularly important as there is evidence to suggest that claimants who are represented have a greater chance of success than those who are not. Welfare rights officers and social workers are sometimes found representing claimants.

1 [1995] 20 EHRR 205.
2 See ch 5, pt 3(8).

## 13. JUDICIAL REVIEW

Judicial review is a procedure by which decisions of many public bodies may be challenged. It differs from appeal in that the right to seek review exists without the express statutory provision which is needed to create a right of appeal; indeed the courts have sometimes reviewed decisions in spite of specific statutory provisions excluding their jurisdiction. This makes review particularly useful in cases where there is no provision for appeal against a decision.

There are, however, two major drawbacks to using judicial review to challenge decisions. The first of these is that actions for judicial review can be dealt with only by the Court of Session in Edinburgh. This is not as much of a problem as it used to be following the introduction of a simpler and quicker form of procedure, though it makes the process more expensive than it would otherwise be. The second drawback is that review can be sought only on restricted grounds. To succeed the applicant must be able to show that the person or body taking the decision acted outwith their powers (that is, *ultra vires*), acted unreasonably, or did not comply with the requirements of natural justice. (For examples and further discussion, see chapter 8).

Despite these drawbacks judicial review has been a valuable remedy in certain areas. The most prominent in recent years has been its use by people who have been refused accommodation under the homelessness legislation, made necessary because there is no statutory provision for appeal against a local authority decision to refuse housing. One example is the case of *Kelly v Monklands District Council.*[1] In this case a 16-year-old girl left home because of violence by her father against her. She had nowhere to stay and had attempted suicide. She applied for housing as a homeless person. One of the cases in which an authority is bound to provide housing is if the applicant is vulnerable. The local authority decided that Ms Kelly was not vulnerable despite a report from the social work department to the contrary. The court decided that the authority had acted unreasonably in arriving at its conclusion on vulnerability and in not taking proper account of the report from the social work department. The council was ordered to house Ms Kelly.[2]

1 1986 SLT 169.
2 See also ch 2, pt 2(3).

## 14. LEGAL AID

Legal aid in Scotland is administered by the Scottish Legal Aid Board. There are three types of legal aid: legal advice and assistance; civil legal aid; and criminal legal aid.

### (1) Legal advice and assistance

This is a means tested scheme which provides free advice and assistance to applicants who qualify on the basis of a means test. Above the qualifying level for free assistance there is a sliding scale for contribution up to the point where full payment must be made. People in receipt of income support or family credit qualify automatically on income grounds, but may be ineligible through their ownership of capital above the permitted limit. The decision as to entitlement is made by the solicitor who is approached for advice.

Legal advice and assistance covers advice about any matter of Scots law and, with very limited exceptions, only covers assistance short of representation before a court or tribunal. One exception is appeals under the Mental Health (Scotland) Act 1984.[1]

### (2) Civil legal aid

Civil legal aid is available to raise or defend actions in the civil courts. Once again it is means tested, and again those in receipt of income support or family credit qualify automatically on income grounds. As with legal advice and assistance there is a sliding scale of contributions above the level of free entitlement, up to the point where the applicant is not entitled to any assistance.

This is the type of legal aid that would be appropriate for actions under the Children (Scotland) Act 1995, for example proof hearings in the sheriff court, and for adoption proceedings.

In urgent cases emergency legal aid can be obtained immediately. This might be necessary, for example, to allow a woman to obtain an interim exclusion order excluding a violent spouse from the family home.[2]

1 See ch 6, pt 5.
2 See ch 3, pt 4(2).

Children are entitled to apply for legal aid in their own right, and there are special rules for calculating their eligibility.

### (3) Criminal legal aid

The operation of this scheme depends on whether or not the first appearance in court is made from custody and whether the prosecution is solemn or summary. Applications for legal aid in solemn cases are decided by the court while applications in summary cases go to the Board. The granting of legal aid is almost automatic in solemn cases. The only ground for refusal is that the accused could pay for his/her defence without undue hardship. Where an accused appears in court from custody that person is entitled to be represented by the duty solicitor assigned to that court.

## 15. THE SOCIAL WORK (SCOTLAND) ACT 1968

### (1) Introduction

The Social Work (Scotland) Act 1968 (the 1968 Act) grew out of two developments. The first was a trend towards generic social work based on the view that social work with all types of people has a common base of values and skills. The second was the recommendation of the Kilbrandon Report[1] for the setting up of a social education department to provide support for the children's hearings which the report proposed. These two developments were brought together in the White Paper *Social Work and the Community*[2] which formed the basis for the 1968 Act.

The 1968 Act was one of the core pieces of legislation, providing much of the framework for the activities of social workers employed by local authorities, as well as setting down specific duties and specific procedures that have to be followed in particular circumstances. Although most of the provisions relating to children have been replaced by the Children (Scotland) Act 1995, the basic provisions of the 1968 Act regarding the overall duties and

1 *Children and Young Persons* Cmnd 2306 (1964).
2 Cmnd 3065 (1966).

powers of social workers remain in place and it is worth undertaking a brief survey of the Act at this point. It must be remembered, of course, that the 1968 Act is only one of a large number of statutes conferring duties and powers on social workers.

The major contribution of the 1968 Act, as far as provision of social work services is concerned, was to draw all of the disparate services provided by local authorities into one department under one overall director and with a council committee responsible for its oversight. This has been changed for the new councils which came into existence in April 1996. These must appoint a chief social work officer, but there is no longer any requirement to have a separate social work committee.[1]

## (2) Persons in need and assessments

In keeping with the interventionist tenor of the times, section 12 of the 1968 Act imposes an overall duty to 'promote social welfare' by making available advice, guidance and assistance and securing the provision of facilities, including residential accommodation.

This section also allows the provision of assistance in cash or kind in certain circumstances[2]. This type of assistance can be provided in an emergency to a 'person in need' (see below) aged 18 or over where doing so would avoid greater cost to the local authority either in the provision of some other service, such as the direct provision of accommodation, or at some future date because of aggravation of the person's need. Social work departments have their own policies and practices in relation to the giving of section 12 assistance. It should be noted that it is not intended to operate as an alternative to the benefits system: indeed consideration must be given to the person's eligibility for assistance from any other statutory body and the availability of that assistance before a payment is made. Section 12 payments can be made conditional on repayment.

Various interpretations in different authorities and within authorities have led to enormous variation in the use of section 12. Strategies which have encompassed the promotional use of these funds and those which have used the funds for preventative services have come and gone over the years. The bureaucratic hierarchical structures of social work departments have also been reflected in

1 Local Government etc (Scotland) Act 1994, ss 45, 180 and Sch 14.
2 See also ch 4, pt 2(10).

the policies of departments regarding the amounts of section 12 money which can be dispensed to the public by various grades of staff. For example, many basic grade social workers can dispense only £10 without authorisation from a higher grade member of staff.

Section 14 deals with the provision of domiciliary services (usually referred to as home helps) for households including a person in need or an expectant mother, and also the provision of laundry services in such cases.

As we have seen these provisions refer to persons in need, defined in the 1968 Act as being persons who:

(a) are in need of care and attention arising out of infirmity, youth or age; or
(b) suffer from illness or mental disorder or are substantially handicapped by any deformity or disability; or
(c) being persons prescribed by the Secretary of State who have asked for assistance, are, in the opinion of a local authority, persons to whom the local authority may appropriately make available the services and facilities provided by them under the 1968 Act.[1]

In addition, for the purposes of section 12 only, the definition is extended to include those in need as a result of drug or alcohol dependence and release from prison or other form of detention.[2]

Section 12A of the Act, added by the National Health Service and Community Care Act 1990, requires the authority to carry out an assessment of need before providing 'community care services'. This provision, which took effect from 1 April 1993, is considered more fully in chapter 6, part 3.

## (3) Reports and supervision of offenders

Section 27 deals with the responsibilities of the social work department in relation to the provision of reports to criminal courts and the provision of supervision to probationers and those released from custody on licence. Chapter 7, parts 2, 4 and 8, looks at this area in more detail.

1 Social Work (Scotland) Act 1968, s 94(1). The Secretary of State has not made use of the power given here.
2 Social Work (Scotland) Act 1968, s 12(6).

### (4) Residential establishments

Part IV of the Act deals with the provision of residential establishments by local authorities and provides a system for registration with the local authority of other residential establishments, for example private residential homes for persons who are elderly.

### (5) Complaints procedure

Local authorities must have a complaints procedure to deal with representations (including complaints) about the authority's performance, or lack of performance, of their obligations under the 1968 Act and various other pieces of legislation, such as the Disabled Persons (Services, Consultation and Representation) Act 1986. There is no national representations procedure: rather, each authority will have developed its own within the context of directions issued by the Secretary of State. In broad outline, these directions require a two-stage process. Intial investigation is carried out by an officer of the local authority. If the service user is dissatisfied with the outcome of this, there is a right to have the complaint considered by a review committee which must include an independent person as the chair.[1]

## 16. THE CHILDREN (SCOTLAND) ACT 1995

The years between the passing of the Children Act 1989, which made major changes to child care law in England and Wales, and the Children (Scotland) Act 1995 were relatively tumultuous ones for child care in Scotland. Initially, the view had been that unlike the position in England and Wales, Scotland did not require a major overhaul of child care law. Many events, including ones in Orkney, Fife and Ayrshire, provided the impetus and the ammunition to thoroughly take stock, adapt some initiatives from south of the border and move beyond those innovations to others designed to take child care law in Scotland into the next millennium. Additionally, a paradigm shift occurred which is seen in the move from parental rights to parental responsibilities and children's rights holding a central position and which reflects the significance of the United Nations *Convention on the Rights of the Child.*

1 The Social Work (Representations Procedure) (Scotland) Directions 1996.

The new law does not codify the law and so other provisions relating to children, for example in the Adoption (Scotland) Act 1978, remain in force. It is a complicated piece of legislation which has generally been welcomed by professionals in the field, in spite of what one commentator refers to as provisions 'which undermine the whole philosophy upon which the Act purports to be based'.[1] Norrie notes that in spite of the shift to an emphasis on parental responsibilities, a third of all fathers who are not married to the mothers of their children are specifically excluded, and that the power of a sheriff to substitute his/her own disposal in the place of one made by the children's hearing challenges the previous acceptance that the children's hearing was the most appropriate venue for long-term decision-making for children in need of supervision.

Part I (sections 1–15) sets out the private law and law in relation to parental responsibilities. Part II (sections 16–93) covers the duties of local authorities to children in their area (chapter 1), provisions for children's hearings and child protection (chapters 2 and 3), and arrangements for parental responsibilities orders (chapter 4). Part III (sections 94–98) and Schedule 2 set out changes to adoption law and Part IV (sections 99–105) sets out miscellaneous provisions.

1 K Norrie *The Children (Scotland) Act 1995* (1995) p 36–5.

# 2. General law relevant to social work

## 1. INTRODUCTION

As well as a knowledge of what has been described as professional law, namely, that law which is central to the professional activities of a social worker, social workers also need to have some knowledge of other areas of law in order to be able to assist service users with some of the problems and concerns they may have. This chapter is intended to give a brief outline of the law in the areas of housing, discrimination, debt, access to information and education. The coverage is not exhaustive and we have attempted to give further references where more detail may be found. It may also be the case that where a service user has a problem in these areas counsel to seek qualified legal advice, perhaps under the legal advice and assistance scheme, would be warranted. The first edition of this text contained a section on welfare benefits. It has been omitted from this edition for a number of reasons, but mainly because of the frequent changes in benefits and because in the space available it was not possible to give proper coverage of the topic. References to various benefits will still be found at various stages in the text as appropriate.[1] This omission is not to deny or undervalue the indisputable link between material deprivation and a range of other factors which bring people to social workers and one which can not be ignored. It therefore follows that a basic understanding of the benefits system is a crucial component in a social worker's repertoire. Social workers have no legal mandate to become involved in benefit matters other than in pursuing the general obligation to promote social welfare, but notions of good practice suggest that until material needs are addressed, other needs are less accessible. In some social work departments there is an expectation that benefits checks will be carried out for new service users.

1 See, for example, CPAG *Rights Guide to Means Tested Benefits* and *National Welfare Benefits Handbook*. Both of these are revised and republished annually.

## 2. HOUSING

Housing problems experienced by social work service users are not always limited to the bricks and mortar. The typology of problems identified by Gill Stewart and John Stewart[1] provides an excellent framework for making sense of and exploring these problems: ones arising from changing personal relationships and family patterns; ones which initially seem to be individually based but relate more to how society views specific groups of service users; and ones which are rooted directly in the quality of the housing. The links between housing problems and other problems which seriously detract from service users' quality of life, such as health and parenting, are undeniable. These links provide the rationale and urgency for social workers to 'think housing'[2] when assessing.

### (1) Rights to repair

Certain obligations are imposed on all landlords whether in the private or public sector to repair rented houses. In this context the public sector consists mainly of houses let by local authorities and by Scottish Homes. Houses let by housing associations are now regarded as being in the private sector, at least as far as most legislation is concerned.

There is a general common law duty to keep premises wind and water tight and in a proper tenantable condition. An example of breach of this duty is *McArdle v City of Glasgow District Council*[3] where a tenant successfully sued the landlord for damages as a result of chronic dampness in the flat.

There are also a number of statutory obligations imposed on landlords:

(a) Properties let for a rent of less than £300 per week (that is, most properties) must be in all respects fit for human habitation at the start of the tenancy and must be maintained in that condition by the landlord. In deciding whether the property is fit for human habitation consideration is given to the extent to which the house falls short of the requirements of the building

1 G and J Stewart *Social Work and Housing* (1988).
2 *Social Work and Housing*, p 21.
3 1989 SCLR 19.

regulations.[1] In *Quinn v Monklands District Council*[2] the local authority was held to be in breach of this obligation. As a result of condensation a number of rooms in a flat were affected by black mould, treatment of which required the tenant to leave the property for a period. She was awarded compensation for property damaged by the mould and for inconvenience and the general depression caused by the state of the premises.[3]

(b) For properties let for less than seven years the landlord must keep the structure and exterior of the house in good repair and inside the house must keep the gas, water and electricity supply, the sanitary appliances, and space and water heaters in good repair and working properly.[4] The restriction on the length of tenancies has little practical effect as most tenancies, including those in the public sector, are for less than seven years.

(c) Where the landlord is responsible for the maintenance and repair of the premises he/she must take reasonable care in carrying out this responsibility so as to prevent danger to people coming into the premises. *Hughes' Tutrix v Glasgow District Council*[5] is an example where a mother successfully sued for damages for her daughter who was injured on a defective toilet bowl.

In addition to the statutory and common law responsibilities other obligations may be imposed on the landlord in the lease of the property. If the landlord fails in carrying out these obligations the tenant has a number of remedies. The tenant may, unless this is excluded by the lease, withhold his/her rent or take legal action against the landlord for damages or for an order requiring the landlord to meet his/her obligations. Where the tenant withholds rent all of the arrears of rent must be repaid when the landlord fixes the defect, unless the property was in such a state that a lower rent was appropriate during the period of disrepair.[6] Public sector tenants also have limited powers to have repairs carried out themselves if their landlord fails to do them and to recover the costs and a small compensation payment from the landlord. This power arises only in respect of a limited list of repairs, including blocked drains, loss

1 Housing (Scotland) Act 1987, Sch 10.
2 1995 SCLR 393.
3 Most of the reported cases in this area concern problems with dampness or condensation, usually caused by poor building design.
4 Housing (Scotland) Act 1987, Sch 10.
5 1982 SLT (Sh Ct) 70.
6 See *Renfrew District Council v Gray* 1987 SLT (Sh Ct) 70.

of electrical power and insecure doors and windows, and then only if the landlord fails to carry out repairs within a specified time after being notified (usually one day).[1]

Councils also have power to take action against properties which are in disrepair or which are dangerous to health. They may, of course, be reluctant to use these powers where they own the property.

Social workers have no mandatory duties in relation to people whose assessed needs relate to the completion of housing repairs other than under the general umbrella of the duty to promote social welfare contained in section 12 of the Social Work (Scotland) Act 1968. However, a social worker may be well placed to advise the service user what legal obligations fall to the landlord and what remedies fall to the tenant.

Using the legal knowledge available to inform social work practice can contribute to the empowerment of the service user in arranging, for example, for repairs to be completed. It may well be agreed that the social worker becomes actively involved taking on the role of liaison or advocate with the housing authority, while continuing to support the service user through what may well be experienced as a very stressful experience.

### (2) Eviction

Generally, tenants cannot be removed from a property until the landlord has obtained an order for recovery of possession of the property from the sheriff court. Before any landlord can commence court proceedings to obtain such an order for recovery of possession of property, he/she must serve a **notice to quit** or, in public sector tenancies, a **notice of intention to start proceedings** on the tenant. This applies to all tenancies, whether or not they enjoy some other form of statutory protection (see below) and must give the tenant at least 28 days notice.[2] In addition, where the tenant enjoys some form of statutory protection, the notice to quit must contain certain specified information including advice to the tenant on possible sources of information and assistance. If the notice to quit does not contain this information it is invalid, and the landlord cannot rely on it in proceedings for recovery of possession. For

1 Secure Tenants (Right to Repair) (Scotland) Regulations 1994, SI 1994/1046.
2 Sheriff Courts (Scotland) Act 1907, ss 37, 38; Rent (Scotland) Act 1984, s 112; Housing (Scotland) Act 1987, s 47.

assured tenancies (basically private sector tenancies starting after January 1989) the notice to quit must be accompanied by a **notice of intention to raise an action for possession**.[1]

Tenancies enjoying statutory protection include nearly all public sector tenancies, as well as most in the private sector. The main exceptions are premises with a resident landlord and tenancies where the landlord is an educational institution. In this context it is perhaps worth noting that housing association tenants enjoy protection as public sector tenants if their tenancy started before January 1989; tenants with tenancies starting after that date are protected as assured tenants.

Where a tenant does enjoy some form of statutory protection the effect is that the court will grant an order for possession only on certain restricted grounds, such as non-payment of rent or causing a nuisance to neighbours. In the private sector, some of these grounds are mandatory, that is, the sheriff must grant an order for eviction if the ground is established. One example is if the tenant owes 3 months' rent arrears both at the time when the notice of proceedings was given and at the date of the court hearing.

Finally, in many cases the sheriff has the power to adjourn the hearing. This power might be used, for example, to allow payment of arrears of rent or to allow a 'bad neighbour' to mend his/her ways. It is an offence for a private sector landlord to evict someone without following the correct legal procedure or to harass a tenant into leaving accommodation.[2] In both cases the tenant has a right to damages assessed on the difference in value between the house without the tenant and its value with a sitting tenant.[3] This can amount to a substantial sum.[4]

If possible, the social worker should help the service user identify the type of tenancy or facilitate the service user getting this information from a specialist agency or solicitor. This will, of course, influence which set of statutory procedures and protections apply. The process of possible eviction is potentially extremely stressful and if a social worker is involved with the person/family threatened with eviction there are a number of things which may prove helpful in diminishing unnecessary stress. For example, it may help the person/family to learn that the notice means that there are at least 28 days before the council (or other landlord) can apply to the

1 Housing (Scotland) Act 1988, s 19.
2 Rent (Scotland) Act 1984, ss 22 and 23.
3 Housing (Scotland) Act 1988, ss 36 and 37.
4 In *Tagro v Cafane* [1991] 2 All ER 235 damages were assessed at £31,000.

sheriff for an order for recovery of possession (an eviction order) and that they cannot be removed until there has been a hearing and the sheriff has issued such an order. If the notice to quit is not in the statutory form designed for this purpose, then the service user may be helped by learning that it is invalid.

So, the social worker should advise the service user not to leave his/her home unless alternative accommodation is already available and he/she wants to leave; to get legal advice under the legal advice and assistance scheme;[1] and to attend the court hearing and/or arrange for an application to be made to the court on their behalf. Tenants who attend the hearing or are represented at the hearing are less likely to be evicted.

The social worker may determine that it would be appropriate to negotiate with the service user to act as an advocate on his/her behalf to the housing authority or the sheriff court. The service user may require the social worker to act as liaison with other agencies for a limited period until his/her level of coping has been restored.

### (3) Homelessness

Homelessness is a growing problem both in Britain as a whole and in Scotland. There are a variety of reasons for this, including the decline in the private rented sector and the decline in the number of public sector houses available for rent. Some people are homeless or threatened with homelessness as defined in law (see below) and some are roofless and living rough. Many of these people have been identified as not in priority need, so the local authority has no statutory duty to secure the provision of accommodation but only to provide advice and assistance which may not be useful in actually finding a roof. The number of young people leaving local authority care who become homeless should be of particular concern to social workers.[2]

Until 1977 the duty to provide for those who became homeless rested on social work departments. In 1977 the Housing (Homeless Persons) Act was passed and this transferred the responsibility to housing authorities. It came into effect in Scotland on 1 April 1978. The law is now contained in Part II of the Housing (Scotland) Act 1987 (the 1987 Act) which operates in conjunction with a code of guidance issued to local authorities by

1 See ch 1, pt 14.
2 For an overview see J Greve *Homelessness in Britain* (1991).

the Secretary of State in 1991, though this is currently under review.[1]

The code of guidance is not binding on authorities or on the courts, but it may be taken into account in any proceedings for judicial review of a decision taken by a local authority in this area. The code emphasises the importance of considering the individual circumstances of each case. Experience under the previous code of guidance (issued in 1980) showed considerable variations in practice, and some practices contrary to the clear terms of the guidance contained in the code.[2]

The text below should be read in conjunction with the flow diagram at the end of the section. When someone approaches a housing authority for assistance the first obligation on the authority is to carry out initial inquiries. These may involve a request for information from the social work department. The code suggests that the investigation should be completed in 30 days. The inquiries are directed towards answering four questions:

(a) Is the applicant homeless or threatened with homelessness?
(b) Is the applicant in this position intentionally?
(c) Does the applicant have priority need?
(d) Does the applicant have a local connection with the authority dealing with the application?

While these inquiries are being carried out and if the authority has reason to believe that the applicant is homeless and has priority need, the authority must provide temporary accommodation.

*(a) Is the applicant homeless or threatened with homelessness?* A person is homeless for the purpose of the 1987 Act if **one** of the following three conditions is satisfied:

> (i) *If there is no accommodation in Great Britain that he/she is legally entitled to occupy together with his/her family or any other person it is reasonable for him/her to live with.* This means, for example, that if a family unit has no accommodation that they can occupy together then they will be homeless. The reference to another person with whom it is reasonable for an applicant to live could extend to a carer, and the applicant would be regarded as homeless if there was no accommodation which could be occupied together with the carer.

1 The Scottish Office *Tackling Homelessness* (May 1994).
2 Scottish Office Central Research Unit *Homelessness in Scotland* (1990).

(ii) *If accommodation is available, but it is not reasonable for him/her to continue living there.* Local housing conditions will be relevant in considering whether it is reasonable for an applicant to continue to live in the accommodation. The code suggests that it would not be reasonable for a person to remain in housing which is below the tolerable standard (for example, it is badly affected by damp, or has no bath/shower, or is structurally unstable, or has an outside toilet); bed and breakfast accommodation; or short-stay hostel accommodation. Violence from neighbours, racial harassment, overcrowding which is not a danger to health, or a danger to health created by the condition of the accommodation, though not mentioned in the code, would also be relevant to deciding whether it is reasonable to stay in accommodation.

(iii) *If accommodation is available to him/her but* either:

—*he/she cannot gain entry to the property;* or

—*occupying the property would lead to violence, or threats of violence which are likely to be carried out, by someone who shares the accommodation with the applicant or someone who has previously shared accommodation with the applicant, wherever that sharing may have taken place.* An example of the second category would be a woman moving from Edinburgh to Glasgow who was threatened with violence at her new address in Glasgow by someone she had lived with in Edinburgh. The code stresses that, if a claim about violence or the threat of violence is not supported by evidence in the normal sense, the expressed fears of the applicant should be accepted, unless there are compelling reasons suggesting the opposite. The code also makes the point that possession of an order under the Matrimonial Homes (Family Protection) (Scotland) Act 1981[1] excluding the violent partner from the home does not by itself mean that it is safe for the applicant to return home; or

—*the accommodation is a houseboat or mobile home but there is no mooring or pitching place available*; or

—*it is overcrowded as defined in the Housing (Scotland) Act 1987*[2] ***and*** *may endanger the health of the occupants.*

A person is threatened with homelessness if he/she is likely to become homeless within the next 28 days.

1 See ch 3, pt 4.

2 Sections 135–137. This consists of a room standard which is contravened if two people of opposite sex over ten who are not married have to share accommodation and a space standard which provides, for example, that a three-room house is overcrowded if more than five people over ten live there.

*(b) Is the applicant in this position intentionally?* For an applicant to be intentionally homeless the following conditions must be satisfied:

(i) The applicant must deliberately have done or failed to do something as a result of which occupation of available accommodation ceased. An example is deliberate failure to pay rent or a mortgage resulting in eviction.[1] There must be a clear causal connection between the act or omission on the part of the applicant and the homelessness. It must be the applicant who is responsible for the deliberate act or omission. The actions of one member of a family which might lead to that person being regarded as intentionally homeless do not necessarily mean that if another member of the family applies for housing that other family member will be so regarded.
(ii) It must be reasonable to have expected the applicant to remain in the accommodation. The physical and personal circumstances of the applicant must be taken into account in deciding whether it was reasonable for the applicant to remain in accommodation. The code suggests, for example, that severe emotional stress or overcrowding may be good reasons for leaving accommodation.
(iii) The applicant must have been aware of the consequence of his/her action, so an act done in ignorance of a relevant fact will not be significant. *Wincentzen v Monklands District Council*[2] illustrates this. In this case a young woman left home temporarily despite her father's warning, which she did not believe, that she would not be allowed to return. When she returned her father refused her access to the house. The Court of Session decided that she was not intentionally homeless as when she left she had acted in good faith and in ignorance of the relevant fact that her father meant what he said.

The concept of intentional homelessness was one of the compromises accepted during the passing of the 1977 Act. It was designed to reduce the demands for housing on local authorities by giving them a ground for refusing permanent accommodation. The status of intentionally homeless is not immutable: it can be reviewed as circumstances change and time passes. Finally, the code suggests that a victim of domestic violence should never be

1 Though the code suggests that where failure is due to real personal or financial difficulties this should not result in a finding of intentional homelessness.
2 1988 SLT 259.

regarded as intentionally homeless. The same considerations are relevant in deciding whether someone threatened with homelessness is in that position intentionally.

*(c) Does the applicant have priority need?* There are four categories of applicant with priority need:

(i) those who have dependent children, that is, children under the age of 16 or those under the age of 19 undergoing full-time education or training or who are unable to support themselves. The children must either be residing with the applicant or it must be reasonable to expect them to reside together. This last proviso ensures that families split up in temporary accommodation will not therefore be deprived of priority status. The code stresses that the normal expectation is that families would stay together under the same roof. Splitting of families should take place only on the basis of advice from the social work department that there are compelling reasons why the family should not live together;
(ii) those whose homelessness or threatened homelessness is due to an emergency, such as flood, fire or other disaster;
(iii) those who are or have somebody who might be expected to live with them who is vulnerable as a result of old age, mental illness or handicap, physical disabilities or other special reasons. The code of guidance suggests that this last category might include battered women without children, people at risk of racial harassment and homeless young people who are at risk of sexual or financial exploitation. In *Kelly v Monklands District Council*[1] a 16 year old girl who had left home because of violence, had nowhere else to stay, had attempted suicide and was described by the social work department as vulnerable was accepted by the court as having priority need although there was no evidence of possible sexual or financial exploitation;
(iv) those who are pregnant or who reside with a pregnant woman. Where a pregnant woman miscarries, her continued treatment as being in priority need depends on the policy of the particular local authority involved.

*(d) Does the applicant have a local connection with the authority dealing with the application?* A local connection is a connection arising from voluntary residence, from employment, from family

1 1986 SLT 169.

connections or from other special circumstances. The issue of local connection is relevant only if the applicant is in priority need and is not intentionally homeless. The question is: does the applicant have a local connection with the authority processing his/her application? If the answer is yes, then that authority must comply with the housing duty set out below. If the answer is no, a further question arises: does the applicant have a local connection with another area in Great Britain? If the answer to this is yes, the applicant's case can be notified to the authority for that area, but only if there would be no risk of domestic violence to the applicant if housed by this second authority. Should no local connection exist with another area, the duties outlined below fall on the council receiving the application.

If the notified authority accepts that there is a local connection and no risk of domestic violence, the obligation to secure housing devolves on it. If this is not accepted the duty remains with the notifying authority, which, in any event, has a duty to provide temporary housing while this decision is made. Note that the legislation refers to a local connection in Great Britain: a local connection in Northern Ireland would therefore be irrelevant.

### *(e) Local authority duties*

Once the authority has carried out its investigation and answered these questions it must notify the applicant of its decision and the reasons for it. Regardless of the decision the authority will have a duty to provide some form of assistance to the applicant. The nature of that assistance will depend on how the questions have been answered:

(i) The authority has a duty to provide advice and appropriate assistance where either:
  (a) it is satisfied that the applicant is homeless or threatened with homelessness but is not satisfied that he/she has priority need; or
  (b) where the applicant does have priority need but became homeless or threatened with homelessness intentionally.

(ii) Where the applicant is intentionally homeless and in priority need the local authority has a duty to secure the provision of accommodation for the applicant for such a period as will give the applicant a reasonable opportunity to secure permanent accommodation. The code of guidance suggests a period of 28 days.

(iii) The authority has a duty to take reasonable steps to ensure that accommodation does not cease to become available to the applicant where he/she has priority need and is threatened with homelessness but this is not intentional.

(iv) It has a duty to secure that accommodation becomes available to an applicant who has priority need and is not intentionally homeless. This obligation is only to **secure** the provision of accommodation: the actual provision may be done by someone other than the housing authority. Any accommodation provided must not be overcrowded and must not pose a threat to the health of the occupants.

### *(f) Challenging decisions*

There is no statutory provision for appeal against any of the decisions a local authority may take in processing an application by someone who is homeless or threatened with homelessness. Instead, the code suggests that local authorities should have an appeals mechanism, and most, if not all, authorities have some form of appeals procedure. Aside from these arrangements, the only way of challenging these decisions is by seeking judicial review of them in the Court of Session.[1]

### *(g) The social work rolew*

The Morris Committee emphasised that homelessness was an area in which 'there is an overwhelming need for effective co-operation between the two services [social work and housing]'.[2] The importance of co-operation is further stressed in the code of guidance which identifies a role for social work in, for example, the initial inquiries, in preventing arrears and evictions, and in providing support for rehoused families.

Since housing is a perpetually scarce resource and housing authorities are normally organised following the rules of large bureaucracies, it may well be justified and acceptable to both service user and social worker for the social worker to take an active role in assisting the service user with an application and in being supportive throughout the process. Prevention of homelessness is clearly preferable to dealing with the trauma associated with having

1 See ch 1, pt 13.

2 *Housing and social work: a joint approach* (1975, SDD), para 8.2.

already lost one's home, and a thorough assessment while co-operating with housing authorities is clearly the key in this respect. Accommodation provided, particularly temporary accommodation, can prove to be an additional source of anxiety and stress for people and so further warrant the involvement of a social worker. Particular difficulties for families centre on 'first, access to mainstream services particularly education, health services and social security benefits; and secondly, personal health and safety'.[1]

Through the provision of a comprehensive initial inquiry report, the social worker may provide relevant information highlighting the factors which are significant in determining the service user's eligibility. Some of these include availability of suitable accommodation, reasons for threatened homelessness or homelessness, responsibility for dependent persons, presence of persons vulnerable through various risks, emergency conditions, pregnancy, and local connection. In light of the decision in *Kelly v Monklands District Council*[2] that housing authorities must take social work reports and information into account in deciding on an application, social workers clearly can play an important part in the process by providing information about and advocating for a service user.

### (h) Conclusion

It should be noted that the statutory framework guiding housing authorities is just that: a framework. It allows considerable discretion to local authorities in how they put the law into practice. Indeed a study of how the legislation operated which was carried out in 1988 and published in 1990 concluded that:

> '. . . local authority discretion appears to be applied arbitrarily rather than flexibly. In other words, how applicants are treated . . . depends, to some extent at least, upon which local authority they apply to rather than upon a consistent evaluation of their circumstances'.[3]

This study also discovered that many authorities operated their policies in breach of the then existing code of guidance. The study formed part of the background to the revised code in 1991, which was intended to create greater consistency between different authorities. Research carried out in 1993 and published in 1994 concluded, however:

1 G and J Stewart *Social Work and Housing* (1988), p 87.
2 1986 SLT169. See also *Wilson v Nithsdale District Council* 1992 SLT 1131.
3 Scottish Office Central Research Unit *Homelessness in Scotland* (1990), para 4.20.

## HOMELESSNESS FLOW DIAGRAM

Is applicant homeless? → No → **No Further Action**

↓

Yes

↓

Yes ← Does Applicant have dependent children?

↓ ↓

No

↓ ↓

Yes ← Is homelessness caused by emergency/disaster?

↓ ↓

No

↓ ↓

Yes ← Is applicant/co-resident vulnerable/pregnant? → No → **Provide Advice/Assistance**

↓ ↓

Yes

↓ ↓

→ Is homelessness intentional? → Yes → **Provide Advice/Assistance & Temporary Accommodation**

↓

No

↓

Does applicant have local connection? → Yes → **Secure Provision of Accommodation**

↓

No

↓

Does applicant have local connection with another area? → No → **Secure Provision of Accommodation**

↓

Yes

↓

Would applicant be at risk of domestic violence in other area? → Yes → **Secure Provision of Accommodation**

↓

No

↓

**Notify Other Authority**

'Overall the research suggests that while there have been substantial improvements between 1988 and 1993 in the extent to which local authorities observe the Code of Guidance, there remain a number of issues where local authorities vary considerably in their adherence to the Code.'[1]

Examples of variation are whether the authority treats living in overcrowded accommodation as equivalent to homelessness; varying views on when an applicant is regarded as homeless; varying views as to priority in non-statutory cases; and variations in the definition of intentional homelessness.

It is therefore clearly the case that local authorities retain considerable discretion. Some authorities will simply provide the bare minimum: others will go beyond their strict statutory obligations and provide a more generous service for homeless people. For this reason a knowledge of how the policy is operated by particular authorities is of as much practical importance as an understanding of the legal framework.

## 3. DEBT RECOVERY

### (1) Court actions

Generally speaking, the process of debt recovery must be initiated by court action. In the vast majority of cases the action will be raised in the sheriff court and will take the form of a small claims action or a summary cause action. The former is available where the sum involved is less than £750, the latter for sums between £750 and £1,500.

Apart from the financial limits there are a number of other differences between small claims and summary causes, principally:

(a) Legal aid is available in summary causes, but not in small claims, although assistance for these can be obtained through the legal advice and assistance scheme.
(b) Procedure in court is intended to be much more informal in small claims cases.
(c) The summons in a small claim can be served by the sheriff clerk, while a summary cause summons must be served by a solicitor or sheriff officer.

1 Scottish Office Central Research Unit *The Code of Guidance on Homelessness* (1994), para 4.47.

(d) An individual can be represented by someone other than a solicitor at all stages in a small claim. Such representation is possible only at the first, largely formal, hearing of a summary cause.
(e) There is a restriction on the amount of expenses that can be awarded against the unsuccessful party in small claims. Currently the position is that, provided the defender has defended the action and has acted reasonably and in good faith, no expenses can be awarded where the claim is for less than £200, and above that there is a ceiling of £75 on the expenses that can be awarded against the unsuccessful party.[1]

Once a creditor has initiated action there are four courses of action open to the debtor. He/she can:

(a) defend the action. This would be appropriate if there was a dispute about the amount owed or the quality of goods or services supplied. In order to defend the action the relevant form attached to the summons should be returned to court by the date specified there. Failure to return this form, indicating an intention to defend, will allow the creditor to obtain a judgment in his/her favour simply by means of a written minute without the need to turn up in court on the appointed day;
(b) apply for a time to pay direction permitting payment by instalments or as a lump sum at some future date. Again, the relevant form must be returned to court with details of the proposal for repayment;
(c) do nothing. The result of this is that the creditor will get a judgment (decree) in his/her favour which will require payment of the whole amount, plus any legal expenses and interest, which is payable upon the service of an extract decree. In this situation, and providing that a warrant has not been granted for a warrant sale (see below), the debtor can apply to the court for a time to pay order, which has the same effect as a time to pay direction;
(d) pay the debt. If the debtor has already received a summons he/she will be liable for the creditor's legal expenses.

Even following the granting of a decree for payment of money to the creditor, the creditor may still decide to write off the debt if there is no realistic hope of payment. Sometimes the decree is sought to satisfy internal or external auditors. However, once a

1 Sheriff Courts (Scotland) Act 1971, s 36B(3). The restriction on expenses does not apply to appeals.

decree for the payment of money has been granted in favour of a creditor and he/she decides to pursue repayment, there are a number of courses of action (collectively known as 'diligence') open to the creditor if payment is still not forthcoming. The main forms of diligence are poinding and sale; arrestment; and arrestment of earnings.[1]

### (2) Poinding and sale

Poinding (pronounced 'pinding') involves the listing and valuation of all moveable property (basically all property except land and buildings) owned by the debtor, or owned jointly by the debtor and another person. This is followed by the sale of this property. There is an extensive list of items exempt from poinding. These include bedding, toys, heating and cooking appliances and floor coverings, all provided that they are reasonably required for use in the dwelling house by someone living in the house.[2]

Once a poinding has been carried out the articles poinded must not be removed or damaged. At this stage the debtor has the right to apply to court for recall of the poinding on the ground that it would be unduly harsh to proceed to a sale, that the total value fixed on the goods is less than their market value, or that the proceeds of the sale would not cover the expense of holding it.[3] In this context it is worth noting that research undertaken for the Scottish Law Commission established that in about 20% of warrant sales the proceeds did not cover the expenses.[4]

If no payment is made and the poinding is not recalled the creditor can then apply to court for a warrant to hold a sale. The sale no longer takes place in the debtor's house unless the debtor consents, but he/she is liable for the costs of removing the goods to the place of sale. Any surplus raised by the sale is returned to the debtor. If part of the debt remains outstanding it is still owed to the creditor. After a lengthy period of decline, warrant sales increased dramatically as local authorities sought to recover arrears of community charge and now council tax. These account for over half of poindings and over two-thirds of sales.[5]

1 These are largely regulated by the Debtors (Scotland) Act 1987.
2 Ibid, s 16.
3 Ibid, s 24. See eg *McCallum, Applicant* 1990 SLT (Sh Ct) 90.
4 Scottish Office Central Research Unit *The Characteristics of Warrant Sales* (1980), p 21.
5 Scottish Courts Administration *Civil Judicial Statistics* (1995), p 25.

### (3) Arrestment

Arrestment involves the freezing of assets belonging to or owed to the debtor, but which for the time being are in the hands of a third party. A common example would be money in a bank account. The effect of an arrestment is to prevent the third party dealing in any way with the property. In order for the debtor to have it released he/she must raise a separate action known as 'an action of furthcoming'. The effect of this is to order the third party to hand over to the creditor assets to the value owed by the debtor.

### (4) Arrestment of earnings

Arrestment of earnings involves an order to the debtor's employer to pay a part of the debtor's pay to the creditor. The order lasts until the debt is paid. There are statutory restrictions on the amount which can be deducted. There are two forms of arrestment of earnings: the earnings arrestment which covers ordinary debts and arrears of maintenance (that is, payments of periodical allowance or aliment); and current maintenance arrestment to enforce current maintenance payments.

### (5) Social work contribution

Increasingly people are finding themselves in debt. It is useful to distinguish between debt which is the result of inability to keep up with and pay for essentials like rent and fuel and debt which is associated with non-essential purchases and commitments. Sometimes the usual coping mechanisms fail. Some people panic and find themselves in a state of crisis. Many go to citizens' advice bureaux and some go to the social work department. The Social Work (Scotland) Act 1968, section 12 umbrella with the duty to promote social welfare and ensure that the local authority is saved greater expense at a later date, requires and enables social workers to become involved with people in debt.[1] Social workers are ideally placed to advise service users about the process of debt recovery:

1 The duties to children and families under s 17 of the Children (Scotland) Act 1995 may also be relevant. See ch 4.

reminding them, for example, that they may be eligible for legal aid; that they must return the summons to the court if they intend to defend the debt action; that they may apply for time to make payment toward the debt; that they may be subject to diligence (poinding and sale of their property or arrestment of assets or earnings); that only certain items of property are liable to be poinded; that they need not agree to have a warrant sale in their home; that any surplus money raised in such a sale belongs to them; and that only a limited amount of money may be arrested from their earnings.

Social workers may well provide support for families suffering from the stress of these procedures. If the debtor is eligible,[1] it may be possible for the social work department to provide material assistance as well. Families who have defaulted on the payment of mortgages may need advice and guidance about alternative accommodation. Increasingly people may be in a position of multiple indebtedness and it may be appropriate for a social worker to advocate on their behalf with creditors and negotiate to combine various debts and arrange feasible payments. Debtors may also be entitled to benefit, about which a social worker might advise them.

## 4. DISCRIMINATION

### (1) History and definitions

The earliest piece of legislation in this field was the Race Relations Act of 1965, which dealt with racial discrimination in places of public resort. A further Act was passed in 1968 and extended coverage to housing, employment, education and provision of services. The emphasis of both of these Acts was on providing a process of conciliation between the parties involved.

The earliest legislation on sex discrimination was the Equal Pay Act 1970, which requires equality of treatment in all matters relating to contracts of employment: it therefore covers such matters as holiday entitlement as well as earnings. This was not brought into force until 1975, at the same time as the Sex Discrimination Act 1975 which dealt with discrimination in other aspects of employment (for example, selection for employment, promotion and dismissal), in education, in provision of accommodation and in the

1 See ch 1, pt 15.

provision of goods, facilities and services. A further change was made in 1983, when a requirement that men and women should be paid equally for work of equal value was added to the existing requirement for equal pay for like work or work rated equally in an employer's evaluation study.

The sex discrimination legislation bans discrimination on the grounds of sex, and in terms of employment also prohibits less favourable treatment of married people.

Following doubts about the effectiveness of the earlier legislation the Race Relations Act 1976 was passed, based on the Sex Discrimination Act. It therefore covers the same areas as that Act but in addition creates a criminal offence of incitement to racial hatred[1] and imposes on local authorities a duty to carry out their functions with due regard to the need to eliminate unlawful discrimination and promote equality of opportunity and good relations between different racial groups. The 1976 Act deals with discrimination against someone on the grounds of their membership of a racial group. A racial group is defined by reference to colour, race, nationality, or ethnic or national origins.

## (2) Direct and indirect discrimination

The legislation prohibits both direct and indirect discrimination.[2] Direct discrimination takes place where someone is simply discriminated against on the basis of their race or sex. Indirect discrimination occurs where a general requirement is made that applies equally to everyone. If this requirement is such that members of a certain sex or racial group have less chance of meeting the requirement than others then the requirement will be indirectly discriminatory provided that it is not justifiable and that it has caused disadvantage to the person complaining. An example of this is a case where employers had agreed with a trade union that part-time workers would be made redundant first. When the case went to an industrial tribunal this was found to amount to indirect discrimination. The reason for this was that the proportion of women who could meet the requirement for avoiding redundancy, full-time employment, was considerably less than the proportion of

1 Now contained in the Public Order Act 1986.

2 For a fuller discussion of this see L Lustgarten *Legal Control of Racial Discrimination* (1980), chs 1 and 2.

men who could comply.[1] It should be noted that separate provision for different racial groups also amounts to discrimination.

### *(a) Exempted areas*

There are a number of areas which are exempted from the scope of the legislation and in which discrimination is still allowed. Examples include: special treatment of women in connection with pregnancy or childbirth; entertainment (where particular characteristics are required to play a role); and provision of personal social or welfare services where this can best be done by a member of a particular sex or racial group. This would allow the appointment of someone of a particular race and sex to provide social work services to a particular group. For example, a recent advertisement appeared in the social work press seeking to appoint a 'male residential social worker' and a 'male family support worker' on the strength of the expectation that the successful applicant would 'address the personal needs of male users of the service' and 'in order to be able to offer gender-appropriate personal care' in accordance with section 7(2)(e) of the Sex Discrimination Act 1975. Another post sought part-time Afro-Caribbean social workers 'to ensure the Department's same race policy can be fully implemented' in accordance with section 5(2)(d) of the Race Relations Act 1976.

In addition, special provision can be made to meet the special needs of a racial group in relation to education, training or welfare. This would, for example, permit the provision of special training to allow people to obtain the qualifications required for a particular job, but it does not allow for positive discrimination in selection for employment.

### *(b) Remedies*

Complaints regarding discrimination in employment are dealt with by industrial tribunals. All other cases are dealt with in Scotland by the sheriff court. In addition, the Acts set up an Equal Opportunities Commission for sex equality cases and a Commission for Racial Equality for race relations. The functions of both of these bodies are similar and are to give advice and assistance to those bringing cases and to carry out formal investigations

1 *Clarke and Powell v Eley (IMI) Kynoch Ltd* [1982] IRLR 482.

into particular bodies or areas of activity. They also have the sole right to enforce the provisions relating to discrimination in advertising, pressure to discriminate and instructions or inducements to discriminate.

## (3) Children (Scotland) Act 1995

Local authorities have a duty to promote the welfare of children in need by, amongst other things, providing appropriate services. In taking decisions they must now take account of the child's religious persuasion, racial origin and cultural and linguistic background.[1] This is a qualified duty in that the social work departments are required only to take account of these factors and not necessarily to provide the specific service indicated. It has also been noted that the 'subsection must not be used to provide either a greater or lesser level of service for those of minority persuasions, origins or backgrounds than is provided for those of the majority in Scotland today.'[2]

## (4) Control of immigration[3]

This brief section looks at an area of law which is closely related to the Race Relations Act. As one commentator has noted: 'Perhaps the most subversive influence on the success of the [Race Relations Act] is the existence of the quite contradictory assumptions of the immigration laws and the kind of racialist propaganda which is associated with them'.[4]

Apart from British citizens[5] and European Union nationals all other entrants into Britain are subject to immigration control. In some cases, for example visitors, this simply requires production of a passport; in other cases, for example those wishing to settle in the United Kingdom, entry clearance must be obtained in the country of origin before coming to the United Kingdom.

1 Children (Scotland) Act 1995, s 22(2).
2 K Norrie *The Children (Scotland) Act 1995* (1995) 36–23.
3 For a full treatment see I Macdonald and N Blake *Immigration Law and Practice in the UK* (4th edn, 1995).
4 I Macdonald *Race Relations: the New Law* (1977), p 8.
5 No attempt is made here to enter the complex area of law relating to nationality.

Apart from visitors without proper documentation and certain classes of student, those refused entry have a right of appeal to an adjudicator and then to the Immigration Appeal Tribunal. These rights of appeal can, generally, be exercised only once the appellant has left the United Kingdom. In addition, the entrant has the right to seek judicial review of a refusal of entry, but this no longer guarantees that the applicant will be allowed to stay in the United Kingdom pending the hearing. Finally, Members of Parliament have the right to ask the immigration service to reconsider a decision to send someone back, but they no longer have the power to prevent removal from the United Kingdom.

Entrants other than those admitted for settlement will be subject to conditions, for example, visitors may stay for only 6 months. Deportation can be ordered for breach of such conditions; it can also be ordered by the Secretary of State if deemed to be conducive to the public good; and it can be recommended by a court following a conviction. There is a right of appeal against a deportation order.

### (5) Social work contribution

The legislative similarity in the treatment of racial and sexual discrimination has been capitalised upon for reasons of simplicity and clarity. For the practitioner, however, matters are never so straightforward. Some would argue that social workers are immersed in patriarchal structures which foster institutional sexism and racism[1] and while there may well be a daily accumulation of evidence for these assertions, what is of interest here is an acknowledgment of the likely effects of such structures upon social work practice.

Although there are no statutory obligations for social workers in the area of discrimination, except for the duty to carry out their functions with due regard to the need to eliminate unlawful discrimination and to promote equality of opportunity and good relations between different racial groups,[2] they are sometimes involved with people who are experiencing deprivation at least in part due to discrimination.

In Scotland, this discrimination may also take the form of sectarianism or even classism, as when individuals from peripheral

1 See, for example, J Dale and P Foster in *Feminists and State Welfare* (1986), and L Dominelli in *Anti-racist Social Work* (2nd edn, 1997).

2 Race Relations Act 1976, s 71.

housing estates are excluded from employment purely on the basis of assumptions made about them as a result of their surname or address. These forms of discrimination are not the subject of specific legislation but can possibly be addressed through more general legislative provisions. One central tenet of social work values is the adherence to the view that men and women are individuals who must be accorded respect regardless of their particular traits or actions.[1] The implementation of this stance requires social workers to maintain a sensitivity and vigilance to matters of discrimination of all description and to use the regulatory and enabling functions of the law in this area to facilitate the improvement of service users' quality of life.

Some areas which social work touches upon have provided particular evidence of discriminatory practice and might require special attention. These include sentencing policy in the criminal justice system,[2] immigration decisions, allocation of council houses, and fostering and adoption policy. The professional qualification for social work, the Diploma in Social Work, requires that social work students

> 'identify and question their own values and prejudices . . .; respect and value uniqueness and diversity . . .; identify, analyse and take action to counter discrimination, racism, disadvantage, inequality and injustice'.[3]

These requirements provide the framework and continuing impetus for social workers to maintain a central focus on social justice. It is also incumbent upon educational establishments and social work agencies providing practice placements for students to demonstrate an adherence to these principles.[4]

## 5. DISABILITY DISCRIMINATION

Discrimination against people on the grounds of their disability is prohibited by the Disability Discrimination Act 1995 (the Act). It outlaws discrimination in employment; provision of goods, services

1 See, for example, R Plant *Social and Moral Theory in Casework* (1970), p 12.

2 See, for example, P Carlen and A Worrall (eds) *Gender, Crime and Justice* (1987).

3 Central Council for Education and Training in Social Work *Rules and Regulations for the Diploma in Social Work* (1995), p 18.

4 For a fuller discussion of these issues see M Payne *What is Professional Social Work?* (1996), ch 4; S Banks *Ethics and Values in Social Work* (1995); or R Hugman and D Smith (eds) *Ethical Issues in Social Work* (1995).

and facilities; disposal of premises; education; and public transport. It is gradually being brought into force. At the time of writing the provisions covering employment and the provision of premises are in force, as are the provisions about discrimination in the supply of goods and services except so far as they refer to the duty to modify premises and practices.

## (1) Definition of disability

A disability is any physical or mental impairment having a substantial and long-lasting effect on the ability of a person to carry out normal day-to-day activities.[1] This definition is supplemented by others, mainly contained in the first Schedule to the Act. 'Long-term' generally means lasting 12 months or more and an impairment is regarded as affecting the ability to carry out 'day-to-day' activities if it affects, for example, mobility, manual dexterity, speech or perception of physical danger. Regulations provide an additional definition of 'disabled', for example, excluding most drug addictions, disfigurement caused by tattoos and hay fever, but providing that in a case of a child under six the impairment is to be assessed in the context of activities that a child over six would undertake.[2] This means that a very young child is not to be prejudiced just because the child is too young to participate in most of the activities which are used in judging whether a person is disabled. People with progressive diseases, such as multiple sclerosis or HIV infection are to be treated as disabled for the purposes of the Act only once the condition has some effect, even though this is not substantial.[3]

## (2) Discrimination and employment

The anti-discrimination provisions affecting employment apply only to those who employ 20 or more people and do not extend to the police or armed services, though they do extend to contract

1 Disability Discrimination Act 1995, s 1.
2 Disability Discrimination (Meaning of Disability) Regulations 1996, SI 1996/1455. See also Department of Social Security *Guidance on matters to be taken into account in determining questions relating to the definition of disability* (1996).
3 Disability Discrimination Act 1995, Sch 1.

workers. There are two aspects of these provisions: a prohibition on discrimination, and a duty to make adjustments.

### *(a) The ban on discrimination*

It is against the law to discriminate against disabled people[1] by treating them less favourably than other people because of their disability, though the employer has a defence if the less favourable treatment is justified. It will be justified only if the reasons for it are material to the circumstances of the case and substantial.

The protection offered by these provisions extends to all stages of employment, including recruitment, terms and conditions of employment and promotion.

### *(b) The duty to make adjustments*

Where arrangements made by an employer (for example, as to timing of the working day or methods of working) or a physical feature of the employer's premises place a disabled employee at a substantial disadvantage compared to non-disabled employees the employer is obliged to make adjustments to the arrangements or premises. The duty is to take such steps as are reasonable in all the circumstances of the case to remove the disadvantage suffered.

In assessing reasonableness, the Act says that the following must be taken into account:

(i) the extent to which the disadvantage will be prevented by the adjustment;
(ii) the practicability of the adjustment;
(iii) the costs and disruption to the employer;
(iv) the extent of the employer's financial and other resources; and
(v) the availability of financial or other assistance to the employer.

Examples of steps which might be taken are adjustments to premises, providing a reader or interpreter, or altering the hours worked by the employee.[2] Finally, this duty to make adjustments applies in respect of job applicants who are known to the prospective employer to be disabled.

1 This is the term used in the Act. See also Disability Discrimination (Employment) Regulations 1996, SI 1996/1456.
2 Disability Discrimination Act 1995, s 6(3).

## (3) Discrimination in the provision of goods, facilities or services

Although the Act refers in the text mainly to provision of services, these sections of the Act also extend to goods and facilities. Reference to services here should be understood to include these and, in particular, it includes services provided by a local authority. As with employment, there are two duties here: a duty not to discriminate, and a duty to alter practices or premises.

### *(a) Discrimination*

It is unlawful to discriminate:

(i) by refusing to provide or deliberately not providing a service to a disabled person which is provided to members of the public;
(ii) by failing to comply with a duty to alter premises with the result that it is impossible or unreasonably difficult for a disabled person to use services provided;
(iii) in the standard of service provided to a disabled person or the terms of that provision.[2]

Examples of services covered by this include access to and use of information services, access to and use of any place to which members of the public are permitted to enter, and facilities for entertainment, recreation or refreshment. These provisions do not apply to education and transport as there is separate provision for them.

In these areas discrimination means less favourable treatment which is not justified, and such treatment will be justified only if the service provider is of the opinion that one or more conditions set out in the Act apply and the holding of that opinion is reasonable in all the circumstances. These conditions include:

(i) Discriminatory treatment is necessary to avoid endangering someone's health or safety.
(ii) The disabled person is incapable of entering into an enforceable agreement.
(iii) The treatment is necessary because otherwise the service provider would not be able to provide a service to the public.
(iv) The increased costs of a service to a disabled person reflect increased costs of provision.[2]

1 Disability Discrimination Act 1995, s 19(1).
2 Ibid, s 20(3), (4).

*(b) Changes of practices/premises*

Providers of services have a duty to take steps to change any policy, practice or procedure which makes it impossible or unreasonably difficult for a disabled person to use the service. The steps are those which are reasonable in all the circumstances of the case.[1]

Secondly, where a physical feature of the premises in which services are provided has the same effect there is an obligation to take such steps as are reasonable in all the circumstances to remove or alter the feature or to provide a means of avoiding the feature or a reasonable alternative means of providing the service to disabled people.

Where provision of an auxiliary aid or service, such as a sign language interpreter, would enable or facilitate the use of a service by a disabled person, the provider has to take such steps as are reasonable in all the circumstances to provide such an aid or service.

Finally, there are other limits on what a service provider is obliged to do. They need not do anything which would fundamentally alter the nature of the service provided or the trade, profession or business of the provider, nor need they do anything involving expenditure above a limit to be prescribed.

### (4) Provision of premises

This prohibits less favourable treatment of disabled people in relation to selling or offering a tenancy of premises. It covers discrimination in the terms on which premises are offered; refusal to offer premises; and discrimination in relation to housing lists.

### (5) Education

The only provision in the Act is a limited duty on universities to publish 'disability statements' setting out their provision for disabled people. Disabled people of school age who have special educational needs are covered by the Education (Scotland) Acts (see chapter 6, part 4).

1 See Disability Discrimination (Services and Premises) Regulations 1996, SI 1996/1836.

### (6) Public transport

There is provision for regulations to be made about the accessibility of taxis, public service vehicles (that is, buses) and trains.

### (7) National Disability Council

The function of this body is to give advice to the Secretary of State and to prepare codes of practice as requested by him/her. Though the Secretary of State can extend the role of the Council, it cannot be extended to allow it to investigate complaints which might be the subject of proceedings under the Act. Unlike the Equal Opportunities Commission and the Commission for Racial Equality, the Council has no power to provide assistance to people in pursuing complaints under the Act or to carry out general investigations.

### (8) Enforcement

Enforcement of employment rights is through the industrial tribunal system. Complaints about discrimination in provision of goods, facilities, services or premises are dealt with by the sheriff court and any claim must be made within 6 months of the alleged incident of discrimination. The accessibility provisions are to be enforced by making failure to comply a criminal offence.

### (9) Social work contribution

Campaigners have fought for many years to see various of the above-mentioned rights included in legislation. Many are disappointed that the Act did not go far enough and others that it was not matched with an increase in resources. Social workers may be in the front line as either providers of specified services which are subject to conditions of the Act or as purchasers of other services also affected. Many people with physical or mental impairments may be unaware of the existence of the provisions of this Act and so social workers have a special responsibility to ensure that there is a raised level of awareness and may need to work with service users to seek compliance.

## 6. ACCESS TO INFORMATION

### (1) Introduction

There are a number of pieces of legislation which allow for access by individuals to records which contain information regarding them[1]. Two of these, the Data Protection Act 1984 and the Access to Personal Files Act 1987, have direct relevance to social work practice and should perhaps be considered as what we have termed 'professional law' in part 1 above. These will be considered in some detail below. The rest of the legislation gives rights of access to a variety of information and will be considered more briefly.

This area of general law is especially important for social workers for a number of reasons. As Phyllida Parsloe[2] so succinctly points out, 'Their [social services agencies'] stock in trade is largely information . . . ' and both the philosophy which guides how social workers handle information and the practice which ensues reflect the basic values which drive social work. The inherent dilemmas which revolve around state intervention and individual liberty are clearly manifest in how social workers understand and use that understanding in this area.[3]

### (2) Data Protection Act 1984

This legislation covers only information held in such a form that it can be processed by equipment operating automatically. It therefore does not cover information which is recorded in written files and records. In general terms, people who hold the former type of information must register with the Data Protection Registrar and must give individuals access to information kept about them. The definition of processing is broad enough so that most social work computerised record systems will be covered.

There are restrictions on access to certain types of information, one of these being information kept for the purposes, or acquired in

1 The government is expected to shortly introduce a Bill to alter the law in this area. It is unlikely to have a substantial effect on the access rules affecting social workers.

2 P Pearce, P Parsloe, H Francis, A Macara and D Watson *Personal Data Protection in Health and Social Services* (1988), p 80.

3 For a very detailed account see T Thomas *Privacy and Social Services* (1995).

the course, of carrying out social work. Briefly, these restrictions prevent the disclosure of information where it would be likely to cause serious harm to the physical, mental or emotional condition of the person applying for access, or anyone else, or where the identity of someone else, other than a social worker or person who has consented to disclosure, would be disclosed as a result of disclosure of the information. In addition, where the information includes information as to the health of the applicant which has been supplied by a doctor or other 'health professional' (see below), that health professional must be consulted before the information is disclosed.

As well as the right of access, individuals who are the subjects of data have rights in connection with inaccurate information and unauthorised disclosure. They are entitled to compensation for any loss to them caused by inaccuracy of the information or unauthorised disclosure. They can also apply to the sheriff court to order correction of inaccurate information.

Complaints about information held on computer are heard at a national level by the Data Protection Registrar who has a duty to investigate alleged inappropriate disclosures or other irregularities which raise 'a matter of substance'.[1] This legislation will be of increasing relevance to social workers as local authority departments establish service user data bases and use computer files as an alternative to paper files.

### (3) Access to Personal Files Act 1987

The Access to Personal Files Act 1987 permits access to what it describes as 'personal information' held either by housing authorities (including Scottish Homes) for the purpose of tenancies[2] or by councils for the purpose of their functions under the Social Work (Scotland) Act 1968. Unlike the Data Protection Act, the Access to Personal Files Act does not extend to voluntary organisations; there is, therefore, no statutory right of access to the information covered by the latter Act which is kept by voluntary organisations, although most operate policies which permit access.

'Personal information' is defined as information relating to a living individual who can be identified from that information or from

1 Data Protection Act 1984, s 36(2).
2 See Access to Personal Files (Housing) (Scotland) Regulations 1992, SI 1992/1852.

that and other information in the possession of the authority. The right of access extends to any expression of an opinion about the individual concerned, but not any expression of intention (for example, plans for future care of or action in respect of the person). Access is not restricted to information kept in a form which can be processed automatically as with the Data Protection Act 1984, but extends to information held in any form. The main restriction is that the right of access does not extend to any information recorded before the date when the regulations filling in the detail of access arrangements came into effect. In the case of social work that date is 1 April 1989. Earlier information may, however, **have** to be disclosed if this is necessary to make sense of information recorded after that date. Local authorities also have the power to disclose such earlier information.

The person entitled to access is the person to whom the information relates. Minor children, that is, boys aged 14 or over and girls aged 12 or over, have a right of access to information about themselves and would have to consent to any application by their parents for information about them.[1]

The detail of the access arrangements for social work is contained in the Access to Personal Files (Social Work) (Scotland) Regulations 1989.[2] In addition, most authorities will have their own procedures and guidelines for dealing with access to information which will, for example, set out their policy on disclosure and the procedure for dealing with requests for information.

Under the regulations the social work authority is obliged to tell anyone who applies in the correct form whether they hold any personal information about the applicant and, subject to the restrictions on access described below, the contents of that information. The information must be provided in an intelligible form. The time limit for supplying this information is generally 40 days from the date of receipt of the application, though this period can be extended, for example if the authority needs further information from the applicant to process the application.

As mentioned, there are certain restrictions on, or exemptions from, disclosure. These release authorities from disclosing only that information which falls within the exemptions: any other personal information held by the authority must be disclosed. This may involve, for example, the deletion of information identifying a

1 See ch 4, pt 3(9).
2 SI 1989/251.

third party from a file before the applicant is allowed to see it (unless, of course, the third party consents to disclosure). The exemptions fall into three categories.

*(a) Information as to the physical or mental health of the applicant.* Where information of this nature is held by a social work authority and has, or is believed to have, originated from or been supplied by a health professional the authority must advise the relevant health board (if the health professional is employed by a health board) or the health professional of the request for information. The term 'health professional' is defined widely and includes not only doctors, dentists, opticians and nurses, but also registered chiropodists and physiotherapists, clinical psychologists, speech therapists, health visitors, and art or music therapists employed by a health board.

The social work authority is exempted from disclosing the information if, within the 40-day period mentioned above, the health board or health professional informs it that disclosure would either:

(i) cause serious harm to the physical or mental health of the applicant or any other person; or
(ii) reveal to the applicant the identity of some other person other than a health professional or someone who has consented to disclosure.

It should be noted that if there is no response within the 40-day period the social work authority must disclose the information, even if it would have one of the effects specified.

*(b) Information from reporters to children's panels.* Before information supplied by or originating from a reporter can be disclosed the reporter must be informed of the request for information. The social work authority will be exempted from the obligation to disclose the information if, within the 40-day period, the reporter advises it that the information should not be disclosed because this would be likely either:

(i) to cause serious harm to the physical or mental health of the applicant or any other person; or
(ii) to disclose to the applicant the identity of another person who has not consented to disclosure; or
(iii) to prejudice the prevention or detection of a crime or the apprehension or prosecution of offenders.

Once again, if there is no response within the 40-day period the information must be disclosed.

*(c) Other information.* The social work authority is also exempted from disclosing information which falls into one of the following categories:

(i) information which, if disclosed, would be likely to prejudice the carrying on of the authority's social work functions because it is likely to cause serious harm to the physical or mental health or the emotional condition of the applicant or any other person; or
(ii) information which would reveal the identity of another individual who is not an employee of the social work department or a provider of services for reward to the department (for example, an approved foster parent in receipt of a fostering allowance) and who has not consented to disclosure; or
(iii) information which, if disclosed, would be likely to prejudice the prevention or detection of crime or the apprehension or prosecution of offenders; or
(iv) information in respect of which a claim of confidentiality between client and professional legal adviser could be maintained in legal proceedings; or
(v) information covered by certain statutory provisions, mainly information to do with adoption and a child's record of needs.

There are three points worth noting briefly about this third category of exemptions. The first is that one of the concerns is the protection of confidentiality. Information which would identify a third party as the source, or which relates in part to that third party, must not be disclosed without his/her consent. The second is that there is no time limit for the consent as there is in the case of responses on health information and information from the reporter. The information cannot therefore be revealed simply because the 40-day period has passed without response. The third is that where there is no response from a health board, health professional, or reporter the authority cannot fall back on one of the exemptions in this category to refuse disclosure. This final category does not extend to information covered by the previous two categories.

### *Rights to correction*

Anyone who has obtained access to information held about him/her can serve a notice on the authority requiring it to correct or delete any information which he/she regards as inaccurate. If it is satisfied that the information is incorrect the authority is not bound to amend its records, but the individual concerned has the right to have a note that he/she regards the information as inaccurate placed with the information. In practice this would, for example, be noted on the file.

Anyone who is the subject of information held by a social work authority and who is unhappy with any decision taken by the authority about access to information or rectification of information has the right to seek review of the decision. The review is carried out by a committee of three councillors. Additionally, judicial review could be sought[1] or a complaint made to the local government Ombudsman.

## (4) Other legislation

### *(a) Access to Medical Reports Act 1988*

This gives a right of access to medical reports prepared for employment or insurance purposes.

### *(b) Consumer Credit Act 1974*

This Act gives a consumer the right to obtain a copy of any file relating to him/her kept by a credit reference agency. The right is to see any information, however it is held. If the consumer considers that any of the information is incorrect and may lead to prejudice, the consumer may serve a notice on the agency requiring it to correct or delete the information. If the agency refuses to do this the consumer can apply to the Director General of Fair Trading to exercise his/her enforcement powers. The information kept by credit reference agencies often turns out to be incorrect and this may be a remedy worth pursuing where someone is refused credit or some other service because of an adverse report from an agency.

### *(c) Access to Health Records Act 1990*

This gives a right of access to health records kept by health professionals (see above). Application is made to the holder of the record, such as a general practitioner or the health board. There is no right of access where the patient is incapable of understanding the nature of the application, where the patient is a child and the grant-

1 See ch 1, pt 13.

ing of access is not in the best interests of the child (unless he/she has consented to the application), and where the information was recorded before 1 November 1991, unless this information is necessary to understand information recorded later. There are also exemptions covering information likely to cause serious damage to the mental or physical health of the patient or another individual, and information identifying a third party who is not a health professional and who has not consented to disclosure. There is provision for application to be made for correction of health records and for a statement of the patient's position to be included in the record if correction is not made.

### *(d) Access to school records*

The School Pupil Records (Scotland) Regulations 1990[1] give a right of access to personal information kept by education authorities in the context of providing school education. There are certain exemptions to the right of access: these include exemptions similar to categories *(a)*, *(b)* and *(c)* (iii) and (iv) noted above in relation to social work information, as well as references for employment and information which would disclose the identities of third parties. The rights to seek correction and review are similar to those noted above for social work information.

## 7. EDUCATION

This section is intended to deal briefly with the rights and duties of parents and discipline in schools. The principal right that parents have in relation to education is the right, subject to availability of places, to choose the school where their child will be educated. The principal duty of parents is to ensure that their child receives a suitable education while of school age. This may be done at home, or by sending the child to an independent school or, most commonly, to a local authority school. Failure to meet this responsibility can result in an attendance order being served requiring the child to attend a specific school, or in prosecution of the parents. Successful prosecution may result in the parents being fined. The child may be referred to the reporter for the children's hearing as

1 SI 1990/1551.

being in need of compulsory measures of supervision if he/she fails to attend school regularly without a reasonable excuse.[1]

A child may no longer be subjected to corporal punishment in school, but may be disciplined in other ways, for example, by being given additional homework or a verbal reprimand. In serious cases the child may be excluded from school. If this happens the parents must be notified right away and there is a right of appeal against the exclusion and against any conditions imposed on the child's re-attendance at school.

Provision for children who have special educational needs is discussed in the context of other special needs in chapter 6, part 4(5).

1 See ch 5, pt 3(3).

# 3. Children and their families

## 1. THE RESPONSIBILITIES, RIGHTS AND POWERS OF PARENTS AND CHILDREN

### (1) Introduction

This section starts with an attempt to explain the powers and rights that a child has at different stages of his/her life. Powers are concerned with the ability or capacity of children to enter into legal transactions, for example contracts, and to give legally effective agreement, such as the giving of consent to medical treatment. Rights are concerned with the child's rights to make choices about his/her life, for example choices about friends, about religious beliefs and about where to stay. The extent of a child's rights is closely connected with the extent of the parent's responsibilities and rights enjoyed by his or her parent(s): the child's power to control his/her own life grows with the decline of the parents' role. For this reason we will also consider the responsibilities and rights of parents and the major changes brought about by the Children (Scotland) Act 1995 (the 1995 Act).

The age of majority, the age at which, technically, one is fully an adult, is 18 in Scotland. There are other age limits relevant for other purposes. For example, at the age of 16 one can marry and enter into other legal transactions (see below). Sixteen is also the age at which compulsory education finishes and below which children can be referred to a children's hearing and be the subject of actions seeking parental responsibilities or rights (see below). Children under the age of eight cannot be guilty of a criminal offence or be referred to a children's hearing on the ground that they have committed an offence.

Below the age of 18 the historically important division was between pupils and minors. Pupils are boys under 14 and girls under 12, minors are those between those ages and 18. Pupils had very restricted powers and were subject to the control and guidance of their tutor, normally their parent. Minors had slightly greater powers, for example to enter contracts and to consent to some types of medical treatment, and acted with the concurrence of a curator, again usually the parent. Where a child had two parents in the legal sense (see below), both were tutor/curator of the child.

The Age of Legal Capacity (Scotland) Act 1991 made some changes to this position. In particular, it made changes which affect the capacity of children and it abolished tutors and curators, creating instead the position of guardian who, in relation to children under the age of 16, was to have the powers of a tutor.[1] The first of these developments is discussed in more detail below, but it should be noted that although the distinction between pupils and minors is generally no longer relevant as far as the powers or capacity of children is concerned it is still relevant as far as children's rights are concerned.

Knowledge and an understanding of the law in this area should prove invaluable to social workers and young persons in such situations as leaving care and planning for independent living; entering into contractual arrangements, for example with catalogue companies; and being on home supervision and perhaps in conflict with parents or being looked after by the local authority and needing to know what rights and responsibilities are relevant.

## (2) Legal capacity of children

The Age of Legal Capacity (Scotland) Act 1991 (the 1991 Act) sets out the rules about the capacity of children. In terms of this Act the important age is 16. Below this age, subject to the exceptions noted below, children have no capacity to enter into what the 1991 Act calls 'transactions'. The term 'transactions' includes contractual agreements, the giving of any consent having legal effect (for example, consent to medical treatment), and the bringing or defending of any legal action in a civil court. It describes, in other words, actions which will have legal consequences for the child.

The main exceptions are:[2]

(a) Children under 16 may enter into transactions of a kind normally entered into by children of the child in question's age and circumstances, provided the terms of the transaction are reasonable.

1 See ch 4, pt 3(9).
2 Age of Legal Capacity (Scotland) Act 1991, s 2.

(b) Children over the age of 12 have the power to make wills.
(c) A child under 16 may consent to any surgical, medical or dental procedure or treatment[1] where, in the opinion of the medical practitioner attending him or her, the child is capable of understanding the nature and possible consequences of the procedure or treatment. This is considered more fully below.
(d) Children over 12 have the power to consent (or withhold consent) to adoption and freeing for adoption.
(e) A child under 16 has the capacity to instruct a solicitor in respect of a civil law matter, provided that the child has a general understanding of what it means to instruct a solicitor. Such children also have capacity to sue and defend in civil court actions.

Children over the age of 16 have full legal capacity in respect of the matters covered by the Act. Sixteen and 17 year olds enjoy some additional protection in that before their 21st birthday they can challenge any transactions entered into at those ages on the grounds that the transaction was prejudicial.

As we have noted, a child can now give effective consent to medical treatment if capable of understanding the nature and possible consequences of the treatment, with the judgment as to ability to understand being made by the doctor or dentist treating the child. This capacity is also regarded as extending to refusing medical treatment,[2] though in England the view has been taken that the parents of a child can overrule his/her refusal of treatment.[3]

A problem might arise where the child is unable to consent and the parents refuse to consent to therapeutic treatment. In such cases treatment may be authorised by the general welfare principle extending to children. There is also the possibility of applying to court for permission for treatment under section 11 of the 1995 Act. Failure on the part of the parent to consent to therapeutic treatment may also give rise to a referral to a children's hearing on the ground of lack of parental care.[4] In emergency cases treatment can be given without consent.

1 This would include consenting to the prescribing of contraceptives.
2 See Norrie's annotation to s 90 of the Children (Scotland) Act 1995; see also *Houston, Applicant* 1996 SCLR 943 and annotation.
3 *Re W (a minor) (medical treatment)* [1992] 4 All ER 627 at 639j-640a. See also *V v F* 1991 SCLR 225 and comment thereon.
4 *Finlayson, Applicant* 1989 SCLR 601. See ch 5, pt 3(3).

## (3) Children's rights

As children get older the responsibilities and rights of their parents diminish, and the rights of the child to manage his/her affairs and take decisions about his/her life increase. Where the exercise of rights involves doing things which have legal consequences for the child the rules in the Age of Legal Capacity (Scotland) Act 1991 explained above apply. Outside these transactions children have certain rights which exist from birth, for example, rights to compensation for injury and the right to express a view about important decisions affecting their life. Some rights are also acquired on reaching the age of minority, for example, the right to choose a religion and the right to seek access to personal files.[1]

Specific rights that children possess include the rights to protection, to the promotion of their welfare and to support from their parents, or, indeed, from anyone who has accepted them as a member of their family. This right to support or aliment lasts until the child is 18, or until the age of 25 if the 'child' is undertaking full-time education.[2]

The 1989 United Nations Convention on the Rights of the Child has proved to be a benchmark influence in the consultation and drafting of the 1995 Act, with some of the new fundamental principles, for example, that a child's views should be taken into account where major decisions are to be made about his/her welfare, arising directly from this trendsetting document.[3]

## (4) Parental responsibilities

In the new language of the 1995 Act, parents now have responsibilities to their children, and the legal emphasis is on these responsibilities rather than the rights that parents have. The responsibilities of a parent to a child under 16 are:[4]

(a) to safeguard and promote the health, development and welfare of the child;

1 Though this view is not uncontroversial: see ch 4, pt 3(9).
2 Family Law (Scotland) Act 1985, s 1.
3 For an extremely detailed account see A Cleland and E Sutherland (eds) *Children's Rights in Scotland* (1996). See also G Schofield and J Thoburn *Child Protection: The Voice of the Child in Decision-making* (1996).
4 Children (Scotland) Act 1995, s 1.

(b) to provide direction to the child appropriate to his/her age (which implies that as the child gets older the responsibility to direct lessens);
(c) in cases where the child is not living with the parent (for example, because the parents are separated or divorced) the parent has to maintain regular contact and 'personal relations' with the child;
(d) to act as the child's legal representative, for example, in relation to entering contracts and managing property. As we have seen above, when the child gets older the capacity to do these things is acquired.

For children of 17 and 18, the parent has a responsibility to provide guidance appropriate to the child's age, though the right to give such guidance expires on the child's 16th birthday. In all cases the responsibilities are to be fulfilled only where this is practicable and in the interests of the child. Fulfilment will also be subject to any court orders about parental responsibilities.

These responsibilities replace any analogous duties imposed by common law, so that the duties of a parent are as described in the 1995 Act and in other statutory provisions, for example, as to aliment and ensuring that children are provided with education, and any duties imposed by common law which are not analogous to those listed above.

There is one further provision of the 1995 Act to be considered under this heading. This is the duty to 'have regard to' the views of the child in taking any major decision involving the exercise of parental responsibilities and rights. The age of the child is relevant to this process and children of 12 and over are deemed to be capable of forming a view. It is not clear what decisions will be major decisions, though presumably an objective standard will be invoked; nor is it clear how a child could enforce this provision and prevent an action in respect of which his/her views had not been sought. Perhaps the only remedy would be for the child to seek an order in relation to parental responsibilities or rights. Finally, the requirement is only to have regard to what the child wants and does not extend to a requirement to do what the child wants.[1]

### (5) Parental rights

Parents have certain legal rights which are conferred on them for the express purpose of enabling them to fulfil their parental respon-

1 1995 Act, s 6.

sibilities. This reflects the views expressed in relation to parental rights before the 1995 Act was passed. For example, Lord Scarman in the case of *Gillick v West Norfolk and Wisbech Area Health Authority* said: 'The principle is that parental right or power of control of the person and property of the child exists primarily to enable the parent to discharge his duty of maintenance, protection and education until [the child] reaches such an age as to be able to look after himself and make his own decisions.'[1]

Parents have the right:[2]

(a) to have their children living with them or to regulate their residence;
(b) to control, direct or guide their children's upbringing in a manner appropriate to the age of the child;
(c) to maintain direct contact on a regular basis with any child who is not living with them and to maintain personal relations with the child;
(d) to act as their children's legal representative.

These rights supersede any analogous common law rights held by parents. One of the rights encompassed in (d) above is the right to manage any property belonging to a child. In doing this a parent must act as a reasonable and prudent person acting on his/her own behalf would act. Parents still have other rights conferred by statute, such as the right to attend a children's hearing involving their child. The rights listed above apply until the child is 16 years old.

Where more than one person has parental rights in respect of a child they may exercise their rights independently of each other. For example, if the parents are separated, the mother can take any decision about the child without consulting the father. Clearly this is one scenario which may well augur conflict and in which social workers may find themselves involved.

### (6) Who holds parental responsibilities and rights?

The mother of a child holds parental responsibilities and rights automatically, as does the father of the child, if he was married to the mother either at the time of conception of the child or subsequently.

1 [1985] 3 All ER 402 at 421d.
2 1995 Act, s 2.

Aside from this, the biological father does not automatically have responsibilities and rights, but can acquire these in one of two ways. He can enter into an agreement with the mother of the child (providing she has not been deprived of any responsibilities or rights) in a form set out in regulations. To be effective the agreement must be registered in the Books of Council and Session.[1] Alternatively, he could apply to court for an order in respect of parental responsibilities and rights under section 11 of the 1995 Act. Other people may come to hold responsibilities and rights as a result of such an order or as a result of another type of court order, for example, an order freeing a child for adoption or a parental responsibilities order made in favour of a local authority.

Parents holding parental responsibilities and rights can appoint a guardian to take over those rights and responsibilities after their death.[2]

Where someone without responsibilities and rights has care or control of a child, that person has the responsibility of doing what is reasonable in the circumstances to safeguard the child's health, development and welfare. Included within this is the power to consent to medical treatment where the child is unable to and the person does not know that the parent would refuse consent to treatment. These powers are not conferred on teachers, but would apply where a child is under the care and control of a foster parent or, possibly, a social worker.[3]

## (7) Court orders and parental responsibilities[4]

Anyone claiming an interest can, under section 11 of the 1995 Act, apply to court for an order relating to parental responsibilities and rights. This includes the child concerned, but local authorities are specifically excluded. An application for an order can also be made by anyone holding parental responsibilities and rights, as well as by someone who previously held them but has lost them, provided they were not lost in a number of specified ways. These specified ways include transfer on an order freeing for adoption or a parental responsibilities order or loss on adoption of the child. For example, a parent of a child who had been adopted would not be able to go to court to seek contact with the child.

1 Parental Responsibilities and Parental Rights Agreements (Scotland) Regulations 1996, SI 1996/2549.
2 1995 Act, s 7.
3 1995 Act, s 5.
4 1995 Act, s 11.

The 1995 Act provides a non-exclusive list of the types of order that may be sought:

(a) an order depriving someone of some or all rights or responsibilities;
(b) an order imposing responsibilities and conferring rights;
(c) a residence order specifying where a child is to live (replacing custody orders);
(d) a contact order, regulating personal relations and direct contact with someone with whom the child is not living (replacing the notion of access);
(e) a specific issue order which is designed to regulate any specific issue which has arisen with respect to parental responsibilities, for example, a question about medical treatment;
(f) an interdict preventing some action in exercise of parental responsibilities and rights.

The application for such an order can be made in a legal action intended to resolve that particular issue or it can form an incidental part of any other proceedings, such as a divorce or separation action. Three principles are set out in the 1995 Act to guide the court in making a decision in this type of case:[1]

(a) The court must regard the welfare of the child as its paramount consideration.
(b) The court must not make any order about parental responsibilities or rights unless it considers that making the order would be better for the child than making no order at all. This emphasises a strategy of minimum intervention.
(c) The child involved must be given an opportunity to indicate if he/she wishes to express a view about any order and if the child does wish to express a view he/she must be given an opportunity to do so and the court must have regard to any views expressed before making an order. In order to allow this to happen, a child must be notified of applications for orders dealing with responsibilities and rights and on the notification there is a form which the child can return indicating whether he/she wishes to express a view. If the child does, the form allows him/her to nominate someone to communicate his/her views to the court or to write to the judge expressing his/her views. The procedural rules also envisage the judge either speaking to the child directly or sending someone to speak to the child on his/her behalf.

1 1995 Act, s 11(7).

If, during the course of the hearing, the judge considers that any of the non-offence grounds of referral to a children's hearing exist, the judge may refer the case of the child to the reporter.[1] The effect of an order conferring parental rights on one person is not, automatically, to remove them from another person having parental rights. For example, if the court were to make a residence order in favour of a wife that would not automatically deprive the husband of the right to have the child living with him. Deprivation of rights occurs only where the court expressly takes them away from someone who previously enjoyed them.[2]

## 2. MARRIAGE, SEPARATION AND DIVORCE

### (1) Marriage

Before two people can get married certain requirements must be fulfilled. Both parties must be over 16, must be single, must not be within the forbidden degrees of relationship and one must be male and the other female. If these requirements are met the parties will generally go through a regular marriage, that is, a religious ceremony or civil wedding. It is, however, possible to become husband and wife without such a ceremony. Such a marriage is referred to as an irregular marriage and the only way in which it can now take place is the process of 'cohabitation with habit and repute'. For this, the parties must live together and be regarded as husband and wife for a sufficient period of time. On its own, cohabitation does not constitute the marriage. This must be formalised by applying to the Court of Session for a declarator of marriage.[3]

Irregular marriage is a true form of common law marriage in the sense that it is not provided for by statute, and should be clearly distinguished from what are often referred to as 'common law' marriages. These situations, where, for example, a man is referred to as being a woman's common law husband, amount to mere cohabitation and do not give rise to the legal consequences which follow from a proper marriage. The father of a child who is actually married to the mother will have parental responsibilities and rights in respect of that child, whereas the 'common law' husband who

1 1995 Act, ss 12 and 54.
2 1995 Act, s 11(11).
3 For a recent example see *Dewar v Dewar* 1995 SLT 467. This is an unusual example as both parties were alive at the time of the action.

fathers a child will not automatically have parental responsibilities and rights and will have to apply to court for them or have them conferred on him by agreement with the child's mother.

After marriage the parties have a mutual obligation of financial support and an obligation to live together as husband and wife. Marriage also provides rights of inheritance or succession to the spouse and children. A wife need not take the surname of her husband. Even while married and living together, a husband may be charged and convicted of raping his wife. In the case deciding this the earlier view that, in agreeing to the marriage, a wife was giving blanket consent to sexual intercourse with her husband was rejected.[1]

To date, there has been little official discussion and consideration of marriage between persons of the same sex and since the assumption in Scots law is that only persons of different sexes can fulfil the legal obligations of marriage, then those who do not fit this description will continue to be deprived of the protections and benefits of the law.[2]

### (2) Separation

It is possible to obtain a formal judicial separation requiring the parties to a marriage to live apart but not releasing them from the other obligations of marriage. So, for example, the couple will still be required to support one another financially and the commission of adultery while separated will still be acceptable as a ground for evidencing the irretrievable breakdown of the marriage. In general any separation will be informal, as will any arrangements for aliment or for residence and contact regarding any children. If such informal arrangements are impossible it may be necessary to take action in the sheriff court to regulate these matters.

### (3) Divorce

The Divorce (Scotland) Act 1976 introduced a single ground for divorce in Scotland: 'irretrievable breakdown of the marriage'. In some ways this simply amounted to a restatement of the then existing grounds of divorce, since they, together with two new

1 *S v HM Advocate* 1989 SLT 469.
2 See J M Thomson *Family Law in Scotland* (3rd edn, 1996), pp 28–29.

grounds based on non-cohabitation, were to be evidence of breakdown.

The five grounds evidencing an irretrievable breakdown are:

(a) adultery;
(b) behaviour – where the defender 'has behaved . . . in such a way that the pursuer cannot reasonably be expected to cohabit with the defender'. This ground would cover violence by the defender, drunkenness or unnatural, excessive or insufficient sexual demands;
(c) desertion – where the defender has left without good cause and has been absent for a period of two years;
(d) two years' non-cohabitation with consent – where the parties have not lived together as husband and wife for two years and the defender consents to the divorce;
(e) five years' non-cohabitation – here the defender's consent is not required.

### (4) Divorce procedure

Provided that one of these grounds can be established, a spouse may seek a divorce at any time following the marriage ceremony. Most cases are now dealt with in the sheriff court. There are two types of procedure by which a divorce can be obtained: ordinary and simplified. The ordinary procedure is similar to that involved in an ordinary court action, for example, in a claim for compensation following a road accident.

The simplified procedure amounts essentially to a do-it-yourself divorce. It is available only where the divorce is based on non-cohabitation, there are no children of the marriage under 16, and no financial provisions are being sought. An application is completed and returned to the clerk of the court (either the sheriff court or Court of Session) who notifies the other party. If there is no dispute, a decree of divorce will arrive through the post after a short while.

### (5) Financial provision on divorce

Financial provision on divorce is often regulated by agreement between the parties: failing which the Family Law (Scotland) Act 1985 (the 1985 Act) sets out a number of rules and principles to guide courts in making financial provision. The general effect of these guidelines is to discourage orders for periodical allowance over a long period of time which would maintain a link between the parties. Instead the 1985 Act favours a clean break. To this end it envisages that the principal form of settlement on divorce will be transfer of property or the payment of a capital sum (though this payment may be staged over time).

Before the court can make any award of financial provision it must first be satisfied that the award is justified by reference to the principles contained in the 1985 Act and is reasonable having regard to the resources of the parties. The basic principle is that the net value of the matrimonial property should be shared fairly between the parties: generally, fair sharing will be equal sharing.

### (6) Arrangements for children

There are children involved in about half of all divorces and normally the arrangements for bringing up the children will be agreed between the parties. Even if they are, the court is obliged to consider whether to exercise its power to make an order about parental responsibilities or rights or to exercise its power to refer the case to the reporter because it appears to it that one of the grounds of referral[1] is satisfied in respect of a child of the marriage under 16. If it concludes that it should exercise one of these powers the judgment in the divorce action can be postponed if it is necessary to obtain more information before exercising the power.[2] This can include obtaining a report from the social work department.[3]

Social workers required to produce such a report will need to complete exhaustive inquiries about the backgrounds and parenting capacities of parents in the form of a matrimonial proceedings report. This will be used by the judge, in conjunction with other information, to make decisions about the arrangements for children. In situations where the court deems it necessary, social workers will be required to supervise the contact visits for children. Some of the most stressful experiences for parents and children arise over contact arrangements and visits. The verdict of research

1 See ch 5 pt 3.
2 1995 Act, s 12.
3 Matrimonial Proceedings (Children) Act 1958, s 11; see *Hardie v Hardie* 1993 SCLR 60.

is clear: children who continue to have close, loving relationships with both parents are least likely to exhibit the worst effects of the divorce and a social worker's attention to alleviating barriers to parental contact may contribute enormously to minimising these effects.

## (7) Cohabitation

In general, simple cohabitation will create no legal relationship between the parties and will have few legal consequences. The principal effects to note will be possible effects on any benefit claimed, and the entitlement of cohabitees to apply for occupancy rights under the Matrimonial Homes (Family Protection) (Scotland) Act 1981.

## (8) Child support

In addition to the arrangements covered above, there are likely to be situations where a child's parents have separated and the non-residential parent is not paying aliment for the child. Since the Child Support Act 1991 came into force in April 1993 it has been possible for the residential parent to apply to the Child Support Agency for a maintenance assessment which the agency will collect and enforce if so required. A person with parental responsibility who is claiming Income Support, Family Credit or any other benefit of a prescribed kind is obliged to pursue such an application unless it can be established that to do so would entail undue risk of harm or distress to the applicant or child. Decisions of the Child Support Agency may be appealed and are reviewed by the Child Support Appeal Tribunal.

The early years of the Child Support Agency were characterised by considerable chaos with media attention focused on fathers who claimed the assessments were excessive and mothers who had sought a clean break becoming ensnared in further contact. These early difficulties have now been mainly resolved and many believe that the original aims of the Agency to enforce the obligations of parents to maintain their children and reduce state support are being met while also improving the quality of life for children by ensuring that they can be better financially supported.

## (9) Implications of demographic changes for social workers

Recent statistics[1] indicate that divorce rates have doubled since 1971 and that nearly four in ten marriages are likely to break down. One in four children will experience the process of his/her parents' divorce by the age of 16. One marriage in three will end in divorce by the time the spouses are 45. The trends in Scotland indicate a relatively stable number of divorces in recent years with a slight lessening year by year. Even so, there are over 12,000 divorces annually and over 8,000 children under the age of 16 affected. There is a sizeable increase in the percentage of people divorcing who have previously been divorced.[2] The figures suggest it is increasingly likely that social workers will have contact with families affected by these changes and that the effects on families are increasingly complicated. Research[3] highlights the probability that parents are least able to cope with the demands being made upon them, especially with regard to their children, during the process of divorce and so most in need of advice, guidance and support which a social worker may be well placed to provide.

Increasingly a range of professionals including solicitors and counsellors are offering to provide some of these services. In April 1990 a rule of court allowed the court hearing a divorce application to refer the parties to a conciliation service for assistance in reaching agreements and so if a case goes to court, the parties can be referred to family mediation. Now family mediation services are available throughout Scotland where agreed decisions can be reached regarding, for example, residence, contact, education of the children, the outline of disposition of the matrimonial home and other financial matters (which must then be referred back to solicitors),[4] and other pending matters outwith the court's adversarial procedure. In family mediation, parents and sometimes children are helped to talk about the problems arising from the separation and divorce. It can provide huge benefits for children and for parents in dealing with conflicts, finding ways of keeping family ties alive and learning to approach their futures more realistically and optimistically.

1 See, for example, DSS Research Report No 6 *Lone Parent Families in the UK* by J Bradshaw and J Millar (1991).
2 General Register Office for Scotland, 1996.
3 See, for example, *Second Chances* by J Wallerstein and S Blakeslee (1989).
4 See the Code of Practice agreed with the Law Society of Scotland.

## 3. ADOPTION

### (1) Introduction

Adoption is a process by which a new legal relationship of parent and child is created by transferring the parental rights and responsibilities of the child's original parent(s) to adoptive parent(s). In broad terms, as far as the law is concerned, the relationship between the child and the adoptive parent(s) is the same as that with his/her original parent(s). The effect of an adoption order therefore is to sever the legal relationship between the child and his/her original parent(s). An adoption order therefore terminates rights of contact and also terminates a parental responsibilities order. Adoption law is contained in the Adoption (Scotland) Act 1978 (the 1978 Act).[1]

About half of all adoptions involve someone who is related to the child, usually the mother whose new partner is applying to adopt. The remaining adoptions are arranged by adoption agencies. All local authorities are adoption agencies, and there are a number of independent adoption societies approved by the Secretary of State.

Slightly different rules apply to related adoptions and those arranged by an adoption agency. These differences will be considered as appropriate. One of the main differences is that adoption agencies must appoint an adoption panel. The functions of this panel are to make recommendations to the agency as to the suitability of prospective adopters, the suitability of a particular placement for adoption, and whether adoption or freeing for adoption is in the child's best interests. The agency must take a decision on any recommendation made by the panel on any of these questions within 14 days of the recommendation, and although it must take the panel's recommendation into account, the agency is not bound by it. Additional functions may also be given to the panel, for example, monitoring and reviewing the implementation of plans for children and reviewing prospective adopters who have not had a child placed with them.[2] The composition of these panels is not dissimilar to that of the fostering panels.[3]

1 See *The Children (Scotland) Act 1995 Regulations and Guidance (Guidance): Volume 3, Adoption and Parental Responsibilities Orders* (1997).

2 Adoption Agencies (Scotland) Regulations 1996, SI 1996/3266, ('Adoption Regs'), regs 7 and 11.

3 See ch 4, pt 4(2).

## (2) The welfare of the child

The paramount consideration in all decisions relating to the adoption of a child, whether the decision is taken by an adoption agency or a court, is the need to safeguard and promote the welfare of the child throughout his/her life. This new formulation, introduced by the 1995 Act, goes beyond the previous provision which referred only to the child's 'childhood'. Those involved in decision making must also take into account the views of the child (children over 12 are deemed mature enough to form a view) and his/her religious persuasion, racial origin and cultural and linguistic background. This last requirement was also introduced by the 1995 Act.[1] Before making a decision about adoption, agencies must also consider whether adoption is the option which is likely to best meet the needs of the child or whether there is some practicable alternative which would be better.[2] Adoption panels, as part of their advisory function, must, if they are recommending that adoption is in the best interests of the child, produce a written report on their consideration of alternatives to adoption.[3]

## (3) Who can adopt?

There are certain restrictions affecting the ability to adopt. If a married couple wish to adopt, both must be 21 or older unless one of the partners is the child's parent, in which case that partner need only be 18 provided the spouse is at least 21.[4] A single individual wishing to adopt must be over 21 and is subject to the further condition that he/she is either:

(a) single; or
(b) married to the natural parent of the child (provided he or she has parental responsibilities and rights); or
(c) married but either separated, or the other spouse is incapable of making an application for health reasons.

Where a single applicant is the mother or father of the child, the other parent (in the sense of a parent having parental responsibilities

1 Adoption (Scotland) Act 1978, s 6 substituted by the 1995 Act, s 95.
2 1978 Act, s 6A added by the 1995 Act, s 96.
3 Adoption Regs, reg 11(2).
4 1978 Act, s 14.

or rights) must be dead, have disappeared, or there must be some other reason justifying his/her exclusion.[1]

The 1978 Act does not prevent an application being made by a person who is living in a relationship (whether heterosexual or homosexual) and where the non-applicant partner is intended to participate in the care of the child.[2] Previously where, for example, a mother remarried and the new husband wished to adopt her child, both parents had to adopt, but now, because of the provision noted in (b) above, this is no longer necessary and the husband can apply on his own. In this case, adoption does not deprive the mother of her parental responsibilities and rights.

Adoptive parents for children placed by an adoption agency must be approved by the adoption agency. The process of approval involves a lengthy and detailed investigation of the prospective adopters, their family circumstances and their motives for wishing to adopt. As in the process of investigation to become foster parents,[3] the investigation by the social worker is likely to be protracted over a period of months. The length of time required to complete a comprehensive assessment has led to some criticism from government ministers and from applicants about unnecessary delays and the Guidance suggests that it should be completed within 6 months of the date of application to be considered.[4] On completion of the investigation a report is prepared which is then considered by the adoption panel who will advise on suitability. The relevant guidance suggests that prospective adopters should be allowed to attend the adoption panel meeting and that, although those involved can make use of the agency's complaints and representation procedure, there should be an procedure for appealing against outcomes of the approval process.

Aside from the above there are no **legal** restrictions on ability to adopt: in particular, homosexuality is no bar to adopting.[5] Agencies are obliged to prepare and make available the criteria to be used in deciding whether to assess someone as a prospective adopter.[6] Agencies and/or the Scottish Office may impose restrictions as a matter of policy. They may, for example, refuse to consider people over a certain age to adopt babies or to place children with parents of a different race or to accept applications from gay couples.

1 1978 Act, s 15.
2 *T, Petitioner* 1996 SCLR 897.
3 See ch 4, pt 4(2).
4 Guidance, vol 3, ch 1, para 80.
5 *T, Petitioner* 1996 SCLR 897.
6 Adoption Regs, reg 10(1).

Restrictions such as these have been criticised as arbitrary, driven by ideology or extremely discriminatory.

### (4) Who can be adopted?

Anyone under the age of 18 who is not and has never been married can be adopted. An adoption order can also be made in respect of someone aged 18 if the adoption application was made before his/her 18th birthday. There are, however, certain requirements as to residence with the proposed adopters before an adoption order can be granted. These are:

(a) Where the prospective adopter is the child's parent, step-parent or a relative or where the placement has been made by an adoption agency, the child must have had a home with the adopters for at least 13 weeks prior to the adoption and be at least 19 weeks old.
(b) In other cases, the child must have had a home with the adopters for 12 months.

Before making the order the court must also be satisfied that the local authority (where the placement is not by an adoption agency) or the adoption agency has had sufficient opportunity to see the child with the adopters in their home environment. This requirement may prolong the periods set out above.[1]

Children aged 12 or over must consent to the adoption and their consent can be dispensed with only if they are incapable of giving it. In addition, the court must have regard to the views of the child regarding the adoption (taking account of his/her age and maturity), so the views of children under 12 are also relevant to the adoption decision.[2]

### (5) Rights of the child's parents

The parents of the child usually have to consent to the adoption, but there is provision for their consent to be dispensed with in the following cases:

1 1978 Act, s 13.
2 1978 Act, s 12.

(a) if the parent is not known, cannot be found or is incapable of giving consent;
(b) if the parent is withholding consent unreasonably;
(c) if the parent has persistently failed, without reasonable cause, to fulfil either his/her responsibility to safeguard and promote the child's health, development and welfare or, in cases where the child is not living with the parent, his/her responsibility to maintain contact and personal relations on a regular basis;
(d) if the parent has seriously ill-treated the child, and as a result of this, or for some other reason, the reintegration of the child into the same household as the parent is unlikely.[1]

The consent of the child's mother to adoption (or to freeing for adoption) is ineffective if it is given within 6 weeks of the birth of the child.[2]

Once a decision has been made by an adoption agency that adoption or an application for a freeing order is in the best interests of the child, the parents of the child must be notified of this, provided with certain information and asked if they agree with the decision.[3] If they do not reply within 28 days, the agreement of the parent is to be treated as unlikely to be forthcoming. In such cases and in cases where parents indicate that they disagree with the decision, an accelerated procedure for applying for the adoption/freeing order comes into play which affects local authorities. This requires an application for a freeing order or for an adoption order to be made within 21 days.[4] Where parental agreement is initially given and is then withdrawn the case is to be treated from the date of withdrawal as one where consent is unlikely to be forthcoming. In the case of other adoption agencies, they are simply required to take such steps as they consider appropriate and in the interests of the child as soon as is reasonably practicable.[5]

### (6) Children subject to supervision requirements

Where an agency intends to place a child who is subject to a supervision requirement for adoption or to seek a freeing order in respect of the child, it must report this to the reporter who will then organ-

1 1978 Act, s 16(2).
2 1978 Act, s 16(4).
3 Adoption Regs, reg 14.
4 Adoption Regs, regs 15, 17(2) and (3).
5 Adoption Regs, reg 16.

ise a hearing to consider the matter. The hearing will then prepare a report to be considered by the court which will have to take the decision.[1] The decision of the hearing is communicated to the agency, which if it is a local authority then becomes subject to specific requirements:

(a) If both the parents and the hearing agree with the proposed action no special rules apply.
(b) If the parents disagree but the hearing agrees then an application for an adoption or freeing order must be made within 21 days of the date of the hearing.
(c) If, regardless of the views of the parents, the hearing disagrees with the proposals, the agency must reconsider its decision within 14 days of receiving notification of the hearing's decision and if it concludes that adoption is in the child's best interests an application for an adoption or freeing for adoption order must be made within 14 days of reaching that decision.[2]

### (7) Freeing for adoption[3]

At a stage before the application for an adoption order is made, a local authority adoption agency can apply for an order freeing a child for adoption. If parental agreement to this is to be dispensed with by the court, the child must already have been placed for adoption or be likely to be placed for adoption. The grounds for dispensing with parental consent are the same as those applying in respect of adoption. One difference, though, is that there is a role in freeing applications for the father of a child who does not have parental responsibilities or rights. Before making the order the court must be satisfied that the father has no intention of seeking an order in relation to parental rights or responsibilities or would be refused such an order if he applied. Further, it must be clear that the father has no intention of entering into an agreement to acquire responsibilities or rights or that no such agreement is likely to be made.

The effect of the freeing order is that parental responsibilities and rights are transferred to the adoption agency. The court can also terminate a supervision requirement if it is satisfied that compulsory supervision is no longer necessary. Once a freeing order has

1 1995 Act, s 73(4)(c)(ii) and (iii), (8), (9), (13), and (14); 1978 Act, s 22A.
2 Adoption Regs, reg 18.
3 1978 Act, s 18.

been made, the child's parent must be notified of any placement for adoption or any adoption order unless the parent has made a declaration that he/she prefers not to be involved in future questions concerning the child.[1] The case of a child freed for adoption must be reviewed after 6 months if the child has not been placed for adoption and then at least every 6 months until a placement is made.[2] Both the child's parents and the agency can apply for revocation of the freeing order.

### (8) Placement with proposed adopters

Placements made by an adoption agency will be the culmination of a number of decisions: approval of the adoptive parents; a decision that the welfare of the child is best met by adoption; and a decision as to the suitability of the particular placement. All of these decisions will have involved the adoption panel. Where the child is subject to a supervision requirement the children's hearing will also be involved.

Placements must be notified to the child's parents and to a variety of others, for example, the education authority and health board for the area where the prospective adopter stays. The child must also be visited within 1 week of the placement and thereafter whenever necessary to supervise the child's welfare. Written reports of the meetings must be prepared.[3] Where the parent has consented to adoption as noted above or where a freeing order is pending, the child cannot be removed by the parent.[4]

### (9) Adoption procedure

The main feature of the adoption process in court is the emphasis on confidentiality. There are strict limits on those allowed to see the court papers which must be sealed at the end of the case. Any court hearings must be held in private unless the court directs otherwise and this is unlikely.

If the child has not been placed for adoption by an adoption agency, the local authority must be informed of the intention to

1 1978 Act, s 19.
2 Adoption Regs, reg 21.
3 Adoption Regs, reg 19.
4 1978 Act, s 27.

adopt.[1] Before an adoption order can be granted a report must then be produced by the local authority. The report will cover such matters as the suitability of the applicant and any matters relevant to the effect of the adoption on the safeguarding and promotion of the child's welfare; relevant matters would include the occupations of the adopters and their ability to look after the child. In addition, the report must comment on the feelings and wishes of the child. Finally, the report must confirm that the placement has not been made contrary to section 11 of the Adoption (Scotland) Act 1978, which permits placements to be made only by an adoption agency, unless the proposed adopter is a relative of the child. Where the placement has been made by an adoption agency it must provide a report covering all of these matters.

Once the relevant reports have been obtained, the petition for adoption can be lodged in court and in virtually all cases the court will be the sheriff court. Along with the petition the report mentioned above will be lodged, together with evidence as to the health of the proposed adopters.

Once the petition is lodged a curator ad litem and reporting officer will be appointed. In sheriff court cases these two posts will be combined unless this is not reasonably practicable. The individual appointed may be drawn from a panel maintained by the local authority, and if this is done and the adoption order is granted the authority will pay his/her fees.

The duty of the curator ad litem is to protect the interests of the child in the proceedings and to produce a report to the court. The functions of the curator are dealt with at length in the court rules. Briefly, they are to protect the child's interests; to ascertain whether the facts stated in the petition are correct; to establish whether the adoption is likely to safeguard and promote the welfare of the child; and to establish the reasons for adoption.

Reporting officers' duties are principally to witness the parents' consent to the adoption and to ensure that they understand the effects of adoption.

Following receipt of the reports a statutory hearing will be held. This may simply be a formality ending with the granting of the petition. The court, however, may wish to clarify matters from the reports and may wish to interview the petitioners and any person making a report to the court. Finally, the child's parent may appear and object to the granting of the order and in such a case a proof

1 1978 Act, s 22. If the child is subject to a supervision requirement the case must be referred to the reporter: 1995 Act, s 73(5).

hearing may be necessary to ascertain whether the consent of the parent can be dispensed with.

At the end of the proceedings a number of options are open to the court. The decision is subject to the welfare considerations discussed above. In addition, the court must not make the order unless it is satisfied that it would be better for the child for the order to be made rather than for the order not to be made. The options are:

(a) to refuse the order;
(b) to grant the order as sought;
(c) to grant an interim order giving parental responsibilities and rights to the petitioners for up to 2 years. This is in the nature of a probationary period at the end of which an additional report will be produced by the curator and the matter resolved. An interim order may be appropriate, for example, where the petitioners appear rather immature or where there is some other problem which may be overcome by the passing of time. Interim orders are very rare in practice;
(d) to grant the order subject to conditions. If open adoptions were to become more accepted a condition could be attached requiring contact by the child's parent;
(e) to exercise its general powers under section 11 of the 1995 Act to make an order in respect of parental responsibilities or rights;
(f) if it considers that any of the grounds of referral,[1] except commission of an offence by the child, is satisfied in respect of the child, to refer the case to the reporter who must then investigate and decide whether the child is in need of supervision. If the reporter decides that this is the case a hearing must be arranged.

The court has the power to terminate a supervision requirement if it considers that, as a result of its order, compulsory supervision is no longer necessary.[2] Once an adoption order is made it will be recorded in the Adopted Children's Register kept in the General Register Office for Scotland in Edinburgh.

1 See ch 5, pt 3(3).
2 1978 Act, s 12(9).

## (10) Adoption allowances[1]

Adoption agencies are now enabled to pay adoption allowances in certain types of cases. These are:

(a) where the adoption agency is satisfied that the child has established a strong and important relationship with the adopters before the adoption order is made;
(b) where it is desirable to place a child with siblings or with a child who has previously shared his/her home;
(c) where the child is disabled or suffering from emotional or behavioural difficulties and extra resources are needed to provide special care or where after placement such a child needs greater resources because the child is older or because his/her condition has deteriorated;
(d) where greater resources are needed because the child has developed an illness or disability since placement, provided the risk of him/her developing this was known at the time of placement.

Before allowances are paid the agency must reach a decision that the placement is not possible without paying an allowance. The amount of the allowance is determined after considering the resources available to the adopters, the financial needs of the adopters (excluding the costs incurred in respect of the child) and the financial needs and resources of the child.

## (11) Access to adoption records

As we have noted, the making of an adoption order is recorded in the Adopted Children's Register. In addition, the Registrar General must keep other registers and information linking the Adopted Children's Register with a child's original birth certificate. Once an adopted child reaches the age of 16 that child is entitled to access to these records. On application the Registrar General must advise the child of the availability of counselling. Counselling is optional but if it is requested it will be provided by an adoption society if it made the original placement; otherwise it will be provided by the local authority for the area where the child resides.

1 1978 Act, s 51A; Adoption Allowance (Scotland) Regulations 1996, SI 1996/3257; Adoption Allowance Schemes Directions 1996.

### (12) Post-placement support

There is a new recognition arising from research findings about the short- and long-term effects of adoption that a much wider access to counselling should be provided. This acknowledgment features in section 1(2) of the 1978 Act, as amended, which fortifies and enhances the duty of local authorities to provide post-placement support in the way of advice, support and guidance to a variety of people affected by adoptions, including children who have been adopted, people who have adopted children, parents whose children have been adopted, and anyone else whose problems relate to adoption. Social workers' knowledge about, for example, identity formation, family dynamics and separation and loss forms a sound basis for providing this increased counselling service.

## 4. MATRIMONIAL HOMES (FAMILY PROTECTION) (SCOTLAND) ACT 1981

The Matrimonial Homes (Family Protection) (Scotland) Act 1981 (the 1981 Act) deals with two main topics: the property rights of spouses who do not own or are not the tenants of the house they share with their spouse; and the provision of greater protection to spouses suffering from domestic violence. In practice, although the legislation refers throughout to spouses, the principal beneficiaries and the most numerous applicants to court under its various provisions are women.

There are four provisions of the 1981 Act which are of particular relevance. These are the provisions relating to occupancy rights; exclusion orders; matrimonial interdicts; and the transfer of tenancies. Cohabiting couples also enjoy some of the benefits of the 1981 Act and their position is considered at the end of this part.

### (1) Occupancy rights

Under the previous law the only person with a legal right to occupy a home was the person who was the owner or tenant of the property, or who enjoyed some other permission from the owner to occupy it. The difficulty in this was that the ownership or tenancy of the family home was usually taken in the name of the husband alone, with the consequence that the wife had no legally recognised right of occupation. She could therefore be ejected from the family home and had no legal power to prevent this or to resume occupation after it had happened.

The 1981 Act remedies this situation. It does so by defining the spouse who is the owner or tenant of the family home (referred to in the 1981 Act as the 'matrimonial home') as an 'entitled spouse' and the other spouse as a 'non-entitled spouse', and by granting all non-entitled spouses what is referred to as an 'occupancy right' in the family home.

The precise content of this occupancy right depends on whether or not the non-entitled spouse is in occupation of the matrimonial home. If she is, the right is to remain in occupation and to have free access to the home. If not, the right is to be allowed to enter and occupy the matrimonial home. Should access be refused or should the non-entitled spouse be excluded from the home, the occupancy right can be enforced only by application to court.[1] While this right is a considerable improvement over the previous situation, it is important to acknowledge and appreciate that the non-entitled spouse (usually the woman) may need support and assistance from a social worker or others to consider this as one alternative living situation, which may or may not be the preferred or most appropriate option.

The situation noted above where the title to the matrimonial home is in the name of only one of the spouses is now fairly rare. It is much commoner now for the title to be taken in the joint names of the husband and wife. Where this is the case both have property rights in the home, including occupancy rights, regardless of the 1981 Act.

Wherever occupancy rights exist either spouse can apply to court for an order enforcing the rights, restricting the occupancy rights of the other spouse, regulating the exercise of the other spouse's occupancy rights, or protecting the occupancy rights of the spouse applying for the order. Either spouse may also apply for an exclusion order barring the other from the matrimonial home.

### (2) Exclusion orders[2]

Either spouse can apply to court for an exclusion order suspending the occupancy rights of the other. This can be done **both** where

1 Matrimonial Homes (Family Protection) (Scotland) Act 1981, ss 1 and 3.
2 1981 Act, s 4.

there is an entitled and non-entitled spouse **and** where the title to the property is joint and both spouses are effectively entitled spouses. It is now clear that the spouse applying for the exclusion order need not be in occupation of the matrimonial home when the application is made.

There are two requirements to be fulfilled before the court can grant the order. First, the order must be necessary to protect the applicant or any child of the family from actual or threatened conduct of the other spouse which would be detrimental to their physical or mental health. Secondly, the court must not make an order if it would be unjustified or unreasonable to do so.

*(a) Need for protection.* In the first place making the order must be necessary. The implication is that there must be no other remedy, such as an interdict, which will provide the necessary protection. On the other hand it does **not** mean that an applicant must proceed in stages: first of all seeking an interdict and then, if that is unsuccessful, applying for an exclusion order.

The threat must come from some conduct on the part of the other spouse. The provision will therefore not cover the case where the upset arises simply from the other spouse's desire to remain in the matrimonial home despite the break-up of the relationship. Finally, it should be noted that actual physical injury need not have occurred for an order to be granted.

The courts have formulated four relevant questions to be considered in deciding on this type of application. They are:

(i) What is the nature and quality of the alleged conduct?
(ii) Is the court satisfied that the conduct is likely to be repeated if cohabitation continues?
(iii) Has the conduct been, or, if repeated would it be, injurious to the physical or mental health of the applicant spouse or any child of the family?
(iv) If so, is the order sought necessary for the future protection of the physical or mental health of the applicant or child?[1]

*(b) Unjustified or unreasonable.* In deciding on whether granting the order would be unjustified or unreasonable the 1981 Act directs the court to consider a number of factors. These include the conduct of the parties, the respective needs and resources of the parties, the needs of any children, and the offer by an entitled spouse

1 *McCafferty v McCafferty* 1986 SLT 650.

to make accommodation available to the non-entitled spouse. In the specific case of tied housing where there is a requirement that the non-applicant spouse reside there, the court must consider that requirement and the possible consequences of making an exclusion order in deciding whether or not it is unjustified or unreasonable to make the order.

When the court makes an exclusion order it must also, if requested to do so by the applicant, grant a warrant for the ejection of the other spouse from the home and/or an interdict preventing the other spouse from entering the matrimonial home without the permission of the spouse applying for the order. The court may also grant an interdict prohibiting the other spouse from entering or remaining in a specified area in the vicinity of the matrimonial home. Pending the granting of a full exclusion order the court may make an interim (temporary) order. This may only be done if the non-applicant spouse has been afforded an opportunity of being heard or represented in court before the interim order is made.

### (3) Transfer of tenancy[1]

Where the matrimonial home is rented in the name of the entitled spouse only, the non-entitled spouse may apply to court for the tenancy to be transferred to her. Before granting such an order the court must consider all the circumstances of the case and, in particular, the conduct of the spouses; the respective needs and resources of the spouses; the needs of any children; the extent of any business use of the home by one of the spouses; and any offer by the entitled spouse to provide accommodation for the non-entitled spouse.

### (4) Matrimonial interdicts

In general terms, an interdict is a court order requiring an individual to desist from a course of conduct which is causing or is likely to cause injury (whether physical, mental or financial) or detriment to another or to interfere with his/her legal rights. Normally, breach of the terms of an interdict is a civil matter and will be punished only if the person who has obtained the interdict takes proceedings

1 1981 Act, s 13.

to bring the offender before the court. If this is done the offender can be punished since he/she is guilty of contempt of court. The 1981 Act, however, introduced a new category: matrimonial interdicts. A matrimonial interdict is one which either:

(a) restrains or prohibits any conduct of one spouse towards the other spouse or towards a child of the family; or
(b) prohibits a spouse from entering or remaining in a matrimonial home or in a specified area in the vicinity of the home.[1]

The peculiarity of a matrimonial interdict is that the court can attach to it a power of arrest which gives the police the power to arrest if there is reasonable cause to suspect that a breach of the interdict has taken place. A power of arrest **must** be attached where the interdict is associated with an exclusion order or an interim exclusion order and the spouse applying for the interdict applies for the power of arrest to be attached. In other cases where the power of arrest is applied for, it **must** be attached to the interdict where the non-applicant spouse has had the opportunity of being heard or represented before the court, unless it appears to the court that in all the circumstances the power of arrest is unnecessary. A matrimonial interdict with a power of arrest attached must be notified to the non-applicant spouse and the Chief Constable.[2] The power of arrest is to the effect that a constable **may** arrest if breach of the interdict is suspected.

Once a spouse has been arrested he may be freed if the officer in charge of the police station to which he is taken is satisfied that there is no likelihood of violence to the other spouse or to any child of the family. If the offending spouse is freed a report is made to the procurator fiscal, and he may be prosecuted for any criminal offence that has been committed. If no prosecution takes place the other spouse must be informed.

If the spouse is not freed a report is made to the fiscal who may prosecute the spouse for any offence committed. If no prosecution takes place a petition is presented to the court and if the sheriff is satisfied that there is a prima facie breach of interdict, that civil proceedings for breach will be taken by the other spouse, and that there is a substantial risk of violence against the other spouse or child of the family the sheriff may order further detention for up to 2 days.

Finally, although the only express provision and mention in the 1981 Act is in respect of interdicts prohibiting entry to the matri-

1 1981 Act, s 14(2).
2 1981 Act, s 15.

monial home and its vicinity, there is no reason, for example, why the husband cannot be interdicted from harassing the wife at work or the wife and children at any other place. Such an interdict, because it relates to the conduct of one spouse towards the other or towards a child of the family, would be a matrimonial interdict and could have a power of arrest attached.

### (5) Cohabiting couples[1]

In the case of couples living together as husband and wife where one has a title to the shared home and the other does not, the non-entitled partner may apply to court for the grant of occupancy rights. This grant may be made for up to 6 months, but is renewable for further 6-month periods. Where such an order is in force or where both partners are 'entitled', the provisions of the 1981 Act in relation to occupancy rights, exclusion orders and matrimonial interdicts apply to cohabiting couples in much the same way as to married couples. Non-entitled partners in rented accommodation may also apply for the transfer of the tenancy.

1 1981 Act, s 18.

# 4. Local authority services to children

## 1. INTRODUCTION

One of the major changes in emphasis found in the Children (Scotland) Act 1995 (the 1995 Act) is the importance placed on providing services to promote the welfare of children and their families and to secure that children are brought up by their families. The provision of services is not seen negatively as being concerned with preventing care being taken over by the local authority, but positively as enabling children to achieve and maintain a reasonable standard of development. This is expressed in a duty to provide services to promote welfare,[1] a duty to plan the provision of services for children[2] and a duty to publish information about these services.[3] The first plans for services for children are to be published in April 1998.

The focus of service provision is not on children generally, but on children in need, many of whom may also potentially be in need of protection or at risk. There is no explicit link between the categories of children at risk and children in need, though the guidance issued under the 1995 Act does say:

> '. . . the Act introduces various powers enabling authorities to provide a range of different types of support for children and their families. The effective use of those powers will help to avoid situations which could lead to children being subjected to abuse and may thus avert the need for child protection intervention.'[4]

1 Children (Scotland) Act 1995 (the 1995 Act), s 22.

2 1995 Act, s 19.

3 1995 Act, s 20.

4 *The Children (Scotland) Act 1995 Regulations and Guidance: Volume 1, Support and Protection for Children and their Families* (1997), ch 7, para 2. The other two volumes, both published by the Stationery Office in 1997, are volume 2 on Children Looked After by Local Authorities and volume 3 on Adoption and Parental Responsibilities Orders. In future they will be referred to as '*Guidance*' with the relevant volume number.

Although there is some evidence from England and Wales, where similar duties are imposed on local authorities under the Children Act 1989, that priority is being given to children at risk,[1] the guidance which applies there makes it clear that the categories of children at risk and children in need should not be regarded as the same.[2] The same view should be taken in Scotland.

Other changes introduced by the 1995 Act are a changed view of the role of accommodation provided by a local authority. It is seen as part of promoting the welfare of children and a resource to support the upbringing of a child by his/her family, and a change in terminology so that children are no longer in care, but are being 'looked after' by the local authority. This second change was made as an attempt to remove the stigma attached to being labelled as in care as well as incorporating the notion of partnership with parents and is accompanied by a clarification of which groups of children are to be regarded as looked after.

A final important change in this area is the replacement of the administrative procedure by which a local authority could acquire parental rights by one which requires application to court for a parental responsibilities order.

In considering these provisions below, three definitions should be remembered. The first is that for the purpose of these provisions a child is a person under 18;[3] the second is that the term 'family' extends not only to someone with parental responsibility, but also to any person with whom the child has been living;[4] and the third is that a 'relevant person' is anyone holding parental responsibilities or parental rights or anyone who ordinarily has charge of or control over a child (unless this is in the course of their employment).[5]

Finally, statutory provision in this area is supplemented by regulations, directions given by the Secretary of State and guidance issued by the Social Work Services Group[6] and by local child protection procedures.[7]

1 Eg *Children Act Report* 1994 Cm 2878 (1995), p 1.

2 *The Children Act 1989 Guidance and Regulations, vol 2, Family Support, Day Care and Education Provisions for Young Children* (1991), para 2.4.

3 1995 Act, s 93(2)(a).

4 1995 Act, s 93(1).

5 1995 Act, s 93(2)(b).

6 The last three are collected together in the three volumes of *The Children (Scotland) Act 1995 Regulations and Guidance*. See above, p 108, footnote 4.

7 *Effective Intervention: Child Abuse* (1989) Social Work Services Group; SWSG Circular 4/96.

## 2. SERVICES FOR CHILDREN IN NEED

### (1) Promoting welfare

Two main duties are imposed on local authorities. They must, first, safeguard and promote the welfare of children in need living in their area. Second, they must promote the upbringing of such children by their families, provided that this is consistent with safeguarding and promoting the children's welfare. Both of these duties are to be fulfilled by providing services to children which are of an appropriate type and at an appropriate level.[1]

This general statement of local authority duties raises a number of questions. When is a child 'in need'? How is the decision about provision of services taken? Are there special provisions for particular groups of children? Can the social work department call on others for help? What sort of services can be provided? How can decisions be challenged? These questions are addressed below.

### (2) Children in need

A child will be considered in need if in need of care and attention for one of the following reasons:[2]

(a) The child is unlikely to achieve or maintain or have the opportunity to achieve or maintain a reasonable standard of health or development unless services are provided.
(b) His/her health or development is likely to be significantly impaired or further impaired unless services are provided.
(c) The child is disabled. In this context 'disabled' means chronically sick or disabled or suffering from a mental disorder as defined in the Mental Health (Scotland) Act 1984.
(d) The child is adversely affected by the disability of another member of his/her family. This could be a sibling or a parent.

This definition is almost identical to that contained in the Children Act 1989, in which context it has been described as 'pregnant with indeterminacy, except in so far as it is clear that we are dealing with a restricted category of children'.[3] More definition is

1 1995 Act, s 22.
2 1995 Act, s 93(4)(a).
3 A Bainham 'Children – The Modern Law' (1993, Family Law), p 338.

given in England and Wales of some of the terms. 'Development', for example, is defined to include 'physical, intellectual, emotional, and social development'.[1] No further definition is offered either in the 1995 Act or in the guidance issued on it. This means that a great deal of discretion is left to local authorities to define their own terms for implementation of these provisions. For example, when is a child 'in need of care and attention', what amounts to significant impairment and what is a reasonable standard? This last particularly begs the question of whether the standard to be used is an absolute standard or is to be judged by the standard of the area in which the child happens to live. One thing, however, is clear: the definition looks not only to past and present disadvantage, but also to possible future disadvantage. In this respect, the 1995 Act has clearly taken into account the link established in research between poverty and deprivation.

### (3) Assessment

The guidance[2] envisages that services will be provided only after an assessment of the needs of the child and his/her family. The assessment process should start with the screening of cases. These cases may be referred to the social work department or come to its attention directly. Screening is designed to identify cases which can be dealt with simply, eg by providing information or advice, and cases which need a fuller assessment. Assessment is required to take account of the child's religious persuasion, racial origin and cultural and linguistic background.[3]

Different cases will call for assessments of differing complexity involving varying groups of professionals. Assessments of the child may need to be carried out for purposes other than the provision of services under the 1995 Act, for example to establish if the child needs the provision of services under the Chronically Sick and Disabled Persons Act 1970.

Where different types of assessments need to be carried out they should, as far as possible, be conducted at the same time. Regardless of the form of the assessment, it should include an assessment of risk to the child as well as the needs of the child and family. This points to the fact that children in need may also be at

1 Children Act 1989, s 17(11).
2 *Guidance,* vol 1, ch 1.
3 1995 Act, s22(2).

risk and that an assessment, and indeed the initial referral triggering the assessment, may indicate the need to take some appropriate child protection measures. Here, assessment is seen as something more holistic and comprehensive than what may be a narrowly focused investigation and it is clear from recent research[1] that an overemphasis on investigation and monitoring has been detrimental to the clear intention of the Children Act 1989 in supporting families wherever possible.

At the end of the assessment the social worker will have to reach a conclusion as to the needs of the child and his/her family. The decision about needs is one for the professional judgment of the worker, operating, of course, within the policies and procedures of the local authority. A further decision then has to be taken about which services are to be provided to meet the identified needs of the child and family. This process, like the assessment, should involve the family fully in the spirit of partnership and empowering practice. As with all these sorts of decisions the question arises whether there is a clear right or entitlement to services once needs have been identified and whether the local authority has discretion, particularly as to whether resources can be considered. The vagueness of the definition of 'in need', referred to above, and the reference to providing 'appropriate' services leaves considerable discretion to the local authority. More specifically, the guidance says:

> 'Once a need has been identified, the local authority should consider whether assistance is appropriate, and if so should plan with the family how best to meet this need *within the resources and services available.*'[2]

This seems to indicate that resources are a relevant consideration in deciding whether to meet needs[3], though it should be borne in mind that in some cases the need will be so great and clear that a refusal to provide services will be regarded by the courts as unreasonable and so be open to challenge.

## (4) Children and disability

Special provision is made for children affected by disability.[4] A child may be affected by disability either because the child is disabled or because he/she is affected by the disability of another fam-

1 Department of Health *Child Protection: Messages from research* (1995).
2 *Guidance*, vol 1, ch 1, para 29, emphasis added.
3 See also *R v Kingston-upon-Thames Royal Borough Council, ex parte T* [1994] 1 FLR 798.
4 1995 Act, s 23; *Guidance*, vol 1, ch 6.

ily member. In general, services provided to such children under the local authority's obligation to promote welfare are to be designed to give the child the opportunity to lead as normal a life as possible and to minimise the effect of the disability.

As well as the obligation to provide services the local authority has specific assessment duties in respect of children affected by disability. The parent or guardian of such a child can request an assessment of the child or of the disabled family member[1] and it is hoped that the family's singular understanding of the needs of the child will be fully appreciated and represented. Although only the parent or guardian has the statutory right to request an assessment, the guidance makes it clear that it is good practice to carry out an assessment if requested to do so by a child affected by disability. The guidance also goes into more detail on the assessment process and suggests that the policy and practice guidance on community care assessment are possible further sources of guidance.

The purpose of the assessment is to identify the needs of the child and so to help the local authority in carrying out its duties as regards provision of services **both** to minimise the effect of the disability and give the child the chance to lead as normal a life as possible **and**, more generally, to promote the welfare of the child. Although the 1995 Act restricts assessments to identifying needs flowing from disability, the guidance goes further and suggests, correctly in view of the general requirement to assess before providing services, that the assessment should 'consider whether services available for children in need . . . should be provided to meet the child's wider needs, in addition to those attributable to his or her disability'.[2]

A final element of the assessment process is that, where a disabled child is being assessed, the child's carer[3] can request an assessment of his/her ability to provide or to continue to provide care for the child.[4] The outcome of the assessment of the carer must be taken into account in taking decisions about service provision.

Duties to disabled children under the 1995 Act are superimposed on other duties owed to people with disabilities, and the relationship between these provisions is unclear. It has been said that

1 1995 Act, s 24.

2 *Guidance*, vol 1, ch 6, para 5.

3 Defined as a person who 'provides or intends to provide a substantial amount of care on a regular basis' for the child: 1995 Act, s 24(1)(b). Volunteer carers operating as part of a voluntary organisation and employed carers are excluded.

4 1995 Act, s 24.

'the statutory provisions . . . are unnecessarily difficult to unravel, and are complex and obscure in an area where clarity and simplicity are appropriate'.[1] Other duties owed by local authorities are considered in chapter 6, but there is one specific statutory provision which should be briefly examined here. Section 2(1) of the Chronically Sick and Disabled Persons Act 1970 imposes a duty on the local authority to provide certain services (which are listed in the subsection) to certain classes of disabled people if it is satisfied that this is necessary to meet their needs.[2] Important consequences follow from this. The first is that disabled children to whom a duty arises under the 1995 Act are one of the classes to which this section applies. The second is that in deciding whether to provide services under this section the resources of the local authority may not be relevant (see the discussion in chapter 6, part 3(1)(d)). Third, even though a specific request for assessment for services under the 1970 Act is not made by the child or his/her parent/guardian, the local authority must be alive to the possibility of duties arising under it. If it fails to consider it and carry out an appropriate assessment considering services under the 1970 Act, any decision on provision of services could be illegal.[3]

Where a child is affected by the disability of an adult in his/her family, the local authority's duties to people affected by disability must be considered.

## (5) Assistance from other bodies

In carrying out its duties a local authority may request assistance from another local authority, a health board or an NHS trust. These bodies must comply with this request unless doing so would either be incompatible with their own statutory or other duties or would prejudice the discharge of any of their functions.[4] The inclusion of this section is significant in recognising the pivotal nature of collaboration and co-operation amongst agencies which has so evidently been at the root of difficulties in service provision in the past.

1 *R v London Borough of Bexley, ex parte B* (31 July 1995, unreported) QB.
2 For a list of these services see ch 6, pt 3(1)(a).
3 *R v London Borough of Bexley, ex parte B* (31 July 1995, unreported) QB.
4 1995 Act, s 21.

## (6) Provision of services

If services are to be provided, then the outcome of the assessment process will be a care plan agreed with the family. This care plan should be a written document and its implementation will have to be monitored and reviewed. Evidence from similar experiences of the use of care plans in England and Wales has demonstrated that these plans need to be concrete and specific if they are to be worth more than the paper on which they are printed.[1]

In providing services the local authority must take account of a number of factors. First it must act in partnership with families and pursue the duty to promote the upbringing of the child in his/her own family. Secondly, the local authority must listen to the child and take into account his/her views. Thirdly, it must 'have regard so far as practicable to each child's religious persuasion, racial origin and cultural and linguistic background'.[2] Finally, for a child away from home, the local authority must promote the child's contact with his/her family.

It is important to remember that the duty to promote welfare is laid at the door not only of the social work department, but is a duty owed by the council as a whole. Because of this, all the services of the local authority should be considered when it comes to identifying and meeting needs, and services provided by the housing and education departments will be particularly relevant.

The relationship between services for children and families and other services provided by the local authority is not entirely clear. When a local authority requests help from an outside body, that body is entitled to refuse if complying with the request would be inconsistent with its statutory duties or detrimental to the performance of these duties. Does the same apply within the same local authority? One area where this may arise is in respect of housing and families who are intentionally homeless. If a family with children approaches the housing department of a local authority to ask for housing as homeless persons they will usually need to be given temporary accommodation. The housing department will then have to decide if it has an obligation to secure the provision of permanent accommodation for the family. This obligation will arise only if the applicant is in priority need and is not intentionally homeless. Because there are children involved, the family will be in priority need, but if they were evicted because of non-payment of

1 Department of Health *Children's Service Plans: An analysis of children's service plans 1993/4* (1995).
2 1995 Act, s 22(2).

rent or anti-social behaviour they may be regarded as intentionally homeless. An approach might then be made to the social work department for assistance and it, in turn, might approach the housing department seeking the provision of accommodation. Can the housing department, though part of the same authority, refuse? There is a suggestion in a case on the Children Act 1989 that they could,[1] because there may be a conflict between the 1995 Act and the obligations of the authority under the Housing (Scotland) Act 1987, for example obligations to people already on the waiting list for council housing. The question may, however, turn out simply to be a technical one of deciding which budget is debited, since it is likely that the local authority has an obligation to provide accommodation for homeless families with children under the 1995 Act.

One argument in support of such an obligation[2] starts with the duty of the authority to promote the upbringing of children by their families by providing appropriate services[3] and then moves on to the obligation to accommodate children where their parents are unable to do so.[4] The argument then is that homeless parents are unable to care for their children and that putting the two obligations together imposes a duty on the local authority to provide accommodation for the whole family. One problem with this argument is a provision in the regulations which prohibits placing a child being accommodated by the local authority with his/her parents,[5] but this, it is suggested by those putting forward the argument, should be challenged as being inconsistent with the express provisions of the 1995 Act. Attractive though the conclusion may be, the means of arriving at it is seriously flawed. The flaw is that it is quite clear from the terms of section 25 of the 1995 Act that it refers only to children being accommodated **apart** from their parents: otherwise, the rights, for example, of parents to remove children are meaningless.[6]

1 *R v Northavon District Council, ex parte Smith* [1994] 2 AC 402 at 408D–E, per Lord Templeman.
2 M Dailly 'Stoking the home fires' *The Herald*, 5 March 1997. See also SCOLAG (1997) Issue 241, p 34.
3 1995 Act, s 22.
4 1995 Act, s 25.
5 Arrangements to Look After Children (Scotland) Regulations 1996, SI 1996/3262, reg 16(2).
6 It is also not entirely clear why this argument is thought to be a product of the 1995 Act. On the face of it the same argument could be put forward under s 15 of the Social Work (Scotland) Act 1968, which imposed a duty to accommodate and a duty to seek to have the care of the child taken over by his/her parents. The emphasis on looking after children separately from their parents is clear in the debates on the precursor of section 15, namely, s 1 of the Children Act 1948.

The other way of approaching this is simply in terms of the duties to children and families under the 1995 Act. These require, as we have seen, that appropriate services are provided to children in need, and we have it on the authority of the House of Lords that the children of homeless families are children in need.[1] As such, the local authority has a duty to provide appropriate services which will promote the upbringing of the children by their family.[2] In the circumstances, the only way that this duty can be appropriately fulfilled is by arranging for the family to be accommodated, whether in local authority housing or elsewhere. Any refusal to accommodate would be open to challenge, and it is clear that a blanket refusal to provide accommodation for children with their parents where the parents are intentionally homeless is illegal.[3]

A final point on the relationship between housing and social work services is that it has been suggested that before a local authority takes a decision which may result in duties being owed to children and families it must consider these potential obligations, and that failure to do this will leave the decision open to legal challenge.[4] This suggests that local authorities, before taking a decision to implement or enforce eviction, will have to consider that they will have a duty to accommodate the family under the 1995 Act.

### (7) Day care and after-school services

Appropriate day care services must be provided for children in need who are under five and have not started school, and after-school/school holiday services must be provided for children in need who are at school.[5] Authorities are empowered to provide these services to other children.

1 *R v Northavon District Council, ex parte Smith* [1994] 2 AC 402 at 406C, per Lord Templeman.

2 This is described as one of the 'essential principles' of the 1995 Act in *Guidance* vol 1, p vii. Assessments of children for service provision must, where appropriate, take into account the need for new accommodation: *R v Tower Hamlets London Borough Council, ex parte B* (13 January 1997, unreported).

3 *Attorney-General, ex rel Tilley v London Borough of Wandsworth* [1981] 1 All ER 1162.

4 *R v Avon County Council, ex parte Hills* (1995) 27 HLR 411.

5 1995 Act, s 27.

## (8) Provision of accommodation to children

A local authority has a duty to provide accommodation to any child who appears to require it for one of the following reasons:

(a) no one has parental responsibility for the child;
(b) the child is lost or abandoned;
(c) the person caring for the child is prevented temporarily or permanently from providing suitable accommodation and care.[1]

Accommodation can also be provided for any child, whether or not these criteria are met, and to people between 18 and 21 if it is considered that this would promote or safeguard the person's welfare. Before accommodation is provided to a child, the authority must have regard to his/her views, having regard to age and maturity, with children of 12 and over being deemed to be mature enough to express a view.

A child can be accommodated in a variety of settings:[2]

(a) with a family, relative or other suitable person. A family consisting of the people who have parental responsibilities for the child or people with whom the child has been living are excluded, so the child cannot be accommodated with them;
(b) in a residential establishment, such placements being governed by their own set of regulations and guidance;
(c) by the authority making other arrangements that appear to be appropriate.

A child cannot be cared for by his/her parents while being accommodated by the local authority.[3] The consequence of this would appear to be that the local authority cannot fulfil its obligation to accommodate a child by providing accommodation for the child and his/her family. There is, of course, no reason why this accommodation cannot be provided under the authority's duties and powers towards children in need.

The demise of the official notion of a child being received into care is welcomed but clearly the popular notion of being taken or received into care will take much longer to die. Hopefully, the new

1 1995 Act, s 25. In considering what a child requires reference should be made to future as well as current needs: *Re T (Accommodation by Local Authority)* [1995] 1 FLR 159.
2 1995 Act, s 26. Placements need not be in Scotland.
3 Arrangements to Look After Children (Scotland) Regulations 1996, SI 1996/3262, reg 16(2).

terminology which implies a partnership of parents, children and the social work department in looking after children will influence practice and the experience of service users.

The provision of accommodation for a child by the local authority is likely to be one of the most stressful events in the lives of all concerned. The social worker's role in these situations can often be contradictory. At its crudest and simplest, there is often a conflict of interest amongst the child, the family and the local authority at the point of accommodation being provided and the child being looked after by the local authority and the resulting tensions must be carefully managed. Social workers will be hard pressed systematically to make assessments, negotiate decision-making and marshall appropriate resources while remaining open to the feelings of all those involved in the process, including themselves.

## (9) Rights to object to provision of accommodation

A child cannot be accommodated against the objection of a person who **both**:

(a) holds parental responsibilities and the parental rights to have the child living with him/her and to control, direct or guide the child; **and**
(b) is willing to provide or arrange the provision of accommodation for the child.

Such a person can remove the child from accommodation provided by the local authority at any time. This power to object to the provision of accommodation and to remove the child is subject to two limitations. In the first place it will not arise where accommodation is being provided to a child of 16 or over who agrees to be provided with accommodation[1] or where a person holding a residence order in respect of the child agrees to the provision of accommodation. Secondly, 14 days' notice must be given of the intended removal once the child has been being accommodated for 6 months.[2]

1 It might be argued that the provision that children over the age of 16 cannot be removed against their will is redundant, since there can be no one with the parental rights needed to remove the child once the child is 16: see s 2(7) of the 1995 Act.

2 It is worth noting that the notice requirement is not part of the Children Act 1989. The view was taken that retaining the notice requirement blurred the distinction between voluntary and compulsory care.

Where a child is being provided with accommodation, his/her care plan, which should be agreed with the child's parents, should contain an express agreement about the ending of the provision of accommodation and may say something about the need to give notice before a child is removed. This agreement, of course, does not override the parent's right to remove the child, though some parents may feel, wrongly, that because they have entered into a written agreement they are bound by it and cannot exercise their rights.

The right of parents to remove children who are being provided with accommodation gives rise to two problems. First, who is to judge whether the parent is qualified to remove the child? It will have to be established that the parent holds responsibilities and the relevant rights, and it should be remembered that unmarried fathers will often not hold these. It will also have to be established that the parent is **willing** and **able** to provide accommodation for the child. Does this mean that if, in the judgment of the local authority, the parent is unable to provide accommodation then the parent has no right to take the child? What criteria might be used in arriving at that decision? Is the nature and suitability of the accommodation relevant? It is notable that the 1995 Act refers only to providing 'accommodation' and makes no reference to the suitability of the accommodation. If the local authority was of the opinion that the accommodation was not suitable, then its objection might come under the heading of the second problem, namely what is to be done when the parent demands that children are returned but the local authority does not think that it is in the interests of the child to comply with this?

In *M v Dumfries and Galloway Regional Council*[1] it was decided that if a local authority considered it not to be in the child's best interests to be returned to the parents it could refuse to do this. If the parents objected, they would have to go to court to seek an order for delivery of the child. Such an application was to be treated as an application under section 3 of the Law Reform (Parent and Child) (Scotland) Act 1986 (the 1986 Act), which meant that the court could not grant it unless it was satisfied that it was in the best interests of the child to do so. The authority of this decision has been doubted[2] on the grounds that the 1985 Act did not allow local authorities to rely on it, being purely a private law provision which could only be relied on by individuals. This seems to have been confirmed by the express provision in section 11(5) of the 1995 Act excluding local authorities from applying for orders relating to parental responsibilities or rights. It is debatable

1 1991 SCLR 481.

2 See K Norrie *The Children (Scotland) Act 1995* (1995), commentary on s 11 of the 1995 Act and *City of Edinburgh Council v M* 1996 SCLR 779.

whether the local authority was in fact 'relying' on the 1986 Act and whether the 1995 Act overrules the decision. However, the precedent set is undesirable for the different reason that it appears to allow the local authority to override the safeguards for parents and children built into the procedures which allow it to exercise compulsory powers over a child. What options then **are** open to the local authority in this situation?

(a) The local authority could apply for a child protection order if it considered that the conditions for this were fulfilled, or it could refer the case to the reporter if it considered that the child was in need of compulsory measures of supervision. Indeed, if it thought the child was in need of such measures it would have a **duty** to make the referral.[1] These powers would not help, however, where instant action was needed as they both take time.

(b) Any foster carer with whom the child had been placed or any individual social worker might be able to rely on section 5 of the 1995 Act. This states that:

> '. . . it shall be the responsibility of a person who has attained the age of sixteen and who has care or control of a child under that age, but in relation to him either has no parental responsibilities or rights or does not have the parental responsibility [to safeguard or promote the child's health, development or welfare], to do what is reasonable in all the circumstances to safeguard the child's health, development and welfare; and in fulfilling his responsibility . . . the person may . . . [subject to certain conditions] give consent to any surgical, medical or dental treatment or procedure . . . .'

This could be supplemented by the duty of the authority to safeguard and promote the welfare of children whom it is looking after. There is considerable support for the view that the equivalent English provision would allow the local authority to refuse to hand over a child, at least temporarily, while some other measures were taken.[2] Indeed, while this provision was going through

1 1995 Act, s 53(1)(b).

2 See eg Hayes and Williams *Family Law: Principles, Policy and Practice* (1995), p 120; M D A Freeman *Children, Their Families and the Law*, pp 67–68; and A Bainham *Children: The Modern Law* (1993), p 347. It should be noted that there is some authority for the view that the right of the parent to remove is unrestricted: *London Borough of Lewisham v Lewisham Juvenile Court Justices* [1979] 2 All ER 297, though this was decided before the 1989 and 1995 Acts and also contains a reference to a 'moral duty' which authorities may consider they have to keep a child temporarily rather than return him/her to an unsuitable parent (Lord Salmon at p 306H). The wording of the English legislation is slightly different from that of the 1995 Act, referring only to a 'person' which can include a corporate body such as a local authority: Interpretation Act 1978, Sch 1.

Parliament reference was made to the use of the provision to refuse to hand over a child to an inebriated parent.[1] It was also suggested that unless a social worker's decision to refuse to return a child to his/her parent was 'wholly unreasonable' the social worker would be protected by this provision.[2] No similar debate took place during the passage of section 5 of the 1995 Act; indeed the section was seen as being entirely a private law matter, and the provisions as to medical treatment were described as concerning 'private law' and not dealing with 'public intervention on behalf of the child'.[3] For this reason it might be difficult to argue that section 5 gives powers to social workers and foster carers. The relevant part of the guidance simply notes that:

> 'Carers will need advice on how to handle those occasional cases in which it may be necessary for the social worker to seek an emergency order to prevent an inappropriate or unplanned removal where this would be likely to cause significant harm to the child (for example, a drunk parent coming to "collect" his or her child in the middle of the night).'[4]

This does not really deal with the question of the legal basis for retaining a child until such an emergency order is obtained and it is suggested, notwithstanding the terms of the debate in Parliament, that section 5 of the 1995 Act does empower social workers and foster carers to refuse to return a child, but only temporarily while other action is taken to protect the child.

Even if we are wrong and no protection is offered by section 5 of the 1995 Act, it would be unlikely that a claim against the worker by the parent(s) for interference with the exercise of their rights would succeed.[5]

(c) The police could be called and asked to exercise their emergency powers to protect children.[6]

### (10) Assistance in cash or kind

The services provided by the local authority to children in need may be in kind or, in exceptional circumstances, in cash.[7] If assis-

1 By David Mellor (HC Standing Committee B, 18 May 1989, col 148) and by the Lord Chancellor (HL, vol 505, cols 370–371).
2 HC Standing Committee B, 18 May 1989, col 152.
3 By Lord James Douglas-Hamilton, HC Special Standing Committee, 23 February 1995, col 279.
4 *Guidance* vol 2, ch 1, para 121.
5 See *F v Wirral Metropolitan Borough Council* [1991] Fam 69.
6 1995 Act, s 61(5).
7 1995 Act, s 22(3)(b).

tance is provided in this way it may be unconditional or subject to repayment, in whole or in part, either of the cash sum or of the value of the benefit in kind. No repayment can be required of anyone receiving income support, family credit or jobseeker's allowance, and any requirement to repay can be made only after full consideration of the means of the child and his/her parent(s).

## 3. CHILDREN 'LOOKED AFTER' BY THE LOCAL AUTHORITY

### (1) Who is looked after?[1]

Children regarded as being looked after by the local authority are:

(a) children being provided with accommodation;
(b) children subject to a supervision requirement made by a children's hearing, even if they are staying at home;
(c) children subject to a variety of authorisations or warrants issued under the 1995 Act, for example, a child protection order, a child assessment order, a warrant for apprehension and/or detention issued by a hearing or sheriff court, or a parental responsibilities order. These children are looked after only if the order or warrant imposes responsibilities on the local authority. The local authority will have responsibilities in virtually every case where such a warrant or order is made. One exception might be where a child protection order is made in favour of someone who is not an employee of the local authority;
(d) children sentenced to detention by the sheriff summary court.[2]

Although these children are all being looked after by the local authority it is important to remember that, with the exception of those children in respect of whom a parental responsibilities order has been made, the child's parent(s) retain parental responsibilities and rights in respect of the child. In some cases, of course, these rights will be limited, as where the sheriff, in making a child protection order, or a children's hearing, in making a supervision requirement, regulate contact between the child and his/her parent(s).

1 1995 Act, s 17(6).
2 Criminal Procedure (Scotland) Act 1995, s 44(3).

## (2) Statutory duties[1]

In terms of the 1995 Act the local authority has a number of duties towards children who are being looked after. These duties are supplemented by further obligations contained in regulations which are further explained in the guidance on the 1995 Act. The regulations and guidance will be dealt with below. The duties directly imposed by the 1995 Act are:

(a) to safeguard and promote the welfare of the child. This is to be the paramount concern of the local authority and includes the duty to provide advice and assistance to prepare the child for when he/she is no longer looked after by the local authority;
(b) to make use of such services for children being looked after by their parents as appear to be reasonable;
(c) to take steps to promote regular contact and personal relations between the child and anyone having parental responsibilities in respect of the child. These steps must only be taken so far as the authority consider them to be practicable and appropriate in light of its paramount duty;
(d) to seek the views of the child, his/her parents, any non-parent holding parental rights and anyone else considered to be relevant before taking any decision with respect to a child that the authority is looking after or proposing to look after. The authority must obtain these views only as far as is reasonably practicable;
(e) to take the views of the child into account before making a decision;
(f) to take the views of those others identified in (d) above into account as far as it has been possible to obtain them;
(g) to take the child's religious persuasion, racial origin, culture and language into account before taking a decision.

Authorities may act inconsistently with these duties only where they consider that this is necessary to protect members of the public from serious harm.

## (3) Regulations and guidance: care plans

The Arrangements to Look After Children (Scotland) Regulations 1996 (the Arrangements Regulations)[2] require that before looking

1 1995 Act, s 17.
2 SI 1996/3262.

after a child the authority must, so far as reasonably practicable, make a care plan which addresses the immediate and longer-term needs of the child with a view to safeguarding and promoting the welfare of the child.[1] Where it is not reasonably practicable to make this plan before the child comes to be looked after it must be made as soon as reasonably practicable afterwards. In making the plan the authority must consider all the information available to it which is relevant to the performance of its statutory obligations towards the child.

The local authority must consider the following in making the plan:

(a) the nature of the services to be provided for the child in the immediate and longer-term future, with particular regard to the information about the child specified in Schedule 1 of the Arrangements Regulations, which includes information about the child's family, the present legal status of the child, previous local authority involvement, contact between the child and his/her family, and the child's personality, development, race, religion, language and nationality;
(b) alternative courses of action;
(c) whether a change in the child's legal status should be sought, for example by obtaining a parental responsibilities order;
(d) the arrangements needed for when the child is no longer looked after;
(e) the views of those who have to be consulted (see above);
(f) anything else relating to the child which appears to be relevant.[2]

The care plan itself must contain certain elements such as the type of accommodation to be provided, any contribution to be made by the child's parents to the day-to-day care of the child, arrangements for family contact and the expected length of time for which the child will be looked after. The care plan should be in writing and should, so far as reasonably practicable, be agreed with the child's parent(s), or if the child has no parent(s), the person who normally has care or control of the child. There are two exceptions to this. The first is that where a child over 16 is being provided with accommodation the plan should be agreed with the child. Secondly, there is no requirement to obtain agreement where the child is being looked after under a warrant, order or supervision

1 Ibid, reg 3.
2 Ibid, reg 4.

requirement, though the guidance indicates that such agreement is desirable. As a result, the main case where agreement will need to be reached is where the child is being provided with accommodation by the local authority under a voluntary arrangement with the parents.[1]

If the local authority is considering placing the child who is to be looked after (or a child who is being looked after) away from home, there are certain additional requirements imposed by the Arrangements Regulations as to the making of the care plan.[2] First, the information required by Schedule 1 (see above) must be recorded in writing. Second, there are some additional matters to which consideration must be given:

(a) whether it is necessary to change the arrangements for family contact;
(b) whether existing health arrangements need to be changed;
(c) how to meet any educational needs and achieve continuity in the child's education, for example when a placement will involve changing schools;
(d) where the placement is to be in a residential establishment, whether the placement is appropriate; appropriateness is to be judged by reference to the statement of functions and objectives prepared by the residential establishment.

Where a placement in a residential establishment is being considered, the views of the child must be obtained and, as far as this is consistent with the statutory duties of the authority outlined above, it must ensure that the child is brought up in accordance with his/her religious persuasion and that siblings are placed in the same establishment or, if this is not possible, that the placements facilitate contact between siblings.[3] Finally, there are special considerations which apply in cases where the placement is to be with foster carers. These are considered below.

The guidance[4] focuses on four aspects of making a care plan:

*(a) Assessment*

The assessment should identify the needs of the child and his/her family. It is stressed: that the information required to be collected by the Regulations is the minimum that should be collected (more

1 SI 1996/3262, reg 6.
2 Ibid, reg 5.
3 Ibid, reg 5.
4 *Guidance* vol 2, ch 1.

will probably be needed for a proper assessment); that the assessment should involve the child and family; and that it should, if possible, be carried out before any removal of the child from home.

*(b) Care plan*

Once the assessment has been carried out a care plan for the child should be produced. It is recommended that the agreement on the plan should take the form of a signed written agreement and that a child of sufficient understanding should also be asked to sign the agreement.

*(c) Range and level of services provided*

This is really part of the preparation of a care plan for the child, considering what services ought to be provided and how others might be involved in the care of the child. If a placement is being made of a child under 12, the guidance states that foster care will usually be the best option for both short-term and long-term care.[1] It then goes on to consider the appropriateness of different types of placements for older children.

*(d) Ending the arrangement*

The care plan should suggest how long the child will be looked after and what steps will need to be taken, both by the family and by the local authority, to end the period of being looked after.

Good and empowering practice has always followed the process described above. These stipulations require to be built on the foundation of good relationships between social workers and service users which are grounded in a focus on strengths and abilities rather than exclusively on deficits and problems.

## (4) Health care

The guidance requires that the authority should work in partnership with the parents when the child stays at home. The parents will retain parental responsibilities and rights which give them control over medical care of a young child, unless, of course, there is a supervision requirement or other order requiring medical assessment or treatment. As children get older they acquire the ability to

1 This is weaker than the advice which appeared in the draft guidance which recommended that children under 12 should, as far as possible, be placed in a foster placement.

consent to treatment themselves, and the authority will have to work with these children. Adequate health care for the child should be part of the care plan for the child.

Where the child is placed away from home, a medical examination and health assessment must be carried out before the placement (or as soon as possible afterwards), subject to a child who has capacity to consent to medical treatment having the right to refuse these.[1] The local authority should act as a good parent would in relation to the health of children placed away from home. This does not confer on the authority any powers of consent, and it would seem from the guidance that none is intended to be implied by the authority's duty to 'ensure that arrangements are made for a child to be provided with health care services, including medical and dental care and treatment'.[2] Instead, it is suggested that the authority should obtain the consent of the parents to allow it to seek and obtain any immunisations and treatment recommended for the child. If consent is withheld or no agreement is reached, the authority does not have the power to authorise treatment, though it may be possible to seek a child protection or child assessment order, to refer the case to the reporter or to get a doctor or other medical professional to apply to court for an order relating to parental rights to allow the treatment to be given[3] (since local authorities will no longer be able to apply for such orders). In cases where no agreement is reached (but not in cases where there is opposition to the treatment) the provisions of section 5 of the 1995 Act may be useful. This allows someone who has care or control of a child to consent to medical treatment in fulfilment of the obligation to do what is reasonable to safeguard the child's health, development and welfare, which would seem to include local authority workers who have care or control of children as part of their job, as well as foster carers (see the discussion above). This consent can be given only if the child is unable to consent and if the person consenting is ignorant of the fact that the child's parents would refuse consent.

## (5) Respite care

Support can be provided to families by offering short periods of care for a child in the form of respite care. Under the general

1 Arrangements Regulations, reg 13.
2 Ibid, reg 13(2).
3 1995 Act, s 11.

provisions of the Arrangements Regulations, every time respite is provided the whole process of assessment, agreeing care plans, etc has to be gone through. In order to avoid this procedure, the Arrangements Regulations provide that short periods of respite care which are repeated on a regular basis do not count as separate episodes of being looked after, so the whole process of assessment and medical examination does not have to be repeated for each period of respite care. Respite placements will be treated in this way if the total duration of the placements in one year does not exceed 120 days, and no single placement is for more than 4 weeks.[1]

### (6) Contact with the child's family

In the case of children placed away from home, the local authority must bear in mind its obligation to 'promote, on a regular basis, personal relations and direct contact' between the child and his/her family.[2] The guidance stresses the point that this imposes a responsibility 'not just to enable contact to happen but to actively encourage and facilitate it.'[3] Contact may, of course, be restricted under the terms of any court order or supervision requirement in terms of which the child is being looked after, and the arrangements made by the social work department must comply with the terms of the order or requirement. The child's wishes in respect of contact must also be taken into account.

Most children looked after by the local authority and placed away from home will be returning to their parent(s) and families to live and so the requirement to encourage and facilitate meaningful contact arrangements works to provide a sound basis for the preparation for a return home.

### (7) Monitoring and review

Children placed away from home must be visited within 1 week of the placement and then at least every 3 months. Visits can be more frequent and a visit must be made in response to a reasonable

1 Arrangements Regulations, reg 17.
2 1995 Act, s 17(1)(c).
3 *Guidance* vol 2, ch 1, para 31.

request by the child or any foster carer.[1] Written reports of visits should be produced.

Children placed away from home must be reviewed within 6 weeks of placement, then after 3 months and then at 6-monthly intervals. Children being looked after at home must be reviewed after 3 months and then every 6 months. Note that these are maximum periods and reviews may take place more regularly. In addition reviews must be held before a local authority decides to refer the case of a child being looked after to the reporter (other than in fulfilment of its investigative duties) and must, if practicable, be held before a children's hearing considering a referral of the child or a review of a supervision requirement.[2] The child should be fully involved in the review process, and children over the age of 12 should normally attend the review meeting. Those with parental responsibilities should normally also attend unless there is some reason why they should not. This may be a practical reason or because there is some legal order preventing contact with the child. Where the child is subject to a supervision requirement the review meeting will not be able to take any final decisions. These must be taken by the children's hearing.

The enormous significance of the overriding principle of the need to consider the views of children is evident here again in the arrangements for children over the age of 12 to attend their reviews. Who Cares? Scotland has argued for the acceptance of this practice for many years and it is now incumbent upon the partnerships of service users and social workers to overcome any past inhibitions and barriers to an open review process.

## (8) Termination of placements

Where the local authority considers that a placement is no longer in the child's best interests, the placement should be terminated as soon as practicable.[3] As we have already seen, where a child is being accommodated, the parent has the right to terminate the arrangement, and where a placement is made by the children's hearing it will be under their control.

1 Arrangements Regulations, reg 18.
2 Ibid, reg 9.
3 Ibid, reg 19(1).

## (9) Records

Authorities must keep a written record for each child looked after by them. The Arrangements Regulations[1] specify what must be contained in such a record, which includes copies of care plans, reports on the child's welfare and a copy of any document considered as part of a review of a child's case. The guidance suggests that it might contain other material provided by the child, such as photographs or school certificates. Access to this record is governed by the Access to Personal Files Act 1987 and the regulations relating to social work records.[2] The guidance makes the rather startling claim that a child under the age of 16 has no right to gain access to his or her records. The basis for this is claimed to be section 2(1)(a) of the Age of Legal Capacity (Scotland) Act 1991 (the 1991 Act). This section in fact states that a child under the age of 16 can enter into transactions of the sort that a child of his/her age would normally enter into. Implicit in this may be a suggestion that if, as a matter of practice, children under 16 were allowed to access their records then they would be legally entitled to do so. However, it is submitted that the advice in the guidance is simply wrong. The 1991 Act is concerned with 'transactions', defined as transactions having legal effect. It is easy to see that entering a contract or that giving medical consent has legal consequences for a child: in the former legal obligations are undertaken, in the latter the doctor is effectively granted a waiver against being sued for assault. It is less easy to see that applying for access to one's record has a legal effect and is, therefore, a transaction within the meaning of the 1991 Act. It might be argued that there are certain legal rights to correction of records, but these rights exist independently and are not triggered or brought into effect by access to the record. In our opinion the better view is that younger children have a right to access their records because accessing a record is not a transaction, as well as for other reasons explained below. A further argument that would deny children the right of access is that since the 1991 Act had the effect of extending tutory to all those under 16, it deprived them of certain rights they previously would have had. Prior to the 1991 Act, parents exercised tutory, sometimes described as a right of control over the person and property of the child, over boys under 14 and girls under 12. After that age the parents simply exercised

1 Ibid, reg 11.
2 See ch 2, pt 6(3).

the more restricted right of curatory and the child had more rights, one of them recognised as being the right to seek access to information. It was argued at the time that the 1991 Act was being passed that this extension of tutory was not intended to deprive these older children of any pre-existing rights and they therefore should be regarded as having the right of access to their files.[1] Another reason for taking this view is that it is more consistent with the overall approach of the legislation and guidance which stresses the need for the child to be involved in decision-making. Denying older children access to records would also sit oddly with other aspects of the law: for example, children over 12 are expected to be able to make the complex decisions involved in consenting to adoption, and children under the age of 16 may very well be able to consent to complicated medical procedures.

## 4. FOSTER PLACEMENTS

### (1) Introduction

Fostering describes the situation where a child is placed in the care of someone other than his/her parent(s). The foster carers have the responsibility for caring for the child, but they do not automatically acquire any parental responsibilities or rights. Fostering is therefore different from adoption, which involves the adoptive parents replacing the child's natural parents in the eyes of the law. There are two types of fostering. The first of these involves children who are being looked after by the local authority. For these children, the local authority is bound both by the provisions about children who are looked after considered above, and by specific provisions on foster care which are considered below. The second type of fostering is private fostering, where parents make their own arrangements for the substitute care of a child. We will look at each of these in turn.

1 See E Clive 'The Age of Legal Capacity (Scotland) Bill' (1991) SCOLAG 71, and the comments made by Lord Fraser of Carmyllie and Lord Macaulay of Bragar during the Bill's passage in the House of Lords at HL, vol 530, cols 878 and 881.

### (2) Placements of children being looked after

This category covers not only placements made by the local authority itself, but also children subject to a supervision requirement including a condition requiring residence with foster carers.

The relevant regulations cover three main areas: the approval of foster carers; the making of placements and the provision of information to children's hearings to enable them to make a placement; and the supervision and termination of placements.

#### *(a) Approval of foster carers*

Certain procedures must be followed before foster carers are selected. Approval will be given only after a thorough investigation by the local authority and after consideration of the prospective foster carers by the local authority's fostering panel. The investigations are normally undertaken by experienced social workers, may continue over a period of months, and will be informed by the guidance.[1] The information which must be collected is specified in Schedule 1 of the Fostering of Children (Scotland) Regulations 1996 (the Fostering Regulations).[2]

Once the investigations are completed, a report is produced which will be considered by the authority's fostering panel. This panel is composed of specialist advisers, social work department managers, representatives of other professions such as doctors and child guidance teachers, and local councillors. One of the panel members must be appointed as medical adviser to the panel. The main function of the panel is to advise on the suitability of prospective foster carers, but it can have other functions relating to fostering given to it by the local authority.[3] The prospective foster carers will normally be at the meeting where this consideration takes place. The panel then makes a recommendation on the suitability of the prospective carer for a particular child, for a particular category of child, or for any children. The final decision on acceptance is then made by the social work department on the basis of this recommendation. Once a foster carer is approved, this individual must enter into a foster carer agreement with the local authority which will cover such matters as the support and training to be

1 *Guidance* vol 2, ch 3, paras 5–40.
2 SI 1996/3263.
3 Ibid, reg 6.

given, complaints procedures, procedures for placement, confidentiality obligations and the foster carer's obligation not to use corporal punishment on any child.[1] After approval the foster carer's suitability must be reviewed at least annually.[2]

There are indirect restrictions on who can be a foster carer, in that local authorities can only place children in households which consist either of a man and a woman 'living and acting together' or a man or woman living and acting alone.[3] The clear implication of this is a prohibition on single sex couples being approved as foster carers.

Payments are generally made to foster carers. There is considerable guidance on how these should be calculated which suggests, for example, that the payments should reflect the true costs of providing care and that it will be relevant to take the foster carer's circumstances into account in calculating the payment.[4]

### *(b) Making placements: placement by local authority*

Children who are being placed in a foster placement will also be being looked after by the local authority, and the provisions relating to such children discussed above will apply. This means that some of the requirements that were previously found in the fostering regulations are now found there, for example the requirements for medical examination of the child and as to the information to be gathered about the child.

There are three types of placement recognised in the Fostering Regulations: emergency placements, immediate placements and what might be described as 'other' placements, though they are not so described in the Fostering Regulations.

Dealing with the last category first,[5] these placements must be made with approved foster carers and the local authority must have satisfied itself that placement with the particular foster carer is in the best interests of the child. The carer must also have entered into a foster carer agreement and must enter into a further agreement covering the specific placement. This agreement (a foster placement agreement) will cover such things as the financial arrangements, arrangements for the delegation of the parental responsibility for consent to medical treatment and to consent to

1 SI 1996/3263, reg 8 and Sch 2.
2 Ibid, reg 8(1).
3 Ibid, reg 12(4).
4 *Guidance* vol 2, ch 3, paras 73–78.
5 SI 1996/3263, reg 12.

undertaking activities such as school trips as well as information about the child, his/her background and the agreed care plan for the child.[1]

Emergency placements can be made only with approved foster parents and can last up to 72 hours.[2] Such a placement might, for example, be used where a child is removed from home under a child protection order. Before making the placement, the authority must satisfy itself that a foster placement is the most suitable way of meeting the child's needs and must obtain the written agreement of the foster carer to comply with certain duties, which include a duty to care for the child in a safe and appropriate manner, to allow visiting by the local authority and to allow contact with the child's family. There is no need for a foster placement agreement, but the foster carer must be provided with information about the child.

Finally, immediate placement for up to 6 weeks can be made with people who are not approved foster carers, for example, where it would not be in the child's best interests to wait while arrangements were made with approved carers.[3] The prospective carer must be interviewed, his/her house inspected, and information obtained about that person and other members of the household. Placements can be made only if the prospective carer is a relative or friend of the child to be placed and, in addition, the authority is satisfied that the person has agreed to carry out those duties listed above in the context of emergency placement and that the placement is the most suitable way of meeting the needs of the child. As in emergency placements, there is no need for a foster placement agreement. If the placement is to last more than 6 months the carer must be approved as a foster carer.

Whatever type of placement is made there are certain requirements imposed by the Arrangements Regulations dealing with children being looked after.[4] These require that placement is with someone of the same religion as the child or, if that is not practicable, that the foster carer agrees to bring the child up in accordance with the child's religious persuasion and that siblings be placed together or in placement as close together as practicable. Both of these requirements are subject to the overall statutory duty of the authority to children being looked after and are to be fulfilled after ascertaining the views of the child.

1 Ibid, Sch 3.
2 Ibid, reg 13.
3 Ibid, reg 14.
4 SI 1996/3262, reg 5.

### (c) Making placements: placement by a children's hearing

In this case the placement is made by a children's hearing rather than by the local authority. The hearing, however, must not make a requirement to reside with a foster carer without first considering a report and recommendation from the social work department.[1] The social work department can make a recommendation for a foster placement only if it has carried out either the procedure for 'other' placements outlined above or that required before an emergency/immediate placement is made. In the latter case it must be satisfied that placement is in the best interests of the child. Where the placement made by the hearing is not with approved foster carers the 6-month limit noted in the context of immediate placements does not apply.[2] In other words the hearing can make an unlimited placement with a relative or friend who is not approved.

### (d) Supervision and termination of placements

Children placed with foster carers are subject to the requirements as to supervision, review and termination which apply to all other children who are being looked after.

## (3) Private fostering

It is possible for fostering to be arranged privately and for situations which are legally defined as private fostering to arise without any necessary intention on the part of those involved.

Private fostering is regulated by the Foster Children (Scotland) Act 1984 and by the Foster Children (Private Fostering) (Scotland) Regulations 1985.[3] These will apply in general to any situation where a child under the age of 16 is being cared for by someone other than a relative or guardian for more than one month. There are certain exceptions to this covering, for example, children at boarding school, children in hospital and children placed for adoption.

Where it is intended to place a child in private fostering, at least 2 weeks' notice must be given to the local authority. The authority then has certain duties, including the following:

1 Children's Hearings (Scotland) Rules 1996, SI 1996/3261, r 20(6).
2 1996/3263, reg 15.
3 SI 1985/1798.

(a) to find out as far as possible, bearing in mind the age and understanding of the child, his/her wishes and feelings in relation to the proposed placement;
(b) to interview the proposed foster parents and satisfy itself as to the suitability of the foster home;
(c) to satisfy itself that the placement will not be detrimental to the child's welfare;
(d) to decide whether the placement is appropriate to the child's needs.

The decision as to whether the placement is appropriate must be communicated to those involved, and the authority may seek to have changes made to make the placement more appropriate or better able to promote the welfare of the child. If necessary the authority can prohibit the placement if it considers that it would be detrimental to the child.

Certain types of person cannot act as foster parents.[1] These include: people convicted of Schedule 1 offences;[2] anyone who has previously had a foster child removed from his/her care; anyone who has had a child removed from his/her care under a supervision requirement; and anyone whose parental responsibilities and rights have been transferred to the local authority by a parental responsibilities order.

Once a placement has been made the authority must visit the child within 7 days, then every 3 months for the first year and subsequently every 6 months. Other visits may be made as the authority thinks necessary. If, as a result of these visits, the authority considers that the placement is no longer in the child's interests it must notify the foster parents of this.

The local authority can apply to the sheriff court, or where the child is in imminent danger to a justice of the peace, for an order removing the child to a place of safety if the child is kept, or is about to be kept, by any person who is unfit to have his/her care, by anyone who falls into one of the categories prohibited from being a foster parent, or in any premises or environment likely to be detrimental to the child.

If a foster carer refuses to allow a visit to the child or to inspect the premises, this is to be regarded as establishing that there is reasonable cause to suspect that the child is being so treated or

1 Foster Children (Scotland) Act 1984, s 7.
2 Ie Schedule 1 to the Children and Young Persons Act 1933 and Schedule 1 to the Criminal Procedure (Scotland) Act 1995.

neglected that he/she is suffering or is likely to suffer significant harm for the purpose of an application for a child assessment order.

The place of safety order will apply until other arrangements can be made for the child, and any child removed from private fostering is to be treated as requiring accommodation under section 25 of the 1995 Act.

## 5. SECURE ACCOMMODATION

### (1) Introduction

Children may be placed in secure accommodation provided by a local authority in a variety of ways. The placement may be a condition of a supervision requirement made by a children's hearing; it may be a condition of a warrant or order to take or keep a child in a place of safety made by a hearing or a court;[1] a child being looked after by the local authority may be placed in secure accommodation; or a child detained under an order made by a criminal court may be placed in secure accommodation.

Regardless of the method of placement the manager of the secure accommodation must promote and safeguard the welfare of the child and make sure that the child is provided with whatever education, provision for his/her development and control as is conducive to his/her interests.[2] The period for which a child is kept in secure accommodation must not exceed a total of 72 hours in any 28-day period **unless** the secure placement has been authorised by a court or a hearing.[3]

### (2) Rules applying to all placements

Certain rules apply to all placements in secure accommodation which are made by the local authority. The chief social work officer of the local authority and the person in charge of the secure accommodation must be satisfied that **either**:

1 1995 Act, ss 66(6), 67(3), 68(11), 69(11).
2 Secure Accommodation (Scotland) Regulations 1996, SI 1996/3255, reg 4.
3 Ibid, reg 5.

(a) the child has previously absconded and is likely to abscond unless kept in secure accommodation and if the child absconds his/her mental, physical or moral welfare will be at risk. Examples of this would be a child subject to a supervision order requiring that the child stays in a residential establishment who absconds, or a child being provided with accommodation by the local authority through a foster placement who continually runs away; *or*
(b) the child is likely to injure him/herself or someone else unless kept in secure accommodation.

The chief social work officer for the authority must also be satisfied that the placement is in the best interests of the child.[1]

### (3) Children subject to supervision requirements[2]

Children who are subject to a supervision requirement which does not contain a condition requiring residence in secure accommodation may still be placed in such accommodation. If this is done the relevant person and the reporter must be told about it 'forthwith', and the child must also be told in a way which is appropriate to his/her age and understanding. Within 24 hours, regardless of whether the child is still in secure accommodation, a full report must be made to the reporter, and a review hearing to consider the supervision requirement must be held within 72 hours of the original placement in secure accommodation.

### (4) Children being looked after[3]

Children who are being looked after by being provided with accommodation by the local authority or because a parental responsibilities order has been made in respect of them may be placed in secure accommodation. This can only happen if, in addition to the general requirements outlined above, the chief social work officer and the person in charge of the secure accommodation are both satisfied that the child is in need of compulsory measures of supervision. Once the child has been put in secure

1 Ibid, regs 6(1), 7(1) and 9(1)(b); 1995 Act, s 70(10).
2 SI 1996/3255, reg 6.
3 Ibid, regs 7 and 8.

accommodation the relevant person and the reporter must be informed 'forthwith', and within 24 hours a full report must be made to the reporter.

The reporter then has to decide what to do, and the decision must be taken within 72 hours of placement in secure accommodation. There are two possible decisions. It might be decided that no hearing is necessary, in which case the child would have to be released from secure accommodation. As a complement to this decision the reporter can refer the child's case to the local authority for advice, guidance and assistance provided by virtue of the local authority's duties to children and families. The second option is to refer the case of the child to a hearing, which is possible only if the reporter thinks the child is in need of compulsory measures of supervision. The hearing must take place within 72 hours, though an extra 24 hours is allowed if the hearing cannot take place or the reporter cannot state the grounds for referral within 72 hours.

### (5) Children in a place of safety

Children may be taken to a place of safety under a warrant or order made by a hearing or a sheriff. Even if the order does not impose a condition requiring placement in secure accommodation such children can still, in general, be placed there. The main exceptions to this are children taken to a place of safety under a child assessment order or a child protection order.

If such a placement is made the relevant person and the reporter must be informed. The procedure then depends on the type of warrant or order to which the child is subject. If the order was issued by a hearing either to secure the attendance of the child at a hearing to consider the child's case or because the child did not turn up to this hearing,[1] a hearing must be arranged, if possible on the next working day.[2] If the warrant was issued by the sheriff to extend a warrant issued by the hearing[3] an application must be made to the sheriff within 72 hours.[4] In all other cases a hearing must be convened within 72 hours of the child being placed in secure accommodation.

1 1995 Act, s 45(4) or (5).
2 SI 1996/3255, reg 9(2)(a) and 1995 Act, s 45(7).
3 1995 Act, s 67(1).
4 SI 1996/3255, reg 9(2)(e).

### (6) Children detained by order made by a criminal court[1]

The criminal courts (with the exception of the district court) may remand children to residential accommodation provided by the local authority. For example, a child found guilty in the sheriff summary court may be detained in residential accommodation for up to 12 months. Subject to the exceptions considered below, such children may be placed in secure accommodation if the general rules noted above apply. Once a child has been placed in secure accommodation he/she must not be kept there for longer than the person in charge and the chief social work officer consider necessary. In addition, the cases of such children must be reviewed within 7 days of the placement (even if the child is no longer in secure accommodation) and then at least every 3 months or more often if this is necessary in light of the progress made by the child. As part of this review the views of a Secure Placement Review Panel, which must include one person independent of the local authority, must be obtained. The secure placement is to continue after review only if the person in charge and the chief social work officer consider that it is in the best interests of the child.

The main exceptions to these requirements are:

(a) children remanded to secure accommodation by the court before trial or sentence.[2] Such children must be kept in secure accommodation;
(b) children sentenced for murder or after conviction on indictment. The conditions for the detention of such children are specified by the Secretary of State for Scotland.[3]

## 6. PARENTAL RESPONSIBILITIES ORDERS

### (1) Introduction

The parental responsibilities order replaces the parental rights resolution by virtue of which a local authority could, simply by passing a resolution, take over parental rights and responsibilities.

1 Ibid, regs 13–15.
2 See s 51(1)(a)(i) of the Criminal Procedure (Scotland) Act 1995.
3 Criminal Procedure (Scotland) Act 1995, ss 205 and 208.

There are significant differences between the two procedures. Application for a parental responsibilities order **must** be made to a sheriff and the sheriff grants the order; the child affected by the order need not be being looked after by the local authority at the time the order is made, though usually the child will be; and the grounds for making the order are significantly different from those involved in justifying a parental rights resolution. These changes have been wholeheartedly welcomed as more in keeping with a commitment to social justice and openness in practice.

Before an application for an order is made the social work department will need to consider if this is the best way of meeting the needs of the child and of safeguarding and promoting his/her welfare. Alternatives to an order should be considered, for example a change in the conditions of a supervision requirement or encouraging long-term foster carers to seek a residence order in respect of the child. Where the child is being looked after, the duties of consultation and taking account of views will apply, and the guidance suggests that it is necessary to make 'serious and substantial efforts' to obtain the views of the person whose responsibilities and rights will be transferred by the order.[1]

Where the child is subject to a supervision requirement, it will be necessary to refer the child's case to the reporter and the reporter must arrange a hearing to review the requirement and to provide advice to the court considering the application for the parental responsibilities order. The court must consider the report from the hearing before making a decision.[2]

### (2) Grounds for application[3]

The sheriff can grant the application for an order if satisfied that one of a number of grounds is established. There are that the relevant person:[4]

(a) agrees to the order being made. The agreement must be made freely and with a full understanding of what is involved;
(b) is not known, cannot be found or is incapable of giving agreement;

1 *Guidance* vol 3, ch 2, para 8.
2 1995 Act, s 73(4)(c)(i), (8)(a)(i), (13) and (14).
3 1995 Act, s 86.
4 The relevant person is the child's parent or a person having parental rights in respect of the child.

(c) is withholding agreement unreasonably;
(d) has persistently failed, without reasonable cause, to fulfil either the parental responsibility to safeguard and promote the child's health, development and welfare, or, if the child is not living with him/her, the responsibility to maintain direct contact and personal relations with the child on a regular basis;
(e) has seriously ill-treated the child and the re-integration of the child into the same household is unlikely because of this or for some other reason.

In the ground similar to (d) in the Social Work (Scotland) Act 1968 (the 1968 Act), the view was taken that the failure need not be deliberate on the part of the parent and that reasonableness should be approached from an objective standpoint, that is by asking how a reasonable parent would behave.[1]

### (3) Procedure[2]

Once the application is made, a curator ad litem and a reporting officer will be appointed, though the same person may fulfil both roles. The function of the reporting officer is to witness any parental agreement; to make sure that each relevant person understands the meaning of the order; and to find out if there is anyone else on whom the order should be served. The curator's function is essentially to look after the interests of the child. The curator must safeguard the child's interests and make sure his/her welfare is paramount; confirm the facts stated in the application; find out if the child wishes to express a view and if so what that view is; establish whether an order would safeguard and promote the child's welfare; and report on the present circumstances and care of the child.

### (4) Effect of the order

The effect of the order is to transfer parental responsibilities and rights to the local authority and to impose on the local authority a duty to fulfil these rights and responsibilities.[3] Not all parental

1 *Central Regional Council v B* 1985 SLT 413.
2 Act of Sederunt (Child Care and Maintenance Rules) 1997, SI 1997/291, ch 2, Pt V.
3 1995 Act, s 87(7).

rights are acquired and the relevant person will retain the right to consent (or refuse consent) to a freeing order or to an adoption order. Parental responsibilities orders appear to have the effect of transferring *all* parental responsibilities/rights to the local authority with the exception of those just listed. In consequence it does not seem that it will be possible, as it was under the 1968 Act, to take away the responsibilities and rights of only one parent.

The relevant person before the making of the order will also have a right to contact with the child. Reasonable contact must be allowed by the local authority both with that person and with anyone in whose favour a residence or contact order had been made before the granting of the parental responsibilities order.

Contact can be regulated by the court, either on application by the authority, the child, someone who was a relevant person, or someone with an interest. Those listed here can also apply for variation or discharge of the order.

### (5) Placement with parents

Even though a parental responsibilities order has been made, the local authority can, if it would benefit the child, allow the child to reside with a parent, guardian, relative or friend.[1] Placements with a relative or friend are regulated by the appropriate regulations for children being looked after and for fostering. The local authority can require the return of the child at any time and failure to return the child is a criminal offence.[2]

### (6) Duration of the order

Once the order is made it will last until the child is 18, unless it is brought to an end before then. It can be brought to an end by an adoption order or freeing order being made in respect of the child and by certain orders made under the Child Abduction and Custody Act 1985. The order can also be discharged by the sheriff if the authority, the child, someone who was a relevant person before the order was made, or anyone claiming an interest applies for discharge.

1 1995 Act, s 87(2).
2 Ibid, ss 87(3) and 89(a).

## 7. AFTER-CARE

The 1995 Act gives authorities greater power to provide assistance to people after they have stopped being looked after. They must provide advice, guidance and assistance to anyone between 16 and 19 who was being looked after at 16 or subsequently, but is no longer looked after, unless they are satisfied that the welfare of the person concerned does not require it, and they *may* provide it to anyone between 19 and 21 who was being looked after at 16 or subsequently, but is no longer looked after who requests advice, guidance and assistance.[1] The assistance may be in cash or in kind.

In addition the authority has the *power* to make grants or contributions to enable someone to meet the expenses of education or training or towards the accommodation and maintenance of an individual who is employed, seeking employment, receiving education or receiving training. To qualify the person must be between 16 and 21 and have been looked after at 16 or subsequently, but no longer being looked after. Payments can continue to be made to someone who is 21 or over to allow this person to complete his/her education or training.[2]

Preparation of the child for the time when the child is no longer looked after by the local authority should be part of the care plan produced for the child, and reviews should consider what needs to be done by way of preparation. Before the child stops being looked after, consideration will need to be given to what aftercare services may be needed and how these are going to be provided.[3] In some cases, as the guidance indicates, support and assistance will need to continue into adulthood and to make use of services provided under section 12 of the 1968 Act and community care services. These new duties and powers recognise the vulnerability and additional needs of many young people who have been looked after by the local authority. Clearly, a disproportionate number of these young people become involved with the criminal justice system and are amongst the ranks of people who are homeless.

## 8. CHALLENGING DECISIONS

Children or their families may be unhappy about decisions made about the provision of services or other decisions taken by the local

1 Ibid, s 29.
2 Ibid, s 30.
3 See ch 5, pt 3.

authority in exercising its powers and duties. Decisions taken can be challenged using the complaints and representations procedure set up under the 1968 Act.

It may also be possible to challenge decisions by seeking judicial review of the decision. The challenge will generally be on the grounds that the local authority has exercised the considerable discretion conferred on it in an unreasonable way, though the very extent of the discretion may make challenges difficult. Grounds for a challenge might include a failure to take proper account of procedures laid out in the guidance[1] or a failure to follow a decision or recommendation resulting from pursuing the complaints procedure,[2] unless proper consideration has been given before doing this.[3] In light of the comments made above about the relevance of resources to decisions involving service provision, it will be difficult, but not impossible, to challenge a refusal to provide services on resource grounds. Generally, no challenge by way of judicial review will be possible until the complaints procedure has been exhausted.[4]

Complaints about council actions can also be made to the Commissioner for Local Administration in Scotland, otherwise known as the Local Government Ombudsman.

1 *R v North Yorkshire County Council, ex parte Hargreaves* (1995) 26 BMLR 121; *R v London Borough of Islington, ex parte Rixon* (1996) Times, 17 April.
2 *R v Avon County Council, ex parte M* [1994] 2 FCR 259.
3 *Re T (Accommodation by Local Authority)* [1995] 1 FLR 159.
4 *R v Kingston-upon-Thames Royal Borough Council, ex parte T* [1994] 1 FLR 798.

# 5. Children in need of supervision or emergency protection

## 1. INTRODUCTION

There is no field in social work practice which has a higher public profile and which engenders more anxiety for those involved than child care. Changing public attitudes and views about what characterises good enough parenting, the rights and responsibilities of parents, the rights of children, the justification for state intervention into family life, and the need to protect children have each contributed to the ongoing debate about the most appropriate role for social workers. The intricacies of the dynamic operating amongst the social work departments, the children's hearings and the courts further complicate an understanding of the duties and responsibilities of social workers. Although social workers continue to have a key role to play, there is no doubt that working together with other professionals with each doing what the professional does best, is increasingly being seen as the most effective means of caring for children. Practice emphasis has shifted round the circle again from protection to prevention and family support.

Child care law has seen substantial changes as a result of the Children (Scotland) Act 1995 (the 1995 Act). These changes affect three main areas. First, there is the introduction of overriding principles which have to be taken into account by the courts and by children's hearings when reaching decisions. Secondly, there are some changes in procedure and terminology affecting hearings, such as the recognition of business meetings and the replacement of references to compulsory care with compulsory supervision. Finally, the most extensive changes are in the area of emergency protection of children, with the introduction of child protection orders, exclusion orders and the conferring of a power on local authorities to provide refuges for children who appear to be at risk of harm. Structurally, there has been reorganisation of the reporters' service brought about by the Local Government etc (Scotland) Act 1994 which replaced the regional departments with a national one. The Principal Reporter is now accountable to the Scottish Children's

Reporters' Administration. What the practical implications of this change will be remain to be seen.

These changes result from a variety of sources. The Review of Child Care Law in Scotland, which reported in 1990[1] is the source of some changes, for example, the power to specify a review date when making a supervision requirement. It is interesting to note that this review saw little cause for concern in the operation of place of safety orders and concluded that giving local authorities the power to seek exclusion orders seemed 'unlikely to offer greater protection to the child at risk than is currently possible'.[2] A second source is the Clyde Report into the events in Orkney.[3] This was highly critical of the operation of the place of safety order. Problems identified included the lack of scrutiny of the grounds for seeking an order, the lack of a time limit on implementation and the failure of the legislation to make clear that the order was for use only in emergencies. The report included proposals for radical change in this area which are reflected in the child protection order.[4] Another source is the litigation involving children in Ayrshire who had been made subject to supervision requirements. The evidence was hotly contested and the outcome of these cases led to the provisions in the 1995 Act for the review of findings that grounds of referral are established.

Our concern here is with the statutory framework for children in need and child protection, though reference will also be made to the guidance issued by the Social Work Services Group.[5] It must not be forgotten that this operates in conjunction with local, multi-disciplinary child protection procedures.

## 2. OVERRIDING PRINCIPLES GOVERNING DECISIONS BY THE COURT OR HEARING

When a court or a hearing is considering a case involving a child they must pay attention to three principles set out in the 1995 Act.[6]

1 *Review of Child Care Law in Scotland* (1990).
2 *Op cit*, para 21.11.
3 *The Report of the Inquiry into the Removal of Children from Orkney in February 1991* (1992).
4 *Op cit*, ch 16.
5 *The Children (Scotland) Act 1995 Regulations and Guidance* (Guidance)*: Volume 1: Support and Protection for Children and their Families; Volume 2: Children Looked After by Local Authorities* (1997).
6 1995 Act, s 16(1).

### (a) Principle I

The overriding principle governing decisions by the courts and by hearings, which applies to all cases, is that the paramount consideration must be the welfare of the child throughout his/her childhood (referred to as the 'welfare principle'). Note that this differs from the standard in adoption where the reference is to the whole of the child's life.

### (b) Principle II

In some cases the court or hearing must give the child the opportunity to express his/her views and take those views into consideration before a decision is made (the 'right to be heard' principle).[1] The situations in which this must be done are:[2]

(1) Cases where a children's hearing is:
  (a) considering whether to make a supervision requirement or reviewing such a requirement;
  (b) considering whether to grant a warrant to apprehend and detain a child or to grant a warrant to detain a child where consideration of a case by the hearing is continued to seek further information. Note that this requirement does not apply when the hearing is deciding whether to continue a child protection order;
  (c) meeting to provide advice to the sheriff who is deciding an application to vary or discharge a child protection order;[3]
  (d) drawing up a report in connection with a proposed parental responsibilities order, freeing for adoption, adoption or placement for adoption.

(2) Cases where the sheriff is considering:
  (a) whether to make, vary or discharge a parental responsibilities order, a child assessment order or an exclusion order;
  (b) whether to vary or discharge a child protection order, but not when considering whether to make a child protection order;

1 1995 Act, s 16(2). These provisions are identical to those in s 11 of the 1995 Act discussed above: see ch 3, pt 1(7). The procedural rules are in the Act of Sederunt (Child Care and Maintenance Rules) 1997, SI 1997/291, ch 3, especially r 3.5.

2 1995 Act, s 16(4).

3 See pt 6(4) of this chapter.

(c) whether to grant a warrant for the continued detention of the child;
(d) whether to substitute his/her own disposal of the case for that of the hearing on a successful appeal against a supervision requirement;
(e) any appeal against the decision of a children's hearing.

A child of any age can have a view but it is presumed that children over the age of 12 **will** have a view which must now be considered. Social workers and others will need to work in close partnership with a child to ascertain if the child has a view and further if the child wants that view expressed. It is in precisely this sort of situation that the child may be full of ambivalence and/or conflict. A child may confuse the right to be heard with the right to obtain whatever he/she wants.

### (c) Principle III

Finally, in the cases covered by (1)(a) and (b) and (2)(a)–(d) above the hearing or sheriff must not make a requirement or order unless they consider that it would be better for the child to make the requirement or order than to make none (a principle of minimum intervention or 'no order' applies).[1]

These three principles have been referred to as the 'overarching principles' by some.[2]

## 3. CHILDREN IN NEED OF COMPULSORY MEASURES OF SUPERVISION

### (1) Introduction

The Social Work (Scotland) Act 1968 (the 1968 Act), following on from the report of the Kilbrandon Committee, introduced a new way of dealing with what were described as 'children in need of compulsory measures of care' (now described as 'children in need of compulsory measures of supervision'). This category covered all of the groups of children who would previously have been dealt

1 1995 Act, s 16(3).
2 K Norrie *The Children (Scotland) Act 1995* (1995).

with in different ways through the court system and whose behaviour the Kilbrandon Committee regarded as being symptomatic of some social or family dislocation. The Kilbrandon Committee concluded that:

> 'In terms of the treatment measures to be applied, the children appearing before the courts, whatever the precise circumstances in which they do so, show basic similarity of underlying situation. The distinguishing factor is their common need for special measures of education and training, the normal upbringing process for whatever reason having failed or fallen short.'[1]

These children are now dealt with by way of referral to the reporter to the children's hearing who, after an initial investigation, decides whether or not the case should go on to a hearing. The courts are only involved in cases where there is a dispute about the grounds for taking action in respect of a child and as the forum for dealing with appeals against decisions of the hearing. In law anyone can refer a case to the reporter if that individual is of the view that a child may be in need of compulsory measures of supervision, so that, for example, a concerned neighbour could report suspicions of child abuse. In practice, however, most referrals (nearly two-thirds) come from the police, followed by the social work department, the procurator fiscal and educational sources.

The 1995 Act makes some slight changes in the criteria for determining which children fall into this category, as well as making changes in rules about attendance at hearings; the grounds for appointment of safeguarders; shrieval powers on appeals against a supervision requirement; and the classification of supervision requirements. In addition, a new order which is appropriate at the stage of investigating reports about children, the 'child assessment order', is created. Fundamental changes in the mechanisms for emergency protection of children are discussed in the next section. In spite of these changes, the children's hearing system and the Kilbrandon philosophy have continued to take centre stage in child care law.

## (2) Duties of the social work department[2]

When a social work department receives a report suggesting that a child may be in need of compulsory supervision, it has a duty to

1 *Children and Young Persons* Cmnd 2306 (1964), para 252.
2 1995 Act, s 53(1).

investigate the report unless it is satisfied that no inquiry is necessary. If it concludes, with or without an investigation, that compulsory measures may be needed in respect of the child, the department must pass on whatever information it has about the child to the reporter. Departments now have a new tool in cases where this investigation is being thwarted. They and only they can apply for a **child assessment order**.[1] The purpose of these orders is to allow an assessment of the health, development and treatment of the child. The application for the order is made to the sheriff who may grant an order if **all** of the following conditions are satisfied:

(a) the local authority has reasonable cause to suspect that the child is being so treated or neglected that the child is suffering or is likely to suffer significant harm;
(b) an assessment is needed to establish whether there is reasonable cause to believe that the child is being so treated or neglected;
(c) an assessment is unlikely to be carried out or carried out successfully without an order being granted.

Although the grounds for the order refer to suspicion of risk, the guidance on the use of the order suggests that every effort should be made to find out whether the child is in fact at risk before an application is made for an order.[2] Clear evidence will also be needed that the parents are acting unreasonably and in relation to the nature of the risk to the child. The need for arranging assessment in advance is stressed. This is so that it can take place quickly if an order is granted and is especially important given the short life of the order.[3]

The order will specify the date on which the assessment of the child is to begin and is effective for a period of 7 days starting with this date. It requires anyone in a position to produce the child to do so and to permit the assessment authorised by the order and may allow the child to be taken to and kept at a specified place to be assessed. Where an order is made allowing the child to be taken to a specified place, the sheriff may also regulate contact between the child and any other person for the duration of the child assessment order. If, when an application for an assessment order is made, the sheriff considers that the grounds for granting a child protection order are established[4] the sheriff must make such an order.

1 1995 Act, s 55.
2 *Guidance*, vol 1, ch 7, para 17.
3 *Guidance*, vol 1, ch 7, paras 13–34.
4 See pt 3(2) of this chapter.

In making an order the sheriff is subject to the overriding principles set out in section 2 above, including the obligation to seek the views of the child. This requirement may avert a potential problem where an assessment order is made but the child has capacity, in terms of the Age of Legal Capacity (Scotland) Act 1991, to consent to medical treatment and, by implication, to refuse treatment. Section 90 of the 1995 Act expressly provides that examinations or treatment under certain provisions of the Act are not to be carried out unless the child consents. Child assessment orders are not covered by this specific provision. Two interpretations of this are possible. One is that, since Parliament did not provide that the child's agreement is necessary, as it did in other cases, there is no need for the child to consent to assessment under an assessment order and that such assessment can be carried out against the wishes of the child. The other view, which is preferred by most commentators (and the Guidance), is that this does not affect the ability of the child to refuse consent to medical examination or treatment under the 1991 Act. The requirement to take the child's views into account may mean that in practice no order will be made if the child would refuse the assessment.

This is a new role for the sheriff which involves him/her at a relatively early stage in the process and, it has been suggested, places the sheriff in an interventionist role but one where it would be very onerous for the sheriff to refuse to grant a child assessment order if the social worker is arguing that it is necessary to protect the child.[1] Social workers may want to consider applying for a child assessment order in situations where there have been suspicions, sometimes accumulated over a period of time, that a child is being neglected or abused and an assessment is necessary to produce evidence of such harm.[2]

Two final issues in respect of assessment orders are the short duration of the order (the equivalent provisions in England have been the subject of adverse comment on this ground[3]) and the vagueness of the grounds for making an order. What is 'reasonable cause', how does reasonable cause to 'suspect' differ from reasonable cause to 'believe', and what is 'significant' harm? These terms are not clarified in the Guidance.

1 Sheriff Brian Kearney in conference papers of a seminar held on 28 November 1996 entitled 'Children's Hearings, the Courts and the Children (Scotland) Act 1995'.

2 B Lister in these same conference papers.

3 See M D A Freeman *Children, their Families and the Law* (1992), pp 180–181; J Dickens 'Assessment and the Control of Social Work: An Analysis of Reasons for the Non-Use of the Child Assessment Order' (1993) 15 JSWFL 88.

Another duty of the social work department is to provide reports on children who have been referred to a hearing. The production of a report for a child referred to a hearing (normally referred to as a 'social background report') can give rise to both opportunities and problems for the social worker. If the child and/or family are known to the social worker or social work department, then more comprehensive material may be available in the compilation of the report. The social worker is well placed to provide information about the children's hearing system, procedures and possible outcomes to the child and family while also collecting and analysing data about the people and situations involved. The report is to be completed before the hearing and the child/family may not accept that the grounds of referral apply and may be unwilling to participate in the preparation of the report. In such cases they cannot be forced to assist, though the social worker may try to persuade them that some level of co-operation is in their interest.

There may also be conflict over the identity of the client. Is it the hearing or is it the child and family with whom the social worker may have to work if the child is placed on supervision? The legal answer is probably that the client is the hearing, much as in the preparation of social enquiry reports the court is considered to be the client. Reports provided to the reporter will be sent to the child's parent(s) (or other relevant person) if a hearing is to be held.

Finally, the department has a number of responsibilities in terms of providing supervision for children when this is required by a hearing, and for carrying out reviews of the cases of children subject to supervision requirements.

## (3) When is a child in need of compulsory measures of supervision?

A child may be in need of compulsory measures of supervision if one of the conditions listed below applies to the child. It is for the children's hearing to decide, if the child is referred to them on one of these grounds, whether he/she is in need of compulsory measures of supervision. The conditions, which are contained in section 52(2) of the 1995 Act, are:

(a) *The child is beyond the control of any relevant person.* The term 'relevant person' is used in several places in the 1995 Act and covers parents enjoying parental responsibilities or rights; anyone in whom parental responsibilities or rights are vested (for example, someone who has had them conferred on him/her by a section 11 order);[1] and anyone who ordinarily has charge of or control over the child even though he/she enjoys no parental responsibilities or rights.

(b) *The child is falling into bad associations or is exposed to moral danger.* Thomson suggests that this ground might exist where the child was associating with prostitutes, drug addicts, alcoholics or homosexuals.[2] One of the reported cases is of the father of the friend of a 6 year old girl shining a torch on her naked private parts.

(c) *The child is likely to suffer unnecessarily or to be impaired seriously in his/her health or development due to lack of parental care.* This replaces the 1968 Act ground that lack of parental care is likely to cause the child unnecessary suffering or seriously impair the child's health or development. Cases decided under the old ground still have some relevance to the new ground. For example, the view was taken that it was sufficient for the ground to exist that lack of care was likely to occur based on the known habits of the carer(s); the child need never have been in their care.[3] The appropriate test for deciding whether lack of parental care was likely to cause these consequences was 'whether a reasonable person looking to the circumstances of the particular case would consider that the child is likely to be caused unnecessary suffering or serious impairment to her health and development through lack of parental care on the part of the mother'.[4] In this case failure by a mother to visit a child in hospital for 5 months was not sufficient to establish likely lack of care where the mother had serious medical problems and lived far from the hospital.

Lack of parental care may exist even where the parents act with the best of motives, even if the child appears to be well looked after, and regardless of whether blame should be attached to the parents.[5] For example, this ground was held to be established in a case where the parents of a haemophiliac child were unwilling to give consent to treatment using Factor VIII, even though the court accepted that the parents were concerned parents and that their refusal to consent to this treatment arose from a fear that the child might

1 See ch 3, pt 1(7).
2 J M Thomson *Family Law in Scotland* (3rd edn, 1996), p 281.
3 *McGregor v L* 1981 SLT 194.
4 *M v McGregor* 1982 SLT 41 at 43.
5 *D v Kelly* 1995 SLT 1220.

become HIV positive as a result of the treatment.[1] Another example is a case where the children were described by the sheriff as well nourished and clean, but on two occasions they had effectively been thrown out of the house and left to fend for themselves. In both instances there were long delays before their absence was reported to the police by their father.[2]

(d) *A Schedule 1 offence has been committed in respect of the child.* This refers to Schedule 1 of the Criminal Procedure (Scotland) Act 1995 which contains a list of crimes and offences which can be committed against children (these are listed in the appendix to this chapter). For this ground of referral to be established it is not necessary to identify the person committing the offence, simply that it has been committed against the child.[3] Questions of identity may, of course, be relevant in considering how to deal with the child's case.

One example of a Schedule 1 offence is section 12(1) of the Children and Young Persons (Scotland) Act 1937 which created a number of offences to do with child neglect, one of them being neglect likely to cause unnecessary suffering or injury to the child's health. In one case[4] a 9 month old baby was left alone in the house for a short period of time by his mother who was very drunk. She was convicted of this offence and appealed. The appeal court held that for this offence to be committed the behaviour had to be wilful, in the sense of being deliberate and intentional; there had to be neglect in the form of failing to do '... what a reasonable parent, in all the circumstances, would regard as necessary to provide proper care and attention to the child';[5] and there must be some evidence that there was a substantial risk to the child. Here the court was not satisfied that the third requirement was met. Their view, which was also applied in the case of a 15 year old girl left alone in the house for an evening,[6] was that leaving a child alone in the house did not automatically mean that the offence had been committed.

It is worth noting that parents still have the right to use force on their children by way of punishment, provided that the force falls within the bounds of reasonable chastisement. Whether or not what a parent does falls within these boundaries will depend on the

1 *Finlayson, Applicant* 1989 SCLR 601.
2 *Kennedy v S* 1986 SLT 679.
3 *McGregor v K* 1982 SLT 293.
4 *H v Lees, D v Orr* 1994 SLT 908. See also *McD v Orr* 1994 SCCR 645, dealing with a case of abandonment under the same provision.
5 *H v Lees* 1994 SLT 908 at 913H.
6 *H v Lees, D v Orr* 1994 SLT 908.

facts of each case, with the courts taking into account whether the parent lost his/her temper, the parent's intention, the blameworthiness of the child's conduct and the degree of force used.[1] Reasonable chastisement will not provide the grounds for a referral to a hearing under this subsection,[2] though if a child is struck deliberately without any justification (such as reasonable chastisement) or other exonerating factor this will constitute a ground of referral.[3] Finally, the Schedule 1 offence need not have been committed in Scotland.[4]

(e) *The child is, or is likely to become a member of the same household as a child against whom a Schedule 1 offence has been committed.* The most notable feature of this ground is the broad approach that has been taken by the courts to the interpretation of 'household'. Their general view is that it is not necessary for all the members of the household to be living together, or even living at the same place at the same time. Two cases illustrate this. In the first, the child who had been the victim of the offence was staying with foster parents separated from his family and his sister was regarded as being in the same household as the fostered child.[5] The term 'household' was 'plainly intended to connote a family unit or something akin to a family unit – a group of persons held together by a particular kind of tie who normally live together, even if individual members of the group may be temporarily separated from it'.[6] In the second,[7] the child who was referred under this ground was born 8½ years after the death of a previous child as the result of a Schedule 1 offence and he was still regarded as being a member of the same household as that child. A household was still considered to exist even if one or more members were separated from it permanently where, as here, there was continuity in the form of the parents of the two children and of an elder sister who had been part of the household when the child died.

(f) *The child is, or is likely to become, a member of the same household as a person who has committed a Schedule 1 offence.* The same extended definition of 'household' applies here, though where

1 See *Stewart v Thain* 1981 SLT (Notes) 2; *Peebles v MacPhail* 1990 SLT 245; *B v Harris* 1990 SLT 208; and *Byrd v Wither* 1991 SLT 206.
2 *B v Harris* 1990 SLT 208.
3 *Kennedy v A* 1993 SLT 1134.
4 *S v Kennedy* 1996 SCLR 34.
5 *McGregor v H* 1983 SLT 626.
6 1983 SLT 626 at 628.
7 *A v Kennedy* 1993 SLT 1188.

there is no evidence that a child normally lives with the offender this ground may not be established.[1] If the child stops living with the offender by the time of the proof hearing there will need to be clear evidence that the household relationship has broken down to avoid the ground being established.[2]

(g) *The child is, or is likely to become, a member of the same household as a person who has been the victim of an offence under sections 2A to 2C of the Sexual Offences (Scotland) Act 1976.*[3]

(h) *The child has failed to attend school regularly without a reasonable excuse.* A child suspended from school cannot be referred under this ground unless, possibly, the exclusion from school was made necessary by his/her behaviour.[4]

(i) *The child has committed an offence.* This follows from the provision that no child under the age of 16 is to be prosecuted except on the instructions of the Lord Advocate. If a child under 16 is prosecuted this may be done only in the High Court or in the sheriff court. Generally, children will be prosecuted only if they have committed serious crimes or offences, such as murder, rape, or robbery (in which case the instructions of the Lord Advocate must be obtained). If prosecution is of a child aged 15 or over and could result in disqualification from driving, the procurator fiscal can proceed without reference to the Lord Advocate. Children may also be prosecuted in other cases with the approval of the Lord Advocate, for example, where conviction could be accompanied by an order for forfeiture or where the child has acted with an adult. It is suggested that this last is unlikely if the child is under 14.[5] This ground of referral is available only in respect of children over the age of 8, which is the age of criminal responsibility in Scots law.[6] For this condition to be established the higher standard of proof used in criminal law applies.

1 *Ferguson v S* 1992 SCLR 866.
2 *Kennedy v R's Curator ad litem* 1993 SLT 295.
3 This provision appears to be redundant. The offences created by these provisions were incorporated in the Criminal Law (Consolidation) (Scotland) Act 1995 and, since the relevant offences under this Act are Schedule 1 offences, they are already incorporated in the grounds of referral.
4 *D v Kennedy* 1988 SLT 55.
5 Renton and Brown *Criminal Procedure* (6th edn, 1996), para 25-01.
6 *Merrin v S* 1987 SLT 193.

(j) *The child has misused alcohol or any drug.* This is a new condition, no doubt reflecting recognition of current trends. The term 'drug' covers all kinds of drugs, not only those which are controlled under the Misuse of Drugs Act 1971. This means that a child could fulfil this condition if, for example, the child was addicted to cough bottle.

(k) *The child has misused any volatile substance by inhaling it, other than for medicinal purposes.* This would cover glue sniffing and inhaling butane gas, for example.

(l) *The child is being provided with accommodation by a local authority or is subject to a parental responsibilities order and special measures are needed in order to supervise the child properly either in his/her interest or in the interests of others.* This mainly applies to children who are considered to be in need of secure accommodation.

### (4) Investigation by the reporter[1]

Once the reporter receives information about a child he/she must carry out an initial investigation. Anyone can give information about children who may be in need of compulsory supervision to the reporter, and the police have particular duties to report offences committed by children to the reporter and to report other cases where they have reasonable cause to believe that a child may need supervision. As part of this initial investigation the reporter may request information from the local authority. This is sometimes referred to as requesting a 'social background report', though there is an argument that this term should be restricted to reports produced once a referral has been made.

At the end of this investigation the reporter may reach one of two decisions. The first is that no hearing is necessary in respect of the child. Where this decision is made the child may be referred to the local authority for provision of advice, guidance or assistance on a voluntary basis.[2] A decision not to refer to a hearing may be taken because the child is already subject to a supervision requirement or because the reporter does not consider that compulsory measures of supervision are necessary. If the reporter decides that a hearing

1 1995 Act, s 56.
2 1995 Act, s 56(4)(b). Debate has raged about the meaning of 'voluntary' in this context as well as an erroneous presumption that use of this type of supervision keeps a child 'out of the system'.

is not necessary a hearing cannot subsequently be arranged based only on the information on which this decision was taken. Around 70% of cases are not referred to a hearing.

The second possibility is for the reporter to arrange a hearing to consider the child's case. A hearing must only be arranged if the reporter considers that the child is in need of compulsory measures of supervision (and, of course, that one of the conditions explained above exists). Once a hearing has been arranged, the reporter will request a social background report on the child from the local authority and the authority has a duty to provide this. If the information originally given to the reporter came from the police or a local authority then, whatever decision the reporter reaches, he/she must notify the police or the local authority, whichever was the original source of the information.

### (5) Children's panel

The children's panel is composed of volunteers from the community who have completed training to equip them to undertake the role. These panel lists are maintained for each local authority area. The children's hearing which is convened to consider the case of a child deemed by the reporter to be in need of compulsory measures of supervision is composed of three of these lay members chosen from the larger children's panel. At least one woman and one man must be present and one member will act as chair.

### (6) Who can attend a hearing?[1]

Conduct of hearings is governed partly by the 1995 Act and partly by the Children's Hearings (Scotland) Rules 1996 ('Hearings Rules').[2]

The child who is the subject of the referral has both a right and an obligation to attend. If the child does not attend, a warrant can be issued to apprehend the child and this will authorise detention in a place of safety until a hearing is convened. Attendance by the child at the hearing can be excused in two cases. First, if the hearing is considering a referral concerning a Schedule 1 offence and it considers that the child's presence is not necessary for the just

1 1995 Act, s 45.
2 SI 1996/3261.

hearing of the case. Secondly, in any other case where the hearing considers that it would be detrimental to the interests of the child to be present.[1] These provisions allow the hearing to **excuse** attendance: they do not allow the hearing to **exclude** the child, who can still attend if wishing to do so. On one view the child cannot be excused attendance at the beginning of the hearing, when the grounds of referral are explained, unless the child is incapable of understanding the grounds. This is because the chair of the hearing is directed to explain the grounds of referral to the child and 'relevant person' at the beginning of the hearing.[2] The implication of this is that the child must be present at this stage. No explanation need be given if the child would be unable to understand it, so, presumably, there is no need for the child to be there to hear the explanation. It should be said that, although there are some differences between the wording of the 1968 Act and the 1995 Act on this topic, it is not entirely clear that the contrary view expressed in *Sloan v B*[3] could not be taken under the 1995 Act. This was that a child could be excused attendance at the explanation of grounds stage if it would not be detrimental to his/her interests because it was obvious that the case would have to be referred to a proof hearing to establish the grounds of referral. The Hearings Rules indicate, rather curiously, that a hearing can consider the case of a child in his/her absence.[4] It is not clear at what stage this consideration starts or if it covers the whole of the hearing. The reference to considering the case harks back to the wording of the 1968 Act, which is different from that used in the 1995 Act.

The 'relevant person' (see part 3(3)(a) above) also has the right and obligation to attend the hearing, though this obligation can be dispensed with if it would be unreasonable to require attendance or if this attendance is not necessary to allow the hearing to dispose of the case. The relevant person can be excluded from the hearing for as long as is necessary in the interest of the child. Exclusion can take place where the hearing is satisfied that this is necessary in order to obtain the views of the child or where the presence of the excluded person is causing the child distress or is likely to cause distress. Social workers will be all too familiar with the family interview scenario in which a parent will answer for the child and it is not until the child is seen on his/her own that sometimes there is the opportunity for the child to speak freely. Where a person is

1 1995 Act, s 45(2).
2 1995 Act, s 65(4).
3 1991 SLT 530.
4 Hearings Rules, r 20(2).

excluded the chair must explain to that person the substance of what took place in his/her absence.[1] The child's father also has a right of attendance if he does not fall within the definition of 'relevant person', and provided that he is living with the child's mother.[2] The child and relevant person are entitled to be represented and this representative has a right to attend, but this is rare. If any person who has a right to attend is in the custody of a constable, prison officer or such official, then that person also has a right to attend. If a safeguarder has been appointed, then that individual is entitled to be present throughout the hearing.

Other people normally attend but have no right of attendance, like the social worker who prepared the social background report. The social worker usually clarifies and updates the contents of the report if necessary, identifies appropriate resources, and when appropriate encourages the child and family to participate in the hearing which may be an unfamiliar system where there is a power imbalance. Members of the press are entitled to attend, but may be excluded on grounds similar to those for exclusion of a relevant person, the important difference being that there is no obligation to explain to the press what happened during the exclusion. Other than these, the chair of the hearing can permit others to attend like people training to become members of the children's panel or social workers, subject to the proviso that the number of persons attending is kept to a minimum.[3]

### (7) Business meetings[4]

The practice of holding a business meeting outwith the presence of the child and parents to discuss aspects of the running of the hearing was recognised as legitimate in the case of *Sloan v B*,[5] even though there was no express provision for such meetings in the Social Work (Scotland) Act 1968. These meetings are now given formal recognition in the 1995 Act. They can be arranged by the reporter and the child and relevant person have to be informed that the meeting will take place and of the purpose of the meeting. They can then make written representations to the reporter which will be passed on to the business meeting. The business meeting can

1 1995 Act, s 46.
2 Hearings Rules, r 12.
3 1995 Act, s 43.
4 1995 Act, s 64 and Hearings Rules, r 4.
5 1991 SLT 530.

decide a number of procedural matters and can give the reporter instructions about how his/her functions should be carried out in connection with the referral. It can, for example, decide whether or not to inform the child or the relevant person about being excused attendance at the hearing. The obvious problem which these meetings may raise for the child and family are concerns about decisions being (all but) reached in advance of the hearing.

### (8) Provision of information

The rules about provision of information to parents at hearings were successfully challenged in *McMichael v United Kingdom*.[1] As a result, the Hearings Rules now provide for the following information to be made available to the relevant person (including the father as noted above): the social background report; the statement of the grounds of referral; any judicial remit or reference or reference by a local authority; any existing supervision requirement; any report prepared by a safeguarder; and any views of the child given in writing to the reporter.[2] There is no requirement to make available any other information, for example, a school report or a report submitted by the manager of any residential establishment in which the child is required to reside, but the substance of such information must be conveyed to the relevant person by the chair of the hearing if it appears to be material and disclosure would not be detrimental to the interests of the child.[3] The only right that the child appears to have to access to information is this last right, simply to be informed of the substance of the reports, and other information received by the hearing, where this appears to the chair to be material and provided it is not detrimental to the child's interests.[4] On the approach to interpretation adopted under the previous rules for children's hearings this would appear to prevent these reports being made available to the child by the hearing or reporter.[5]

1 [1995] 20 EHRR 205.
2 Hearings Rules, r 5(1) and (3).
3 Hearings Rules, r 20(3) and (4).
4 Hearings Rules, r 20(4).
5 *Kennedy v A* 1986 SLT 358 at 362B.

### (9) Procedure at the hearing[1]

The hearing starts with the chair explaining the grounds of referral to those present and finding out if the grounds of referral are accepted by the child and the relevant person. If the grounds are not accepted the hearing can either discharge the referral or instruct the reporter to apply to the sheriff for a finding that the grounds are established. This procedure is also followed if the child is not capable of understanding the explanation given (for example, because the child is very young) or if the child has not in fact understood the explanation. If the grounds are accepted in part the hearing can either proceed on the basis of those grounds accepted or proceed as if the grounds were not accepted. The hearing is also obliged to consider if it is necessary to appoint a safeguarder to protect and secure the interests of the child and the reasons for making any appointment must be stated in writing by the chair of the hearing.[2] If a safeguarder is appointed he/she must produce a report which will be considered by the hearing. If the appointment is made at the beginning of the hearing it will presumably be necessary to continue the hearing for further investigation, as described below, in order to allow the preparation of the report.

If the grounds of referral are accepted or if they are established before the sheriff the hearing moves on to consider the case. This takes the form of a discussion involving all of the participants (except those excused attendance or excluded). The discussion is not limited to the grounds of referral. Anything which is relevant to a consideration of the case can be taken into account,[3] the sole possible exception being allegations which have been found not to be established by the sheriff at a proof hearing.[4] Hearings have the task of investigating the case as far as is necessary for a complete consideration of what is in the child's best interests, and this includes taking account of information which is not included in the grounds of referral which were accepted or established. Indeed, it has been decided that the hearing can consider allegations which were deleted from the grounds of referral which were then accepted by the child or relevant person at the proof hearing[5] and information

1 1995 Act, s 65 and Hearings Rules, r 20.

2 The grounds for appointing a safeguarder are broader than under the 1968 Act, which required actual or possible conflict between the interests of the child and his parents as a ground for appointing a safeguarder.

3 *O v Rae* 1993 SLT 570.

4 *M v Kennedy* 1991 SCLR 898.

5 *O v Rae* 1993 SLT 570.

which may disclose grounds of referral additional to those established at a proof hearing or accepted by the child or relevant person.[1] There is no need for the hearing to seek to have these additional grounds accepted or established before they can be taken into account. Overall, then, once consideration of a child's case has been triggered by the acceptance or establishment of any ground of referral, the hearing can consider any relevant information, by which is meant information relevant to the issue of what should be done in the child's best interests.

The views of the child have to be considered by the hearing before reaching a decision. His/her views can be conveyed to the hearing by the child or his/her representative in person, by the child in writing or by any safeguarder. When the child is notified of the hearing, that notification will ask the child if he/she wishes to express his/her views to the hearing and give an opportunity to state those views in writing to the reporter at that stage.[2] If the child is already subject to a supervision requirement that requirement must be reviewed in the course of the hearing. In an ideal world, the relatively informal atmosphere of a children's hearing would prove to be an environment in which all participants, including the child and relevant persons or parents would contribute fully and freely. In practice, the structures may be experienced as intimidating and/or individual's attitudes towards authority may be such that the inherent power imbalances are insurmountable. Here, the social worker who has established good working relationships with the child and others may work to facilitate their full participation. After the discussion the hearing reaches a decision.

Three decisions are possible: to discharge the referral; to make a supervision requirement; or to continue the case for further investigation.[3] This further investigation may require the child to go to a clinic, hospital or anywhere else for investigation and to stay there for up to 22 days. The child can be kept in a place of safety during this period if the hearing is satisfied either that keeping the child there is necessary in the interests of promoting or safeguarding the interests of the child, or that there is reason to believe that the child will not attend on the next hearing date. A child can be kept in a place of safety for only 22 days.[4] Once the further investigation is completed a decision must be made to impose a supervision

1 *R, Petitioner* 1993 SLT 910.
2 Hearings Rules, r 6.
3 1995 Act, s 69(1).
4 1995 Act, s 69(2)–(11).

requirement or to discharge the referral. A note of the decision and of the reasons for the decision (which must be clear, unambiguous and intelligible to the person receiving them) is sent to the child and the relevant person. It may sometimes be appropriate for the social worker to spend time with the child and family following the hearing's decision to clarify the meaning of the decision, to discuss the practicalities and to make arrangements for future contacts. Hearings can be fraught with tension and may even contribute toward the precipitation of a crisis in the family, and so the intervention of a social worker may be welcomed and necessary.

If the hearing is unable to dispose of the case it can grant a warrant to find the child or to keep him/her in a place of safety for up to 22 days.[1] Conditions can be attached regarding medical treatment or examination and about contact with other people. This type of warrant can be issued only where either there is reason to believe that a child will not attend a future hearing (or comply with a condition requiring attendance for further investigation), or where it is necessary to keep the child in a place of safety in order to safeguard or promote his/her welfare.[2] The warrant can be renewed by the hearing subject to a maximum of 66 days and can be further renewed by the sheriff without any upper limit of time.[3] One instance where use of this power would be appropriate is where the grounds of referral are denied, the case goes to a proof hearing and the proof hearing is delayed pending a criminal trial. In this sort of case, the hearing will be unable to dispose of the referral until after the proof hearing has taken place. In his commentary on the 1995 Act, Norrie notes that this power to issue a warrant should not be used where there are other, more appropriate powers, for example, to issue a warrant where the child fails to attend the hearing or to have a child kept in a place of safety while further investigation takes place.[4]

### (10) Proof hearings[5]

The hearing before the sheriff must take place within 28 days of the application to the sheriff being made and the sheriff has to consider

1 1995 Act, s 66.
2 1995 Act, s 66(2).
3 1995 Act, s 67.
4 K Norrie *The Children (Scotland) Act 1995* (1995), commentary on s 66.
5 1995 Act, s 68. The procedural rules are in the Act of Sederunt (Child Care and Maintenance Rules) 1997, SI 1997/291, ch 3, Pt VII.

whether or not to appoint a safeguarder to look after the interests of the child in the proceedings. Any safeguarder appointed by the hearing will continue through the court hearing. The safeguarder must make a report to the court if not intending to appear at the court hearing, and may make a report in other circumstances. The report may contain recommendations.[1]

In general, the proof hearing will take place in the sheriff court that covers the geographical area of the children's hearing. The exception to this is where the ground of referral is commission of an offence by the child, in which case the proof hearing will take place in the sheriff court which would have had jurisdiction in any prosecution of the crime. The child can be represented by someone other than a qualified lawyer and can be excused attendance on the same grounds as at a children's hearing.

After hearing evidence and considering the terms of any safeguarder's report, the sheriff may find the grounds not established and discharge the referral. Alternatively, the sheriff may find the grounds established and the matter will be referred back to the hearing for consideration and disposal. If the ground is that the child has committed an offence, the sheriff must be satisfied beyond reasonable doubt that the child has committed the offence; in other cases the sheriff must simply be satisfied that the ground is established on the balance of probabilities.[2] In making a finding, the sheriff may delete from the statement of facts in the grounds of referral, but cannot amend it.[3]

Where the ground of referral is that a Schedule 1 offence has been committed by a named individual, the court hearing on establishing the ground of referral should not, unless there are exceptional circumstances, be adjourned pending the outcome of any criminal trial.[4] Evidence at the proof hearing should not be restricted because of the possible trial of the alleged perpetrator.[5] An acquittal of a Schedule 1 offence in criminal proceedings does not indicate that a supervision requirement which was made on the basis that the offence was established as a ground of referral should automatically be terminated.[6] Where the evidence establishes that a Schedule 1 offence has been committed, but the sheriff is unable to

1 *Kennedy v M* 1989 SLT 687.

2 1995 Act, s 68(3)(b). See *B v Kennedy* 1987 SLT 765; *Harris v F* 1991 SLT 242. The higher standard of proof cannot be avoided by a referral of what is really an offence on one of the other grounds: *Constanda v M* (25 April 1997, unreported), Inner House.

3 *S v Kennedy* 1996 SCLR 34.

4 *Humphries, Petitioner* 1982 SLT 481; *Ferguson v P* 1989 SCLR 525.

5 *P v Kennedy* 1995 SCLR 1.

6 *Kennedy v B* 1992 SCLR 55.

decide **which** Schedule 1 offence, the ground of referral should be held to be established.[1]

It is also clear now that the sheriff should not, in most cases, rule on any procedural objections without hearing the evidence first. The only exceptions are where the objections, if successful, would mean that the grounds of referral could never be established.[2] An example of this would be a case where the referral was of a child under 8 accused of an offence.

If, during the course of the hearing, the child and the relevant person accept the grounds of referral, the sheriff has to stop the hearing and deem the grounds to be established. Where only the relevant person accepts the grounds the sheriff can either do this or hear the evidence if satisfied that this should be done. If the grounds of referral are established, the case is remitted back to the reporter to arrange a hearing. If not, the referral is discharged.

If grounds of referral are established and the case referred back to the hearing for disposal, the sheriff may issue a warrant for the child's detention if it is likely that the child would run away before the hearing or if detention is in the child's own interests (for example, if the ground of referral was commission of a Schedule 1 offence against the child). Such detention may last, at most, 3 days.

## (11) Supervision requirements[3]

The 1995 Act abolishes the distinction between residential and non-residential supervision requirements. There is now only one type of supervision requirement which can contain a wide variety of conditions, including a condition specifying where the child is to stay, requiring medical examination or treatment, or regulating contact between the child and any other person. It is also possible for the hearing, when it is making a requirement, to fix a time for its review.[4]

Before a condition can be imposed requiring the child to stay in a foster home, the hearing must have considered a report from the local authority which deals with the needs of the child and the suitability of the proposed placement to meet those needs.[5] The report will also need to confirm that either:

1 *M v Kennedy* 1996 SLT 434.
2 *Sloan v B* 1991 SLT 530.
3 1995 Act, s 70.
4 1995 Act, s 70(7).
5 Hearings Rules, r 20(6); Fostering of Children (Scotland) Regulations 1996, SI 1996/3263, reg 15.

(a) the proposed foster carer is an approved foster carer; or
(b) the local authority is satisfied that a supervision requirement providing for a specific foster placement is in the child's best interest and either:
   (i) fostering is the most suitable way of meeting the needs of the child and the proposed carer has agreed to carry out a range of duties, including caring for the child and permitting visits by the local authority; or
   (ii) the proposed carer is a relative or friend of the child who has been interviewed and whose home has been visited and who has agreed to carry out the duties noted in (i).

The same procedures apparently have to be gone through before a recommendation for placement in residential accommodation is made.[1] Many social work departments have adopted procedures which will not permit the social worker to recommend residential accommodation in his/her report without the agreement of a committee of more senior workers, known sometimes as 'area resource groups' or 'admissions and support units'. The social worker's assessment as to the child's situation and needs should guide the decisions concerning the appropriateness of a recommendation for placement in residential accommodation and permit matching with suitable resources. Resources may not be available in the local authority and so may require to be purchased from a neighbouring authority, or a voluntary or private agency.

The requirement can also involve placement in secure accommodation, providing that one of two conditions are met:

(a) that the child has previously absconded, is likely to abscond again and if the child does, this will put his/her physical, mental or moral welfare at risk; or
(b) that the child is likely to injure him/herself or someone else unless kept in secure accommodation.

The local authority can make a recommendation that the child be placed in secure accommodation only if these two conditions are met and if it is in the child's best interests to be placed and kept in secure accommodation.[2] Before any child is placed in secure accommodation a full assessment of his/her needs must be made and any placement will normally include screening procedures within the social work department. For example, a screening group

1 Hearings Rules, r 20(6).
2 Secure Accommodation (Scotland) Regulations 1996, SI 1996/3255, reg 10.

may be set up which may include a senior psychologist, a senior person from the child care section and the head of the establishment. A requirement with a condition that the child be kept in secure accommodation must be reviewed within 3 months,[1] and a child kept in secure accommodation can require a review of the condition if he/she has not been placed in secure accommodation for 6 weeks.[2]

Supervision requirements impose limits on the parental rights and responsibilities of the parents of the child, not least because a child who is subject to a requirement is treated as a child being looked after by the local authority. A requirement to stay away from home clearly suspends the right to have the child staying with the parent(s). This requirement also affects the exercise of the responsibility or right to maintain contact and personal relations: the requirement may make express provision about contact as one of its conditions or the question of contact may be left to the discretion of the local authority.[3] On the basis of cases decided under the 1968 Act it will not be possible for anyone to seek a contact or residence order while a supervision requirement is in force.[4]

Once a supervision requirement has been made, the main duty of the local authority is to give effect to its requirements. Where it provides that the child is to stay at a specified address other than residential accommodation or a foster placement, the authority has to visit the child to make sure that he/she is staying there and that the conditions of the requirement are being fulfilled.[5]

In all cases the local authority must refer the case back to the reporter if the conditions of the requirement are not being complied with, for example, if a fostering placement breaks down or the child cannot be placed in the specified residential establishment. The child also becomes a child being looked after by the local authority, which imposes on the authority all the duties which exist in respect of such children.[6] Social workers would probably take a different view in seeing these duties as important but that the actual contact with the child and family members, foster family members, residential workers and other professionals is the core of work with the opportunities to engage with the child and significant others to effect change for the better.

1 SI 1996/3255, reg 11.
2 Ibid, reg 12.
3 The requirement must be specific, or it will be too vague: *D v Strathclyde Regional Council* 1991 SCLR 185.
4 See eg *A v G* 1996 SLT (Sh Ct) 123.
5 1995 Act, s 71.
6 See ch 4, pt 3; *Guidance* vol 2, ch 2.

## (12) Duration and review of supervision requirements[1]

The guiding principle is that the requirement should last no longer than is necessary in the interests of promoting or safeguarding the welfare of the child. Once a requirement is made there are several means through which it can come to be reviewed. The child or the relevant person can require a review 3 months after the requirement was made or 3 months after any previous review. Reviews can be initiated at any time by the local authority if it is satisfied that the requirement ought to be ended or varied; that a condition of the requirement is not being complied with; or that the best interests of the child would be served either by applying for a parental responsibilities order, by placing the child for adoption or by seeking a freeing order. The special provisions for reviews of children required to reside in secure accommodation are noted above.

In addition, the reporter must arrange a hearing if the requirement will expire within 3 months. The requirement will expire automatically on the 18th birthday of the child or after 1 year from the date on which the order was made or last continued. The reporter must therefore arrange a hearing both once the child reaches the age of 17 years and 9 months and once 9 months have elapsed from the making of the order or the last review.

At the review hearing the case can be continued for further investigation, the requirement can be terminated or the requirement can be varied, for example, by adding to or altering the conditions attached to the requirement. Where the hearing is considering a requirement which is to lapse within 3 months, it has a specific obligation to consider whether, if the requirement is terminated, the child will still require supervision or guidance. If the decision is that such guidance or supervision is necessary it must be provided by the local authority, but only to the extent that the child is willing to accept it.[2]

Since the child who is the subject of a supervision requirement is treated as being looked after by the local authority the review requirements set down for children being looked after apply to him/her.

1 1995 Act, s 73.
2 1995 Act, s 73(12).

## (13) Rights of appeal[1]

There is a right of appeal to the sheriff against any decision of the children's hearing, for which legal aid is available. The appeal must be made within 3 weeks of the decision and if it concerns a supervision requirement made by the hearing, an application can be made to the hearing asking it to suspend the requirement pending the appeal. Although the 1995 Act suggests that any decision can be appealed against, it will not be possible to appeal against decisions which involve procedural steps. An example of this is the decision to instruct the reporter to apply to the sheriff for a finding that the grounds of referral are established. Appeal will therefore usually be possible only against those decisions involving a final disposal of the case.[2] Exceptionally, it is possible to appeal against a warrant issued by the hearing to find a child or to keep that child in a place of safety. Where the appeal is against a warrant, it must be dealt with within 3 days or the warrant will lapse.

At the appeal the sheriff will hear evidence and may question anyone who has compiled a report for the hearing and seek a further report. If the appeal is unsuccessful the decision of the hearing stands. If the appeal is successful the sheriff has a number of options, depending on the decision which is being appealed:

(a) where a warrant is appealed against, the warrant will be recalled;
(b) where the appeal is against a condition attached to a supervision requirement which means that the child has to stay in secure accommodation, the condition will be removed from the requirement;
(c) in other cases the sheriff can either:
    (i) send the case back to the hearing for reconsideration with a note of the reasons for his/her decision;
    (ii) discharge the referral; or
    (iii) impose a supervision requirement in terms that the sheriff thinks appropriate to replace the requirement made by the hearing. This is a new provision which seems to conflict with the ethos of the hearings system that decisions about what steps to take are best taken after discussion in the relatively informal setting of the hearing.[3]

1 1995 Act, s 51.
2 *H v McGregor* 1973 SLT 110.
3 1995 Act, 51(5)(c)(iii). See A Kelly *Scottish Children's Panel* (1996), p 108 for an example of discussion about this development and the disquiet about a radical shift from the principles of Kilbrandon.

The appeal is to be allowed if, in the words of the 1995 Act, the sheriff is satisfied that the decision of the children's hearing is not justified in all the circumstances of the case. No further indication is given as to the grounds of appeal, but it is clear that it includes procedural irregularities at the hearing.[1] If an appeal to the sheriff results in the sheriff ordering that the case is remitted to a hearing for reconsideration, such a hearing need not be arranged if the sheriff's decision is itself being appealed.[2] In such cases care must be taken not to act in a way which might cause difficulty if the appeal was successful. There is a right of appeal from any decision of the sheriff to the sheriff principal or to the Court of Session, and if the initial appeal is made to the sheriff principal his/her decision can be appealed to the Court of Session. This right of appeal covers not only the decision of the sheriff in an appeal from a decision of the hearing, but also other decisions made by the sheriff, for example, a finding that the grounds of referral are established. Once an appeal has been lodged, the original decision of the sheriff need not be implemented pending the outcome of the appeal. If this appeal is successful the case will be sent back to the sheriff with instructions as to disposal.

Even though an unsuccessful appeal has been made against a finding that grounds of referral are established, it is still possible to re-open the question of the existence of these grounds. Under the 1968 Act this was possible in exceptional cases through application to the *nobile officium* of the Court of Session, as happened in the Ayrshire cases.[3] The 1995 Act introduces a new procedure allowing an application to be made for a review of a finding that grounds of referral were established.[4] This review can take place both where the grounds were found to be established by the sheriff against the opposition of the child and/or relevant person and where the grounds were deemed by the sheriff to be established following acceptance by the child and/or relevant person as described above. Either the child or a relevant person may make the application, and it must be based on the following grounds:

(a) there is evidence which might have had material effect on the outcome of the proof hearing which was not considered by the sheriff;

1 *M v Kennedy* 1995 SCLR 15.
2 *Kennedy v M* 1995 SCLR 88.
3 *L, Petitioners (No 1)* 1993 SLT 1310; *L, Petitioners (No 2)* 1993 SLT 1342; see also *JL v Kennedy* (6 March 1995, unreported) IH.
4 1995 Act, s 85.

(b) the evidence would have been admissible at the proof hearing and is likely to be credible and reliable; and
(c) there is a reasonable explanation for the failure to bring this evidence to the proof hearing.

If these three conditions are met the sheriff will consider the new evidence. There are three possible outcomes. First, the sheriff may be satisfied that none of the original grounds of referral are established and that no other grounds are established. If so, the supervision requirement will be terminated either immediately or on a date fixed by the sheriff. The question of whether the child will need some supervision and guidance after the ending of the supervision requirement must be considered by the sheriff and he/she may direct the local authority to provide such guidance or supervision. The social work department must comply with this direction, except where a child is old enough to understand the supervision or guidance being offered and refuses it. Where the requirement is not to be terminated immediately the sheriff can vary conditions in the requirement. Secondly, the sheriff may be satisfied that none of the original grounds of referral are satisfied but that the evidence establishes some other ground which was not the subject of the original proof hearing. If so, the sheriff may find that ground established and remit the case back to the hearing for disposal. Finally, if one of the grounds of referral at the original proof hearing is established the sheriff may refer the case back to the hearing for disposal or can take no action. The decision of the sheriff can be appealed to the sheriff principal and then to the Court of Session or direct to the Court of Session.[1]

## 4. REFERRALS FROM THE COURT SYSTEM

A child under the age of 16 not subject to a supervision requirement who pleads or is found guilty in a criminal court may be referred to a hearing for advice or for disposal. After considering the advice of the hearing the court may refer the case to it for disposal. Where a child under 16 who is subject to a supervision requirement pleads or is found guilty the High Court may, and sheriff courts must[2] ask the reporter to arrange a hearing to consider the case and give advice on the treatment of the child. On

1 1995 Act, s 51(11).
2 The district court cannot deal with the cases of children under 16.

receipt of the advice the case can be referred back to the hearing for disposal.

Summary courts can also refer cases of people between 16 and 17½ to a hearing for advice if they plead or are found guilty. After receiving the advice the case can be referred to a hearing for disposal. None of these provisions apply in cases where there is a fixed penalty, for example, murder or for certain minor traffic offences.[1]

If a court convicts someone of a Schedule 1 offence it may refer the child who was the victim of the offence or a child who is or is likely to become a member of the same household as the offender to the reporter.[2]

If, during the course of a variety of court hearings, including actions for divorce, actions under section 11 of the 1995 Act in relation to parental rights and responsibilities, adoption proceedings or petitions to free for adoption, it appears to the judge that any of the non-offence grounds of referral to a children's hearing exist in respect of a child involved in the hearing, the judge may refer the case of the child to the reporter. The reporter must then investigate and decide whether a hearing is necessary. If a hearing is arranged, the ground of referral found to exist by the judge is regarded as being established.[3]

## 5. COURT ORDERS SENDING CHILDREN TO LOCAL AUTHORITY ACCOMMODATION

Children remanded in custody by criminal courts are to be remanded to the care of a local authority. If the child is between 14 and 16 and the court certifies that the child is unruly or depraved he or she may be held in a remand centre if the court has been notified of the availability of a place there.[4]

Where a child is convicted in a summary court he/she may, provided someone over 21 could have been imprisoned by the court, be sentenced to detention for up to 1 year with the place and conditions of detention to be decided by the local authority.[5] A child so sentenced is to be treated as subject to a supervision requirement.[6]

1 Criminal Procedure (Scotland) Act 1995, s 49.
2 Ibid, s 48.
3 1995 Act, s 54.
4 Criminal Procedure (Scotland) Act 1995, s 51.
5 Ibid, s 44(1).
6 Ibid, s 44(3).

A child who has been arrested and not liberated is to be detained in a place of safety unless the child is so unruly that he/she cannot be so detained, it is impractical to detain the child in a place of safety, or it is inadvisable to detain him/her in a place of safety because of his/her health or mental or bodily condition.[1] In common with others detained the child must be brought to court on the next lawful day.

Social work involvement includes the negotiation for the most appropriate resource for the child. Detention of a child through court proceedings may be experienced as especially traumatic by the child and family and so there may be a need for a social worker to become further involved with them, for example, in supporting them through the court process, in clarifying the meaning and implications of any order made, and in making practical arrangements for visits.

## 6. EMERGENCY PROTECTION OF CHILDREN[2]

The 1995 Act introduces an entirely new means of protecting children in an emergency by way of the 'child protection order' which is granted by the sheriff.

### (1) Grounds for application[3]

Like the place of safety order which it replaced, anyone can apply to the sheriff for a child protection order (CPO), which the sheriff may grant provided that the following conditions are met:[4]

(a) the sheriff has reasonable grounds to believe that the child either:
   (i) is being so treated or neglected that he/she is suffering significant harm; or
   (ii) will suffer significant harm if not removed to and kept in a place of safety or if he/she does not remain in the place where presently accommodated; and

1 Criminal Procedure (Scotland) Act 1995, s 43.
2 See *Guidance*, vol 1, ch 7.
3 1995 Act, s 57.
4 1995 Act, s 57(1).

(b) a CPO is necessary to protect the child from the actual or anticipated harm.

There is no further guidance in the legislation (or in the SWSG guidance) as to what are 'reasonable grounds' and what is 'significant harm' and these terms will be further elaborated in practice. Norrie distinguishes significant harm from harm of a minor, transient or superficial nature and suggests that harm will be significant only 'when it is clearly more serious than the potential trauma removal from the home will almost certainly cause the child'.[1] This seems consistent with the approach adopted in England where significant harm has been described as harm which is 'considerable, noteworthy or important'[2] and the point has been made that significance can exist in the nature of the harm itself or in the implication of it.[3] Significant harm can relate to both physical and psychological harm.

The reference to a child suffering harm if removed from the place where currently resident would allow the granting of an order, for example, for a baby to remain in hospital if it would be dangerous to go home or in the situation that arose in *M v Dumfries and Galloway Regional Council*[4] where a child disclosed abuse by her father while in the voluntary care of the local authority and the authority wished to keep her in care.

As well as these general grounds there is a further set of grounds which can be used only by a local authority to apply for a CPO.[5] These are that the authority:

(a) has reasonable grounds to suspect that a child is being or will be so treated or neglected that he/she is suffering or will suffer significant harm;
(b) is either making inquiries or having inquiries made to allow it to decide if it needs to do anything to safeguard the child's welfare; and
(c) has reasonable cause to believe that access to the child is needed as a matter of urgency, but that it is being unreasonably denied and this is preventing it from completing its inquiries.

Social workers and their managers take decisions about children believed to be at such a degree of risk of significant harm that they

1 K Norrie *The Children (Scotland) Act 1995* (1995), commentary on s 57.
2 *Humberside County Council v B* [1993] 1 FLR 257.
3 Department of Health *The Children Act 1989 Guidance and Regulations: Volume 1* (1991), para 3.19.
4 1991 SCLR 481.
5 1995 Act, s 57(2).

must urgently be protected, in some cases by removal from their homes. The power to intervene so intrusively in the private lives of families is the subject of much debate and misunderstanding. The quality of information processing, decision-making and the interaction skills of the social workers all contribute toward a child being believed to be in need of protection and set the scene conducively for future work towards either the child's return home or placement in a permanent alternative. The unresolved societal conflicts about the role of social workers are perhaps most clearly seen in the consideration and use of CPOs. Although the overriding principles of obtaining the views of the child and seeking the most minimal intervention do not pertain legally to the making of a CPO, good practice would suggest that they are still relevant.

In applying for a CPO, it is clear that the social worker's request will be rigorously scrutinised by the sheriff and the social worker may even be required to be put on oath.[1] The old place of safety orders were never taken lightly, but the new arrangements for application for a CPO are likely to mean that social work departments will find it necessary to tighten their procedures further for preparation of such applications. Guidance suggests that social work departments will need to clarify who will have responsibility for preparing CPO applications, whether the legal department is involved or not; how social workers will be prepared for going before a sheriff; and what the procedure will be if and when the order is granted. The appearance before the sheriff is not a full proof hearing although the social worker will have to convince the sheriff of the necessity for such an order by providing supporting evidence in the application, in supplementary documents and in discussion with the sheriff. This will require preparation and confidence on the part of the social worker.[2]

## (2) Effect of the order

The order can, at the discretion of the sheriff, contain one or more of these requirements or authorisations:[3]

1 Sheriff Brian Kearney in conference papers of a seminar held on 28 November 1996 entitled 'Children's Hearings, the Courts and the Children (Scotland) Act 1995'.
2 *The Children (Scotland) Act 1995 – A Training Programme* (1996, The Scottish Office and BAAF), p 39.
3 1995 Act, s 57(4).

(a) a requirement addressed to whoever is in a position to produce the child to do so;
(b) authorisation for removal of the child to a place of safety and to keep the child there;
(c) authorisation to prevent the removal of the child;
(d) a provision that the location of the place of safety should not be disclosed to a particular person or group of people.

In addition the sheriff has to consider whether to attach directions to the CPO concerned with regulating contact with the child and this would include prohibiting contact. A second type of direction, concerned with the exercise or fulfilment of any parental right or responsibility, can be made only if it is applied for, and application should be made only where the direction is necessary to safeguard and promote the welfare of the child.[1] This type of direction can cover examination and treatment of the child or any assessment or interview.

Once an order is made, the reporter must be notified.

### (3) Implementation

Once an order is made, it must be implemented only if the person who applied for the order has a reasonable belief that this is necessary to safeguard or promote the child's welfare.[2] In any event, an attempt must be made to implement the order within 24 hours of it being made: otherwise the order will lapse.[3] Note that this only requires an attempt to implement the order. An unsuccessful attempt will continue the order in force. This requirement does not apply where the order is to keep the child in the place where he/she is already resident. A child taken to a place of safety is owed the same duties by the local authority as a child being looked after by it.

### (4) How long does the CPO last and what happens next?

There are a variety of possible routes that can be followed after a CPO has been implemented and which may result either in dis-

1 1995 Act, s 58.
2 1995 Act, s 57(6).
3 1995 Act, s 60(1).

charge of the CPO or in other measures being taken in respect of the child.

(a) *Discharge by the reporter.* The CPO can be discharged by the reporter if, on the basis of new information or of a change in circumstances, the reporter considers that the conditions for making a CPO are no longer satisfied. In taking that decision the reporter must have regard to the welfare of the child. Conditions and directions attached to the CPO can also be varied by the reporter on the same grounds.[1] These powers can be exercised only (i) if no initial children's hearing has been arranged, and (ii) before the beginning of any hearing before the sheriff of an application to set aside or vary the CPO.[2] If this power is exercised both the applicant for the CPO and the sheriff who granted it must be notified.[3]

(b) *Arranging an initial hearing.*[4] If the CPO is not discharged and if the reporter has not been notified of an application to set aside or vary the CPO, an initial meeting of the children's hearing must be arranged to consider the child. This meeting must take place on the second working day after implementation of the CPO. Where the CPO authorises removal of the child to a place of safety implementation occurs when this is actually done. When the CPO prevents removal it is deemed to be implemented on the day it is made. The discretion which reporters had been permitted to exercise in the scheduling of the initial hearing is now entirely gone and so the possibility to postpone this hearing to 'take account of the parent's mental state, or alcohol or drug induced condition'[5] no longer exists. The purpose of this hearing is solely to consider whether to continue the CPO.[6] Continuation can be ordered only where this is in the interests of the child and where the hearing is satisfied that the grounds for making a CPO are established. This latter requirement presumably means that it must be satisfied that the grounds exist on the day when it meets to consider the case. Where the hearing continues a CPO its terms can be varied and it will be continued to a further hearing arranged to consider the child's case, which must take place on the eighth working day after implemen-

1 1995 Act, s 60(3).
2 1995 Act, s 60(4).
3 1995 Act, s 60(3) and (5).
4 1995 Act, s 59.
5 B Lister in conference papers of a seminar held on 28 November 1996 entitled 'Children's Hearings, the Courts and the Children (Scotland) Act 1995'.
6 1995 Act, s 59(2).

tation of the CPO.[1] This hearing will take the same format as any other hearing to consider the case of a child referred to it, and the CPO will lapse at the beginning of this hearing, so that if the hearing wishes to continue the case and keep the child in a place of safety other powers must be used.

The CPO will lapse if not continued by the initial hearing and also, presumably, if the hearing is not held on the second working day. If the CPO is continued by the initial hearing, the reporter still has to exercise his/her discretion in deciding whether to refer the child to the second hearing. If the decision is taken not to proceed with such a referral the CPO will lapse.

There is an appeal to the sheriff within 2 working days against the continuation of a CPO by the hearing,[2] and the reporter, on being notified of such an appeal, may arrange a hearing to give advice to the sheriff. The time limits and powers of the sheriff in dealing with the appeal are the same as those when dealing with an application to set aside or vary the order.

(c) *Application to vary or set aside the order.* Such an application can be made by the child, anyone having parental rights, a relevant person or the person who applied for the order.[3] The application is made to the sheriff and must be made before the initial hearing, arranged as described above, has begun.[4] The reporter is notified of the application and can arrange an optional hearing to give advice to the sheriff.[5] The application must be disposed of by the sheriff within 3 working days.[6] Although it is not clearly stated the CPO would, presumably, lapse if this time limit was not complied with.

After hearing evidence, at which stage the reporter has the right to make representations, the sheriff has to decide if the conditions for making a CPO are satisfied or if any direction attached to the CPO should be varied. In the latter case the sheriff can make any necessary modification. If the conditions for making a CPO are not satisfied the CPO is recalled.[7] If the conditions **are** satisfied the sheriff has 4 options which **may** be taken:[8]

(i) the order can be confirmed or varied;

1 1995 Act, s 65(2).
2 1995 Act, s 60(8).
3 1995 Act, s 60(7).
4 1995 Act, s 60(8).
5 1995 Act, s 60(10).
6 1995 Act, s 60(8).
7 1995 Act, s 60(13).
8 1995 Act, s 60(12).

(ii) any direction attached to the CPO can be confirmed or varied;
(iii) a new direction can be attached to the CPO;
(iv) the order may be continued in force until the beginning of the second children's hearing described in (b) above, that is, the hearing which takes place on the eighth working day.

### (5) Emergency protection when there is no time to apply to the sheriff[1]

In emergencies, authorisation to remove a child or to keep him/her in a particular place can be granted by a justice of the peace. This is possible, in the words of the 1995 Act, where 'it is not practicable in the circumstances to apply to the sheriff for a CPO or for the sheriff to consider such an application'. The authorisation can be granted on either of the sets of grounds set out above for granting a CPO, but only if the order granted would probably have contained authorisation to remove the child to a place of safety or authorisation to prevent the child's removal. As well as authorising removal or retention of the child, the authorisation issued by the JP may require production of the child by whoever is in a position to do this. The authorisation must be implemented as soon as reasonably practicable[2] and in any event will lapse 12 hours from the time it was made if no arrangements have been made to prevent removal of the child or if he/she has not been or is not being taken to a place of safety. Otherwise the authorisation will lapse 24 hours after being granted or, if this is earlier, when there is a disposal of an application for a CPO.

Police constables have the power to take a child to a place of safety if they have reasonable cause to believe that the conditions for making a CPO are satisfied; it is not practicable to apply for a CPO or to have the application considered by a sheriff; and that it is necessary to remove the child to a place of safety to protect him/her from significant harm or significant further harm. A child can be kept in the place of safety for 24 hours unless an application for a CPO is disposed of earlier.

If either of these emergency measures is taken the reporter must be informed.[3] Both of these types of emergency action will terminate if the reporter forms the view that the grounds for them no longer exist or that it is no longer in the child's best interests to be

1 1995 Act, s 61.
2 Emergency Child Protection Measures (Scotland) Regulations 1996, SI 1996/3258, reg 4.
3 Ibid, regs 3 and 8.

kept in the place of safety. At all times the general principle is that a child should not be detained unnecessarily in a place of safety and the reporter has broad powers to liberate or discharge a child, for example, when there is a change of circumstances.[1]

## 7. EXCLUSION ORDERS[2]

The traditional approach to the emergency protection of children involved the removal of children from the danger. The 1995 Act introduces the possibility of removing the alleged source of the danger and leaving the child at home. This is done by the introduction of exclusion orders which are, to some extent, based on the exclusion orders provided for in the Matrimonial Homes (Family Protection) (Scotland) Act 1981. One significant difference is that these exclusion orders can be applied for only by the local authority. Questions have been raised about where the excluded person will live;[3] what financial provisions might be made available; and significantly about the principle of excluding a person who is only just alleged to have been the cause of a child suffering. These concerns may be reduced given that the person accused has the opportunity to appear and be represented at court hearings. Many social workers and others have long held the view based on their experience, research and their value base that removing a child from his/her home environment and primary carer just at a time of trauma and stress is illogical, enormously damaging and counterproductive in both the short and long term. In spite of what may prove to be insurmountable practical and civil rights problems, these new orders provide the possibility to consider an alternative which may prove to be much more in keeping with the three overriding principles of the paramountcy of the child's welfare, the child's right to be heard and that no order should be made if this would be better for the child.

1 B Lister in conference papers of a seminar held on 28 November 1996 entitled 'Children's Hearings, the Courts and the Children (Scotland) Act 1995'.

2 1995 Act, ss 76 to 80. See *Guidance*, vol 1, ch 7. The procedural rules are in the Act of Sederunt (Child Care and Maintenance Rules) 1997, SI 1997/291, ch 3, Pt V.

3 The Children Act 1989 makes specific provision for assisting someone who has left accommodation to protect a child: Sch 2, para 5. It could be argued that the same sort of assistance could be provided by the local authority in Scotland under the terms of s 22 of the 1995 Act, given that a service can be provided to another member of the child's family if it will safeguard and promote the child's welfare.

### (1) When can an exclusion order be made?

Exclusion orders can be made if these **three** conditions exist:[1]

(a) the child has suffered, is suffering or is likely to suffer significant harm as a result of any actual conduct by the person named in the application for the order (who is referred to as the 'named person'), or conduct by this named person which is threatened or reasonably apprehended;

(b) the order is necessary to protect the child regardless of whether he/she is living in the family home and would better safeguard the child's welfare than removal from the family home; and

(c) the application identifies someone who is capable of looking after the child and any other family members left in the family home properly (the 'appropriate person').

No final exclusion order can be made until the named person has been given an opportunity to be heard by the sheriff, but until this is done an interim order can be made and this order has the same effect as a final one.[2]

Even if the grounds are made out, the sheriff still has to take account of the overriding principles set out above before making an order and must also not make an order if doing so would be unreasonable and unjustified.[3] This has two aspects. First, the order may be unreasonable and unjustified in all the circumstances of the case. The sheriff must, in particular, look at the conduct of members of the child's family; the needs and resources of members of that family; and the extent to which the family home and anything in it is used in connection with a trade, business or profession. The second aspect to be considered are the possible consequences of making an order if the home involved is an agricultural tenancy or tied accommodation.

If the sheriff dealing with an application for an exclusion order thinks that the conditions for granting a CPO have been established he/she may instead of making an exclusion order make a CPO.

1 1995 Act, s 76(2).
2 1995 Act, s 76(3).
3 1995 Act, s 76(9) and (11).

### (2) The effect of an order[1]

The effect of an exclusion order is to exclude the named person from the family home, which he/she can enter only with the permission of the local authority. Additional orders can be attached to the exclusion order, for example, a warrant to eject the named person; an interdict preventing this named person from entering the home or entering the vicinity of the home; an interdict preventing the named person from taking any step in respect of the child; and an order regulating contact between the child and the named person. The power of arrest can be attached to these orders,[2] as it can be in orders under the Matrimonial Homes (Family Protection) (Scotland) Act 1981. The procedure for dealing with someone arrested for breach of interdict is effectively the same as under the 1981 Act.

### (3) How long does the order last?

The exclusion order will last for 6 months.[3]

## 8. SHORT-TERM REFUGES

Local authorities can provide short-term refuges for children (who for this purpose are those under 18) who appear to them to be at risk.[4] The provision of accommodation is triggered by a request from the child and can be either in a residential establishment or with a foster family approved for the purpose. Refuge can be provided for up to 7 days, or up to 14 days if the authority has been unable to find a responsible person in relation to the child and has no suitable accommodation for the child. The main categories of 'responsible person' are the child's parent; a non-parent with parental responsibilities; someone who ordinarily has charge or control of the child; a local authority looking after the child; and anyone providing accommodation for the child under the 1995 Act.

1 1995 Act, s 77.
2 1995 Act, s 78.
3 1995 Act, s 79(1).
4 1995 Act, s 38(1)(a).

The local authority must notify the 'authorised officer' of the fact that the child is being provided with refuge, of the child's name, of his/her last permanent address, of the address of any responsible person and of a contact telephone number. Notification must be made as soon as reasonably practicable and at the latest within 24 hours of providing refuge. An 'authorised officer' is a police officer identified by the Chief Constable for the purposes of these provisions. The local authority may approve residential establishments run by others for the purpose of providing refuge. If refuge is provided in one of these establishments, the local authority and the authorised officer must be notified as soon as practicable and, in any event, within 24 hours.

As soon as reasonably practicable after providing refuge, or being notified of the provision of refuge by an approved establishment, the local authority must notify the responsible person and the local authority in which the child had his/her last permanent address.

This provision permits social work departments to listen to and respond more appropriately to the views of children who are saying they are at risk and can no longer stay in the place where they believe themselves to be in danger. It provides the time for the social worker to complete a full assessment of the child and his/her whole situation with a view to ensuring as high a quality of life for the child as possible. While, clearly, there may be occasions when children's motivations for claiming to be at risk may be questionable, at least with the possibility of short-term refuge, children who are genuinely at risk can be accommodated.[1]

## APPENDIX

### Offences under Schedule 1 of the Criminal Procedure (Scotland) Act 1995

**NB** These offences qualify as Schedule 1 offences only if they are committed against a person under the age of 17.

*(a) Any offence under Part I of the Criminal Law (Consolidation) (Scotland) Act 1995.* These offences include:

(1) procuring for the purposes of prostitution or unlawful intercourse;

1 See also *Guidance*, vol 1, ch 8; Refuges for Children (Scotland) Regulations 1996, SI 1996/3259.

(2) procuring by the use of threats, intimidation or false pretences, or using drugs to facilitate unlawful intercourse;
(3) a group of offences related to incest. These offences include sexual intercourse within the forbidden degrees of relationship; intercourse with a step-child under 21 or who has lived in the same household as the step-parent while under 18; and intercourse by a person in a position of trust (for example, a foster parent) with someone under 16 living in the same household as him or her;
(4) intercourse with a girl under 13;
(5) intercourse with a girl between the ages of 13 and 16. The difference between this and (4) above is that certain defences are available in this case;
(6) indecent behaviour towards a girl between 12 and 16. This is now covered more comprehensively in paragraph (*d*) below;
(7) abduction of a girl under 18 with the intention of having sexual intercourse;
(8) unlawful detention in a brothel or for the purposes of having unlawful intercourse;
(9) permitting a girl under 16 to use premises for the purposes of unlawful sexual intercourse;
(10) causing or encouraging the seduction or prostitution of, unlawful intercourse with, or indecent assault on, a girl under 16;
(11) allowing a child between the ages of 4 and 16 to reside in or frequent a brothel;
(12) the commission or procuring of a homosexual act –
    (i) otherwise than in private;
    (ii) without the consent of both parties;
    (iii) with a person under 18.

*(b) Any offence under ss 12, 15, 22 or 33 of the Children and Young Persons (Scotland) Act 1937.*

(1) Section 12 makes it an offence for someone over 16 having custody, care or charge of a child to assault, ill-treat, abandon, or expose the child in a manner likely to cause unnecessary suffering or injury to the health (including mental health) of the child. Procuring the commission of any of these acts is also an offence. Aside from any other circumstances where it might be established, neglect is deemed to take place in two cases. First, where the person legally liable to maintain a child has failed to provide or procure the provision of (for example, by obtaining

available benefits) adequate food, clothing or medical aid for the child. Secondly, where the death of a child is caused by suffocation (other than that involving a foreign body) and the child at the time of death was sharing a bed with someone over the age of 16 who was under the influence of drink when he or she went to bed.

(2) Section 15 makes it an offence to cause or allow a child to beg or be used for begging.

(3) Section 22 deals with the situation where a child under 7 is left in a room with an improperly guarded open grate fire without reasonable precautions being taken against the risk of burning or scalding. An offence is committed if the child is killed or suffers serious injury.

(4) Section 33 makes it an offence to allow a child under 16 to take part in a performance where his or her life or limb is endangered.

*(c) Any offence involving bodily injury to a child under 17.*

*(d) Any offence involving the use of lewd, indecent or libidinous practices or behaviour towards a child under 17.*

In addition, section 52 of the Civic Government (Scotland) Act 1982 provides that references to Schedule 1 offences in the 1995 Act are to include the offences which it creates in relation to the taking, distribution, possession or publication of indecent photographs of children under 16.

# 6. Special needs

## 1. INTRODUCTION

This chapter is concerned with the law relevant to those who have special needs arising from some form of disability, either physical or mental, from mental health problems, or as a result of advancing age. Although the chapter has been divided into a number of headings for ease of presentation, this is an area, particularly in relation to people who are elderly, where any of the pieces of legislation might provide options for a range of individuals. The statutory provisions should, therefore, be viewed as a whole. It is also recognised that although there are some transferable concepts concerning the value base, the sources of knowledge and the various skills required for social workers working with persons with special needs, there are also some important differences and specific skills and knowledge which are necessary.

Legal terminology in this field differs significantly from social work terminology which reflects the value base and current thinking. While social workers may refer to persons with a mental handicap as persons with a learning disability, the obvious point is that it is necessary to know the appropriate legal terminology in order to locate and use the relevant law.

## 2. COMMUNITY CARE[1]

Community care in the contemporary sense was introduced by the National Health Service and Community Care Act 1990 and associated guidance, regulations and financial transfers. Its introduction followed a number of reports, particularly *Community Care: Agenda for Action* (the Griffiths Report) and the government White

1 For an overview of early implementation in Scotland see A Petch and others *Delivering Community Care* (1996).

Paper *Caring for People.*[1] A variety of impulses contributed to the introduction of this legislation. One was the feeling that provision for people in need was service-led rather than needs-led, that is, that services were being provided on the basis of what was available rather than what the user needed. Another was that changes in the benefits system allowing payments to be made for private residential care had led to spiralling costs.

According to *Caring for People*, the objectives of the new system are:

(a) to promote the development of domiciliary, day and respite services to enable people to live in their own homes wherever feasible and sensible;
(b) to ensure that service providers make practical support for carers a high priority;
(c) to make proper assessment of need and good case management the cornerstone of high quality care;
(d) to promote the development of a flourishing independent sector alongside good quality public services;
(e) to clarify the responsibilities of agencies and so make it easier to hold them to account for their performance; and
(f) to secure better value for taxpayers' money by introducing a new funding structure for social care.[2]

Following the views expressed by Griffiths, the White Paper identified local authorities as the lead agency in provision of community care with the remit to organise and co-ordinate the provision of packages of care for persons in need.[3] The overall system is sometimes described as care management, since after the assessment has taken place and a service package (care plan) has been agreed, the social worker manages that care plan. This may involve purchasing from and monitoring a range of providers. This highlights the difficulties inherent in the situation when the local authority has a duty to provide various services and is also the body responsible for upholding the rights of users. Conflict of interest and difficulties of enforcing such statutes additionally complicates this situation.[4] Social workers employed by the local authorities have become the care managers. There has been much discussion about whether care management is real social work but the reality

1 Cm 849 (1989).
2 Para. 1.11.
3 See ch 3.
4 See, for example, *Care Management and the New Social Work – A Critical Analysis* by Sheppard (1995).

is that real social workers are taking on the role of care managers and bring a rich tradition to this role, as well as the values, knowledge base and practice skills which characterise social work.[1] From a practical point of view the following are the main consequences of community care:

(a) assessments of need have to be carried out before services are provided;
(b) a split between purchasers of services and providers of services is encouraged;
(c) a mixed economy of care is to be encouraged; and
(d) the responsibility of paying for people in residential care is transferred from the Department of Social Security to local authorities, with an associated transfer of resources.

## 3. ASSESSMENTS

### (1) Assessments under section 12A of the Social Work (Scotland) Act 1968 (the 1968 Act)

Local authorities have a duty to carry out assessments of needs in respect of anyone who appears to be in need of 'community care services'.[2] Indeed, the carrying out of an assessment is made a prerequisite for the provision of such services, except in emergencies, and even then an assessment must be carried out as soon as practicable. In practice these assessments will be carried out by social workers who must consider the person's needs, the views of other relevant organisations and whether the person may have a right to a disabled person's assessment under section 4 of the Disabled Persons (Services, Consultation and Representation) Act 1986. Good practice suggests that community care assessments resemble any other social work assessment rather than being regarded as a technical exercise. Individuals whose needs are being assessed and their carers should be in partnership with the social worker in compiling a holistic assessment.[3] Once the assessment has been carried

1 See discussion in *Contracting and Case Management in Community Care – The Challenges for Local Authorities* by Edward Peck, Pete Ritchie and Helen Smith (CCETSW Paper 32, January 1992).
2 Social Work (Scotland) Act 1968, s 12A.
3 See discussion in *The Care Maze* by Colin McKay and Hilary Patrick (1995), pp 12–14.

out a decision has to be made as to whether, having regard to the assessment, the needs of the individual concerned call for the provision of any of the community care services.

The term 'community care services' covers services, other than services for children,[1] provided under Part II of the 1968 Act or under sections 7, 8 and 11 of the Mental Health (Scotland) Act 1984 (the 1984 Act). The services provided under Part II of the 1968 Act include those provided by virtue of section 12;[2] provision of residential care; provision of residential accommodation with nursing care (though this cannot be directly provided by the local authority); provision of domiciliary and laundry services, probation and supervision services; and burial and cremation of people in the care of or receiving assistance from the local authority. The provisions of the 1984 Act cover local authority functions; provision of aftercare services for those suffering from mental disorder; and training and occupation for those with a mental handicap.[3]

The process of assessment is governed both by the provisions of the 1968 Act and by more detailed guidance issued by the Secretary of State. The guidance is contained in, for example, *Care Management and Assessment: Practitioner's Guide*,[4] as well as various Social Work Services Group (SWSG) Circulars such as 'Community Care in Scotland: Assessment and Care Management'.[5]

Assessments and their outcomes in service provision can be challenged through the local authority complaints procedure or judicial review.

### *(a) Statutory provisions*

There are a number of interlocking pieces of legislation relevant to the assessment process. The first of these is section 12A referred to above, which sets out a number of requirements. One of these is that no decision that a person requires nursing care can be made without consulting a medical practitioner. Another is that if it appears that any person being assessed may be in need of services provided by the health board or a housing authority, the social work department must discover from them what services are likely to be made available to the person being assessed and take that

1 It is not entirely clear whether this was intended to refer to any services provided to a child or only to services of a type provided to children.
2 See ch 1, pt 15.
3 See pt 8, below.
4 (1990, HMSO).
5 Circular SWSG 11/91.

information into account in making the assessment. The Disabled Persons (Services, Consultation and Representation) Act 1986 is also relevant. When a community care assessment is being carried out and the person being assessed appears to be a disabled person, the assessment must be carried out in terms of this Act (its other provisions are considered briefly below). This has two consequences. First, the assessment is directed towards considering whether the disabled person's needs call for the making of arrangements under section 2 of the Chronically Sick and Disabled Persons Act 1970. Section 2 requires authorities, where they are satisfied that it is necessary to meet the needs of an individual, to make arrangements for the provision of a variety of services. These are: provision of practical assistance in the home; provision of, or assistance in obtaining, wireless, television, library or other recreational facilities; provision of lectures, games or other recreational facilities outwith the disabled person's home; provision of assistance in taking advantage of educational facilities; assistance with travel to make use of services provided by the local authority; assistance in adapting the home or in the provision of additional facilities designed to secure the greater safety, comfort or convenience of a disabled person; assistance in taking holidays; provision of meals; and provision of assistance in obtaining a telephone and any adaptation necessary to allow its use.

Secondly, the assessment must take into account the ability of the disabled person's carer to continue in that capacity. In other types of assessment the position of carers has been strengthened by the Carers (Recognition and Services) Act 1995, which allows carers to request that an assessment takes into account their continuing ability to provide care. The local authority must honour any such request.

Finally, the Children (Scotland) Act 1995 (the 1995 Act)[1] allows the parent or guardian of a disabled child to request an assessment of the child or anyone else in the family to determine the needs of that child resulting from the child's disability or the needs of another family member resulting from the disability of the child. In terms of the 1995 Act[2] the local authority has the duty to promote the welfare and upbringing of children in need by providing appropriate services to the child and the family. The purpose of this assessment is to identify appropriate services for the individual case.

1 1995 Act, s 23. See also ch 4, pt 2(4).
2 1995 Act, s 22.

### *(b) Guidance*

According to the guidance in *Care Management and Assessment: Practitioner's Guide*, care management, of which assessment is part, involves a seven-stage process:[1]

(1) publishing information about community care services;
(2) determining the appropriate level of assessment for any prospective service user;
(3) assessing need;
(4) care planning (that is, identifying services to be provided to meet assessed need);
(5) implementation of the care plan;
(6) monitoring of the implementation; and
(7) review of needs and of the care plan.

It also, as this list indicates, identifies a number of different levels of assessment depending on the circumstances of the individual case.[2] These range from a simple assessment, which it is suggested might be carried out by reception staff and result, for example, in the issue of a bus pass, to comprehensive assessments involving a number of agencies. It is suggested that assessments under the Disabled Persons (Services, Consultation and Representation) Act 1986 (the 1986 Act) should be comprehensive.[3] In taking decisions about need and about the provision of services, workers will be guided by the eligibility criteria established by the local authority. These criteria will set out conditions to be met for the provision of services.[4] Regardless of the type or level of assessment being carried out, the guidance stresses that it is to be needs-led not service-led; that it is to involve the prospective service user and the carer fully; that it should embrace physical, mental and social functioning; and that it should be non-discriminatory.[5]

Once services have been provided, they cannot be withdrawn without a reassessment of the service user's needs being carried out. After Gloucester County Council had illegally withdrawn ser-

1 *Care Management and Assessment: Practitioner's Guide* (1990), p 11.
2 For a discussion of the difficulties of operating this number of levels of assessment see J Lewis and H Glennister *Implementing the New Community Care* (1996), ch 8.
3 But see the comments on the usefulness of this aspect of the guidance in *R v Gloucestershire County Council, ex parte RADAR* (21 December 1995, unreported) QB.
4 See the discussion in M Mandelstam and B Schwer *Community Care Practice and the Law* (1995), pp 143-153.
5 Circular SWSG 11/91, para 5.

vices without a reassessment, the Council wrote to all those people (there were over 1,000) who had had services withdrawn, offering them a reassessment. This decision was successfully challenged.[1] It is clear that if it is intended to withdraw community care services from a user or to alter the services provided, this must be preceded by a reassessment. The opportunity to ask for a reassessment is not enough because, as noted above, the obligation to carry out an assessment is triggered by the appearance of need not a request from a prospective user. Those already receiving services must obviously appear to be in need of such services.

Finally, the legal significance of the guidance should be noted. By law, the local authority must carry out its social work functions under the general guidance of the Secretary of State.[2] Failure to follow the general policy guidance on community care[3] without good reason is unlawful and will result in a successful challenge to any care plan prepared in this way. The practice guidance contained in *Care Management and Assessment: Practitioner's Guide* must also be taken into account in carrying out the assessment process and failure to do this could lead to a successful challenge.[4]

A final element of the assessment procedure may be, and if residential care is being provided must be,[5] a financial assessment to set the level of contribution, if any, to be made by the person to whom the service is being provided. The local authority is entitled to charge an amount which is considered to be reasonable for the services it provides. If a charge is made for a service, and the user is not in a position to pay it, the guidance makes it clear that this is not in itself a reason to refuse to provide the service.[6]

### *(c) Care plans and provision of services*

Once the assessment is completed, a care plan is made up for the person involved setting out the services to be provided and the

1 *R v Gloucestershire County Council, ex parte RADAR* (21 December 1995, unreported) QB.

2 1968 Act, s 5.

3 Contained in SWSG 11/91. This is the equivalent of the English guidance in *Caring for People: Community Care in the Next Decade and Beyond* which is referred to in the cases noted below, and is expressed in similar terms.

4 *R v North Yorkshire County Council, ex parte Hargreaves* (1995) 26 BMLR 121; *R v London Borough of Islington, ex parte Rixon* (1996) Times, 17 April.

5 There are detailed rules about the calculation of contributions for residential care: see C McKay and H Patrick *The Care Maze* (1995), chs 9 and 10. It should be noted, however, that the detailed rules change regularly.

6 Circular SWSG 11/91, para 11.

social worker, as care manager, is responsible for its implementation, monitoring and review.

If services are to be arranged or provided as part of a care plan they will generally be paid for directly by the local authority and provided by the authority, a private sector provider, or a voluntary organisation. In some circumstances, however, the authority may make direct payments to the service user to allow the purchase of services required.[1] Use of any money provided is monitored by the local authority. At present, direct payments can be made only to adults under 65 who are able and willing to manage such payments, though people subject to a variety of statutory and other conditions relating to mental health and addiction are excluded.[2] The relevant guidance goes into detail about the assessment of a person's ability to manage a direct payment, pointing out that it is no barrier to the making of such a payment that the person receiving it needs help to manage it, and sets out monitoring, review and termination guidelines. Two restrictions on the use of direct payments are that the payments cannot be used to pay the recipient's partner or member of the family living in the same household as the recipient,[3] and that they can be used only to purchase short periods of residential care.[4] Finally, it should be remembered that payments can be made only to those entitled to community care services, that the ability to make payments is a power conferred on the local authority and that the service user must agree to service provision by direct payment.

Increasing acceptance of the concepts of user involvement and empowering practice point to the desirability of the use of direct payments when possible as an additional means of shifting the balance of power to service users to control the resources which affect them most and increase their quality of life. An alternative view likens the increasing use of direct payments to the former government's provision of nursery vouchers in which services which previously had been provided by local authorities without additional payment are now available only upon direct payment which is partially funded by the voucher scheme.[5]

1 Community Care (Direct Payments) Act 1996, inserting new ss 12B and 12C into the 1968 Act. See also the policy and practice guidance issued with Circular SWSG 3/97.

2 Community Care (Direct Payments) (Scotland) Regulations 1997, SI 1997/693, reg 2(2).

3 Ibid, reg 3.

4 Ibid, reg 4.

5 For a very full discussion of the position in England which is mainly relevant in Scotland see *Disability and the Law* by Jeremy Cooper and Stuart Vernon (1996) pp 92–119.

*(d) Resources and the assessment process*[1]

One issue which has arisen in a number of challenges to community care decisions taken by a local authority is the relevance of available resources to the assessment process. *R v Gloucestershire County Council, ex parte Mahfood*[2] involved the removal of services which had previously been provided, because of budget cuts. The individual involved here, Mr Mahfood, was disabled and so the assessment had been carried out under the 1986 Act as explained above. The court concluded that resources were relevant both at the stage of assessment of need and, in terms of the Chronically Sick and Disabled Persons Act 1970 (the 1970 Act), in deciding whether it was necessary to make arrangements to meet these needs.

This decision was appealed successfully in *R v Gloucestershire County Council, ex parte Barry*.[3] There the Court of Appeal held that the availability of resources was not relevant either at the stage of assessment of need or at the stage of deciding whether provision of a service was necessary to meet the need identified. A further appeal was taken to the House of Lords,[4] which overturned the Court of Appeal decision. They held that in making assessments under the 1970 Act the resources available to the local authority were a relevant consideration in assessing a person's need. The resources would be fed into the process through the eligibility criteria set by the local authority for access to services. This decision has been met with a variety of responses which include relief on the part of some local authorities, shock that a sense of a person's right or entitlement to have need met has been removed and disappointment that rationing of resources has been supported by the judgment.

It should be noted that this decision is subject to two limitations. Once the local authority making an assessment under the 1970 Act has decided that it is necessary to make arrangements to meet the needs of an individual, it has a legally enforceable duty to make those arrangements and lack of resources will not relieve it of this duty. In addition, decisions in the assessment process, regardless of which statutory provision is involved, will still be open to review

1 See T Guthrie 'The Relevance of Resources in Community Care Assessments' (1997) SLPQ 149 and 'The House of Lords and Community Care Assessments' (1997) 2 SLPQ 225.
2 (1995) 30 BMLR 20.
3 [1996] 4 All ER 421.
4 [1997] 2 All ER 1.

and there will be clear cases where a refusal to provide services because of resource constraints will be unreasonable and so challengeable. This is reflected in comments made in the House of Lords to the effect that the assessment must be carried out in a responsible fashion and that resources and cost will not always be an element in determining need. In other words, if a local authority's decision that a person is not in need is utterly unreasonable it will be open to challenge.

In assessments not carried out under the 1970 Act, resources will also be relevant to the decision about service provision. This is explicitly recognised in the legislation, which treats the assessment of need as something which simply has to be taken into account in deciding on service provision.[1]

## (2) Disabled Persons (Services, Consultation and Representation) Act 1986

In addition to its relevance to community care assessments, this Act allows a person who has a mental and/or physical impairment or someone who cares for that person to request an assessment by the local authority of the need for services provided under section 2 of the Chronically Sick and Disabled Persons Act 1970 (see above). The assessment must take into account the ability of the present carer to continue to provide care. The 1986 Act also contains detailed provisions allowing challenge of the assessment and the authority's proposals in relation to the provision of services. The former government indicated that this section will not be brought into force, taking the view that the complaints and representation procedure under the Social Work (Scotland) Act 1968 is adequate for this purpose. The needs and interests of persons who are disabled were to have become much more recognised through this statute and through appropriate social work advocacy, but for a number of reasons, including lack of resources and the low priority that work with persons who are disabled has in social work departments, this has not happened to the extent intended.

1 1968 Act, s 12A.

## 4. GENERAL PROVISIONS ON DISABILITY

### (1) Chronically Sick and Disabled Persons Act 1970

The introduction of this Act marked a turning point in the provision of services and facilities for persons with special needs with a shift in thinking about persons with sometimes quite overwhelming disabilities being supported and empowered to live as independently as possible in the community.

The legislation imposes a number of duties on social work authorities and others. A large part of it is taken up with the provision of access to buildings for disabled people, with the main provisions of relevance here being found in sections 1 and 2.

Section 1 imposes a general duty on local authorities to investigate the need for services to persons with handicapping conditions in their area. This requires the authority to find out the number of such people in the area and assess the need for services for them. A curiosity of the Act is that there is no definition of handicap or disability. Section 2 is discussed above.

### (2) Disabled Persons (Employment) Act 1944

This provided for a quota system for the employment of disabled people, and required that at least 3% of the workforce employed by employers of more than 20 people should consist of people registered as disabled. This has been abolished with the coming into effect of the employment provisions of the Disability Discrimination Act 1995 (see chapter 2, part 5). The other aspect of the Act is the provision for training of disabled people and provision of employment rehabilitation centres. Assistance for disabled people should be available through the employment service and its network of disability employment advisers. This assistance includes various aids which can be lent to employers and grants to help with travel to work, adaptation of the employer's premises and personal readers. In addition, many local authorities provide sheltered employment for people with disabilities.

### (3) Disability Discrimination Act 1995

This gives disabled people protection against discrimination in a wide range of situations. It is fully discussed in chapter 2, part 5.

## (4) Services provided under the Social Work (Scotland) Act 1968

Local authorities can make use of the wide powers to promote social welfare conferred on them by section 12 to provide services for persons who are disabled. This includes providing assistance in cash or kind to prevent future greater expense to the department, since the 'persons in need' to whom such aid is available include people 'suffering from a mental disorder or substantially handicapped by any deformity or disability' as well as those in need of care and attention arising out of infirmity.[1] More specifically, local authorities have a duty to provide domiciliary services and laundry services to households where these are necessary because a person in need lives there or is proposing to live there.[2] These services might include any which contribute to a person being able to continue living at home, such as help with cooking, shopping, cleaning or even respite care.

## (5) Special educational needs

The Education (Scotland) Acts 1980 and 1981 require education authorities to make provision for special educational need. The term 'special educational need' covers children who either have learning difficulties or who suffer from a disability or handicap which prevents them from making use of normal educational provision.

The education authority has a duty to carry out assessments of children aged two or over who come to their attention as having or appearing to have special educational needs. The object of the assessment is to discover if the child has pronounced, specific or complex special educational needs which require continuing review. The assessment involves medical and psychological examination and if, on conclusion of the assessment, the authority considers that the child falls into one of the categories listed, a record of needs will be opened for the child. This record of needs will identify the special needs of the child and specify the provisions which the authority will make for the child. Parents have rights of appeal, for example, against a decision to record a child and against

1 1968 Act, s 94(1).
2 1968 Act, s 14.

the assessment made of a child. Having a record of need opened for a child may access resources, but it may also be possible to access resources, such as a school auxiliary, on the basis of a medical or psychological diagnosis without going through this formal process.

The parents of children have the right to make a placing request for their child to be enrolled in a school of their choice, including a private school, anywhere in the United Kingdom. The local authority can refuse the request for a number of defined reasons, for example, that the authority can cater adequately for the child's needs at a school of its own.

In the period starting two years and finishing nine months before the 16th birthday of a child with a record of need, a 'future needs assessment' must be carried out for the child. The objective of the future needs assessment is to identify educational and training provision which would benefit the child on leaving school. It is not a community care assessment, though duties of assessment and service provision might arise under the Children (Scotland) Act 1995 as a result of this assessment. The assessment involves both the education department and the social work department. As part of the process reference must be made to the latter for an opinion as to whether the child is disabled. If it considers that the child is disabled it must then carry out its own assessment of the child's needs. Typically, a social worker will meet with the parents and the young adult involved shortly before the school leaving date. The young person has the right to say he/she does not want a future needs assessment to be completed. If the young person is under 16 or is unable to consent, the parents may refuse social work attention on his/her behalf.[1] It is important that the social worker discuss the projected needs of the young adult with all persons concerned and that includes the young adult. It is also crucial for the social worker to recognise that this interview may well be viewed as an intrusion and unwelcome intervention, particularly in situations where the social work department has had little previous contact with the family.

Similar reference to the social work department is necessary where the education authority intends to record a child for the first time within the period noted above. The social work department must be notified 6 months before any person, on whom it has given an opinion concerning disability, ceases full-time school education.

1 Disabled Persons (Services, Consultation and Representation) Act 1986, s 13(8).

## 5. MENTAL ILLNESS AND HANDICAP: COMPULSORY ADMISSION TO HOSPITAL

### (1) Introduction

It is vital that all local authority social workers understand the powers which enable them to intervene in the lives of persons who are experiencing mental health problems or persons with learning disabilities. The limits of these powers are equally significant in acknowledging and upholding the civil liberties of service users. This area of work is considered to be especially complex and difficult not least in that social workers become involved in the process of persons losing their liberty. A local authority social worker will undertake further education and training to become a recognised mental health officer before being authorised to use such powers. Local authority duties include providing after-care services for anyone who is or has been suffering from mental disorder (including anyone who has been discharged from compulsory detention in hospital)[1] and providing suitable training and occupation for any person over the age of 16 who has some form of learning disability.[2]

Before anyone can be made subject to compulsory admission to hospital or guardianship that person must be suffering from a mental disorder. 'Mental disorder' is defined as any 'mental illness or handicap however caused or manifested'.[3] With two exceptions, no further legal definition of mental illness or mental handicap is offered. The first exception relates to the definitions of mental handicap amounting to mental impairment and severe mental impairment. Secondly, it is specifically provided that a person is not to be treated as suffering from a mental disorder **by reason only** of promiscuity or other immoral conduct, sexual deviancy, or dependence on drugs or alcohol. There is no lower age limit for compulsory admission to hospital.

Compulsory admission (and some aspects of guardianship: see below) is governed by the Mental Health (Scotland) Act 1984. In practice, well over 90% of those admitted to hospital suffering from mental illness or mental handicap are admitted as voluntary patients, although there are arguments that local authorities have not sufficiently used their powers to intervene to protect some of the most vulnerable and needy people in the community.

1 Mental Health (Scotland) Act 1984, s 8.
2 1984 Act, s 11.
3 1984 Act, s 1(2).

## (2) Grounds for admission

Compulsory admission to hospital can take one of two forms: admission following application to the sheriff court[1] or emergency admission.[2] However, before either of these can take place certain grounds relating to the patient's mental condition and need for treatment have to be established.

In the case of admission following application to the sheriff the requirements are:[3]

(a) that the person is suffering from a mental disorder of such a nature and degree as to make hospital treatment appropriate; **and**
(b) it is necessary for the health and safety of that person or for the protection of others that such treatment should be given, and it cannot be given without compulsory admission and detention.

There are two qualifications to the first requirement. Where the disorder is persistent and shows itself only in the form of abnormally aggressive or irresponsible behaviour (what is sometimes referred to as 'psychopathy'), the disorder must be susceptible to treatment. Secondly, where the disorder takes the form of mental handicap, the handicap must amount to a treatable mental impairment or severe mental impairment.

In the case of emergency admission the requirements are:[4]

(a) that because of the patient's mental disorder it is urgently necessary for his/her health or safety or for the protection of others that the patient should be admitted to a hospital; **and**
(b) that to proceed with an application under section 18 would involve unreasonable delay.

## (3) Procedure: application to sheriff[5]

Applications to the sheriff must be made either by the patient's nearest relative or by a mental health officer (MHO). The nearest relative is essentially the spouse or relative caring for the patient or, if the patient is not being cared for by a relative, is the relative in the

1 1984 Act, s 18.
2 1984 Act, s 24.
3 1984 Act, s 17.
4 1984 Act, s 24.
5 1984 Act, ss 19–21.

highest category on a list starting with children, parents and siblings. An MHO is a social worker, employed by a local authority, who has experience of dealing with people with mental health problems, who represents an independent professional perspective and has received appropriate training. The nearest relative has the power to require the local authority to direct an MHO to investigate the case of an individual with a view to taking proceedings for compulsory admission.

The MHO's investigations will include an interview with the patient, and in arriving at the decision as to whether or not to apply for compulsory admission the MHO must take into account the wishes of the nearest relative. If the MHO is satisfied that the detention of the patient in hospital is the most appropriate way of providing for care and treatment, the MHO may apply for compulsory admission, and must apply in the circumstances noted in the next paragraph. The nearest relative must be notified of the intention to apply and is entitled to object and be heard at the court hearing. If the MHO decides that it would not be appropriate to apply for compulsory admission, the nearest relative must be informed and this relative may then exercise the power to make the application for admission. Whatever the recommendation, it is crucial that the MHO has communicated this and the reasons for the recommendation to the patient and nearest relative so that the basis for reciprocal and mutually agreed goals may be established as soon as possible. The MHO will also, when appropriate, make inquiries about alternative provision of services outwith the hospital setting.

The applicant for admission must have seen the patient within 14 days of the application. In addition, the applicant must have obtained two medical recommendations indicating the form of mental disorder suffered by the patient and which of the grounds of admission applies to him/her. One of these medical reports will normally be given by the patient's general practitioner, and the other by a specialist from the intended place of treatment. The later of the reports must be based on an examination of the patient which took place within 7 days of the application, and the earlier examination must be no more than 5 days before the later. Both reports must agree as to one form of mental disorder suffered by the patient. The MHO must apply for compulsory admission if requested to by one of the doctors providing a report, even if the MHO considers compulsory admission unnecessary. These reports will normally be obtained by the MHO as part of the investigation of the case.

The application is presented to the sheriff court accompanied by the medical reports and a statement as to the MHO's opinion, which will state the reasons for that opinion. In deciding on the application the sheriff may make any inquiries thought necessary and must hear any objecting nearest relative, the MHO (if opposing the application), and the patient or patient's representative.

The application for admission must be approved or a hearing on it held within 5 working days of the submission of the application.

Where the patient is admitted to hospital as a result of an application by the nearest relative, the local authority must be notified of the admission within 7 days, and the MHO must interview the patient within a further 21 days and produce a report on the patient known as a 'social circumstances report'. A copy of this report is sent to the responsible medical officer (RMO, that is, the doctor responsible for treating the patient) and to the Mental Welfare Commission.[1] Although the statutory requirement to produce a social circumstances report arises only where the application for admission is made by the nearest relative, the code of practice issued under the 1984 Act suggests that it is good practice to prepare such a report in respect of all patients compulsorily admitted.

### (4) Procedure: emergency admission[2]

Provided that the grounds for emergency admission are established, the recommendation for admission is made by a single medical practitioner who must have seen the patient on the same day as the recommendation is made. Before making the recommendation the doctor must obtain, where practicable, the consent of a relative **or** the MHO. Although the wording of the 1984 Act is not entirely clear, it appears that the accepted interpretation is that only one of these consents is needed, and admission can proceed in the face of opposition from the other person able to consent. It also appears to be competent to seek the consent of an alternative MHO or relative if the first one approached refuses consent.[3] The Mental Welfare Commission must be notified of the patient's admission, as must the nearest relative or a responsible person living with the patient, if this has not already happened.

1 See below, pt 7(15).
2 1984 Act, s 24.
3 Mental Welfare Commission, Annual Report 1994-95, p 11.

### (5) Duration of detention following application to sheriff[1]

If the sheriff grants the application for admission this is warrant for the detention of the patient for 6 months. This can be renewed for a further period of 6 months and, thereafter, for periods of 1 year.

The procedure for renewal of detention is that the RMO either examines the patient or obtains a report concerning his/her condition, carries out various consultations with others concerned with the patient's treatment, and then assesses the continued need for detention of the patient. For continued detention to be necessary the grounds for admission must still apply to the patient. If continued detention is considered necessary a report is made to the hospital managers and this, without reference to the sheriff, renews the authority for the patient's detention.

In addition, a review of a patient's case must be undertaken between the third and fourth week of detention to determine the need for continued detention.[2]

### (6) Duration of detention: emergency admission[3]

An emergency recommendation is authority for the detention of the patient for up to 72 hours only. This period can, however, be extended for a further 28 days.[4] Such further detention can only take place where a report has been produced on the patient which indicates the need for continued detention for a limited time. The consent of the nearest relative or MHO must be obtained, if practicable.

Unless the MHO has consented to the continued detention, the local authority must be notified. The MHO must then, within 21 days of the continuation of detention, produce a social circumstances report on the patient. Although the statutory requirement arises only where the MHO has not consented, good practice suggests that such a report should be prepared in all cases.

The patient cannot be detained under the emergency admission procedures immediately after the expiry of the 28-day period.[5] However, the patient may be detained for a further 3 days on the

1 1984 Act, s 30.
2 1984 Act, s 22(4).
3 1984 Act, s 26.
4 1984 Act, s 26.
5 For interpretation of 'immediately after' see *R v Hay* 1993 SCLR 112.

lodging of a report with the sheriff clerk. This detention is available only where no application has been made under section 18 or it is not practicable to make such an application within the 28 days, **and** the patient's condition has deteriorated so that he/she needs to be detained in the interests of the patient's own safety or that of others. The consent of the nearest relative or MHO must, if practicable, be obtained. There is a right of appeal to the sheriff.

In addition, an application to the sheriff for admission under section 18 of a patient detained under the emergency provisions outlined above is authority for the patient's detention for a period of 5 days after the submission of the application. Courts must deal with such applications within 5 days.

Concerns have been expressed by MHOs about the use of this emergency detention as an administrative expedient rather than as outlined above and that all the inclusions of the phrase 'where practicable' in gaining the consent of the MHO have served, in practice, to marginalise and even exclude the use and contributions of MHOs.[1]

### (7) Rights of appeal

The patient has the right to appeal against a report authorising continued detention for 28 days following emergency admission and against renewal of the authority for detention where the patient has been detained following application to the sheriff. In the latter case there is a right of appeal once during every period of renewed detention. It should be noted that there is **no** right of appeal against a sheriff's decision to admit the patient to hospital or against an emergency recommendation.[2] In such circumstances it would be open to the patient to seek judicial review of the decision[3] or to exercise the right, which he/she has at all times, to make representations to the Mental Welfare Commission, which has the power to order the patient's discharge from hospital.

### (8) Consent to treatment

In general, patients detained following application to the sheriff or for the period of 28 days following emergency admission can be

1 See 'In the Margins' by Nick Clayton in Community Care 4/6/92.
2 See *F v Management Committee and Managers, Ravenscraig Hospital* 1989 SLT 49.
3 See, for example, *R v Hay* 1993 SCLR 112.

treated for their mental disorder without their consent.[1] There are two categories of exception to this:

(a) *Treatments requiring the patient's consent and a second opinion.*[2] The treatments involved here are psychosurgery and the surgical implantation of hormones to reduce the male sex drive. The patient must consent, and if incapable of informed consent or refusing to consent, the treatment cannot be given. Even if the patient consents, a second opinion supporting the treatment must be obtained from a practitioner appointed by the Mental Welfare Commission. Treatment in this category is very rare.
(b) *Treatment requiring the patient's consent or a second opinion.*[3] The treatments referred to here are administration of medicine for more than 3 months and electro-convulsive treatment (ECT). The patient must either consent or, if the patient refuses or is incapable of giving consent, the treatment must be supported by a second opinion.

Certain urgent treatment, for example, to prevent violent behaviour or to prevent deterioration in the patient's condition, may be given without consent, even if it falls into one of these categories. If such treatment is given it must generally be non-hazardous and reversible.

It should be noted that, even if a patient is compulsorily detained, the patient must consent to any treatment which is not treatment for the mental disorder.

### (9) Detention by nursing staff[4]

Voluntary patients can be detained by a hospital nurse for up to 2 hours to prevent them from leaving hospital. This can be done only when it is necessary in the patient's interests or for the protection of others and where the immediate attendance of a doctor (who could recommend emergency admission) cannot be obtained.

1 1984 Act, s 103.
2 1984 Act, s 97.
3 1984 Act, s 98.
4 1984 Act, s 25.

## (10) Discharge of patients

Discharge of patients can be ordered:

(a) by a sheriff on appeal;
(b) by the RMO or the Mental Welfare Commission if satisfied **either** that the patient is not suffering from a mental disorder of a type which requires him/her to be liable to be detained in hospital for medical treatment **or** that it is not necessary for the health or safety of the patient or the protection of others that such treatment should be received;
(c) by the nearest relative. The procedure for this is that the nearest relative gives at least 7 days notice to the hospital managers. The RMO can object if satisfied that the grounds of admission still exist, and this objection will prevent discharge. The nearest relative can appeal to the sheriff against the prevention of discharge.

In respect of the second type of discharge it was held in *AB and CB v E*[1] that for a patient to be liable to be detained that patient must require actual rather than potential in-patient treatment. Therefore, a patient who might require such treatment at some future date if refusing to co-operate with treatment would not be liable to be detained and would therefore have to be discharged. The waters have been muddied by a later decision, discussed below, suggesting that compulsory detention is appropriate where the patient is 'generally' in need of in-patient treatment.

Social work departments must provide after-care services for people who are or have been experiencing either a mental illness or a learning disability.[2] This duty applies to people who have been in hospital as well as those who have not. 'After-care' is not defined in the 1984 Act and has yet to be tested in court, but it could well include any of the myriad needs people have in settling back into the community or staying in the community. Probably in the light of high-profile cases in England where people have been discharged from long-term psychiatric hospital care with little support in the community, the Scottish Office has issued guidance[3] which emphasises that the social work department should be notified prior to discharge in order to assess the individual's needs.

1 1987 SCLR 419.

2 1984 Act, s 8.

3 *Guidance on care programmes for people with severe and enduring mental illness including dementia* – Circular SWSG 16/96.

## (11) Leave of absence

Patients detained under section 18 can be allowed to leave hospital for periods of leave of absence. This may be for a specific occasion or it may be for a longer period of time. Leave can last for 6 months initially and be continued for a further 6 months but cannot last longer than 1 year.[1] The judgment in *AB and CB v E* was felt to cause problems for leave of absence. Following the logic of that decision, if a patient is not in need of actual in-patient treatment he/she should be discharged rather than on leave of absence. Leave of absence is therefore potentially open to challenge. The legal doubt was cited as the reason for introducing community care orders into Scotland.[2] It is worth noting that the restriction of leave of absence to 1 year which accompanied this introduction does not entirely remove the possibility of challenge through the courts by a patient on leave of absence, though in one unreported case the view was taken that there was no problem in renewing the detention of a patient who was on leave at the time of the continuation. The view was taken that where a patient was generally in need of in-patient treatment that was enough to permit renewal of authority for detention.[3]

## (12) Community care orders

The reason for the introduction of these, contrary to the views of the Mental Welfare Commission,[4] is referred to above. After a patient has been detained for more than 28 days following admission under section 18, a community care order can be applied for in respect of the patient. The application is made by the RMO who must consult the patient's nearest relative (provided the patient does not object to this); those who have been principally concerned with the medical treatment received by the patient in hospital; the medical practitioner in charge of that treatment (the special medical officer or SMO); and the social worker who is to be the patient's after-care worker. A report by the after-care officer setting out the social circumstances of the patient and the care or after-

1 Mental Health (Patients in the Community) Act 1995 now inserted in the Mental Health (Scotland) Act 1984 as ss 35A–35K.
2 See Baroness Cumberledge in HL, vol 562, col 937.
3 *K v Murphy* 1997 SLT 248.
4 See their 1994–95 Annual Report at pp 20–22.

care available and on offer must be lodged with the application. It is also necessary to lodge two medical recommendations including a statement that the medical conditions for the making of a community care order are present. These medical conditions are:

(a) that the patient is suffering from a mental disorder of a nature and degree making treatment appropriate, but the grounds for compulsory admission to hospital do not apply; and
(b) that the patient requires to be subject to a community care order (i) with a view to ensuring that medical treatment and after-care services are received; and (ii) in the interests of his/her health and safety or with a view to the protection of others.[1]

Applications are considered by the sheriff and if granted the order will last for 6 months, renewable for 6 months and then for further periods of 1 year. Renewal is accomplished by the SMO, following examination of the patient and consultation with those identified above, certifying to the Mental Welfare Commission that the SMO is satisfied that the medical grounds still exist. There is provision for altering any conditions attached to the order and for change of the SMO or after-care officer.

Granting an order brings the section 18 detention to an end. There is no provision for compulsory medication of those subject to an order. However, if the condition of the patient deteriorates to such an extent as to give grounds for serious concern about his/her health and safety or the protection of others, a procedure exists for temporary readmission to hospital and this allows compulsory treatment. Readmission is to be for a maximum of 7 days, though if an application for detention under section 18 is then made, the patient can be detained for 21 days.

Revocation of the order can be effected either by the SMO or the Mental Welfare Commission where, after consultation, it is considered that the patient does not need to be subject to the order to ensure that the patient receives treatment or other care or in the interests of his/her own health or safety or that of others.

## (13) Detention by a police constable

Police constables have the power to remove to a place of safety anyone found in a public place who appears to be suffering from

1 For interpretation of these grounds and their relationship to the grounds for discharge from compulsory detention see *K v Craig* 1997 SLT 748.

mental disorder and to be in immediate need of care and control. Once taken to a place of safety that person can be detained there for up to 72 hours. In this context a place of safety is a hospital or residential home for those suffering mental disorder, or another suitable place. Those detained are not to be kept in a police station unless in an emergency where there is no other suitable place available. The nearest relative of anyone detained must be informed as soon as possible.

### (14) Place of safety orders

MHOs have the power to enter any premises where a person suffering from a mental disorder is living if the MHO believes that this person has been ill-treated or neglected, is not being kept under proper control, or is living alone and uncared for and is unable to care for him/herself. If entry is refused a warrant can be obtained authorising a police officer to enter the house with a doctor. Following such entry the mentally disordered person may be removed to a place of safety and kept there for up to 72 hours.

## 6. MENTAL ILLNESS AND HANDICAP: GUARDIANSHIP

As an alternative to admission to hospital, people over the age of 16 can be received into guardianship under the Mental Health (Scotland) Act 1984. This is sometimes referred to as 'mental health guardianship'.

### (1) Grounds[1]

The grounds for application are that the patient is suffering from a mental disorder of a nature or degree warranting reception into guardianship **and** that it is in the interests of the patient's welfare that he/she should be so received. The first ground must be certified by two medical practitioners; the second is the province of the MHO.

1 1984 Act, s 36.

### (2) Procedure[1]

The procedure is similar to that involved in compulsory admission and the application can be made either by the MHO or by the nearest relative. An additional duty is imposed on local authorities to satisfy themselves as to the suitability of the proposed guardian. In practice nearly all guardians are local authorities, their social work departments or chief social work officers.

Once the application is approved it must be forwarded to the local authority. The powers of the guardian are then to specify the place of residence of the patient and to require the patient to attend for education and medical treatment. These powers are limited and exclude, for example, the ability to consent, on the patient's behalf, to beneficial medical treatment. Where it is necessary to seek greater authority to provide day-to-day help, guidance and supervision, it is possible to apply to the Court of Session for the appointment of a tutor-dative.[2]

Patients subject to guardianship are to be supervised by the local authority and this requires at least one visit every 3 months. The authority can also issue directions to guardians (in the odd case where it is not the guardian) and require them to supply information and reports on the patient.

### (3) Duration and appeal[3]

Initially guardianship lasts for 6 months, but it can be renewed for further periods, initially of 6 months, and then of 1 year. The procedure for renewal requires that the patient is examined by the RMO who reports on his/her condition. If the RMO is satisfied that the first of the grounds noted above still applies to the patient, the RMO will forward the report to the MHO. The MHO will consider whether the second ground still applies, and if it does will report to that effect to the local authority. The report renews authority for guardianship. There is a right of appeal against renewal of authority for guardianship.

1 1984 Act, ss 37–40.
2 See pt 7(5) below.
3 1984 Act, s 47.

### (4) Discharge[1]

Discharge can be ordered by:

(a) the RMO or the Mental Welfare Commission, if satisfied that the first ground no longer exists;
(b) by the local authority or the Mental Welfare Commission, if satisfied that the second ground no longer exists;
(c) by the sheriff on appeal if satisfied that either or both grounds no longer exist;
(d) by the nearest relative. Fourteen days notice must be given and if the RMO and the MHO agree that the grounds of guardianship still exist they can refuse discharge. The nearest relative can appeal to the sheriff.

### (5) Use of guardianship

The numbers involved in guardianship are small: only about 4% of those who were in the same sort of position in 1960. A variety of reasons have been put forward for its unpopularity, for example, the limited powers conferred on guardians, lack of use leading to lack of familiarity and the vagueness of the welfare ground.[2]

## 7. MENTAL DISABILITY

### (1) Definitions

In its discussion paper on *Mentally Disabled Adults: Legal Arrangements for Managing their Welfare and Finances*[3] the Scottish Law Commission offers the following definitions of legal incapacity and legal disability:

'A person who is mentally incapable or lacks mental capacity is incapable in the legal sense of entering into a transaction or making a decision. This is because the person, due to his or her mental state, cannot understand the nature of the transaction or decision or comprehend its consequences

1 1984 Act, ss 50, 51.
2 See C Moore, A Connor, P Martin and J Tibbit *The Hidden Safety Net?* (1992); H Richards and C McGregor *Guardianship in Scotland* (1992).
3 Scottish Law Commission Discussion Paper No 94 (1991).

or effects. Transactions or decisions by a mentally incapacitated person are legally ineffective. Few people with a mental illness or mental handicap are so incapacitated that they are unable to make even the simplest decision. The majority have the ability to make some decisions and may be said to be disabled. We use the term "mentally disabled" as a convenient way of referring to those individuals who suffer from total or partial mental incapacity.'[1]

Following on from this there are three important points to note. First, as far as the law is concerned, mental disability has to do with the ability to understand the meaning and consequences of decisions, whether these are to do with personal matters, such as medical treatment, or financial matters, such as renting accommodation. Secondly, the degree to which mental disability affects individuals varies markedly. Some are only incapable of dealing with decisions which are relatively complex; others are incapable of making, or communicating, **any** decision, however minor. Finally, the way in which the law is used to intervene in the lives of mentally disabled people must be sensitive to these differences in competence and must allow them the greatest say possible in how they live their lives.

## (2) The relevant law

This section will concentrate on three areas: personal guardianship; management of affairs; and consent to medical treatment. There are, however, a number of other statutory provisions which are relevant in this context. These include the Disabled Persons (Services, Consultation and Representation) Act 1986 with its provision for assessments; the Education (Scotland) Act 1980 with its provisions for special educational need; the Chronically Sick and Disabled Persons Act 1970; the provisions of the Mental Health (Scotland) Act 1984 regarding compulsory admission; the provisions for assessment introduced by the National Health Service and Community Care Act 1990; and the general provisions of the Social Work (Scotland) Act 1968 under which a person suffering mental disorder (which includes mental handicap) is defined as a 'person in need'.

1 Scottish Law Commission Discussion Paper No 94 (1991), para 1.2.

## (3) Personal guardianship

Personal guardianship is concerned with decisions affecting the personal life of an individual. This includes decisions about residence, education, employment, medical treatment and with whom that person may associate.[1] As we have already seen, parents have, subject to some exceptions, certain rights in respect of these types of decisions as they affect children.[2] Therefore the parents of a mentally disabled person are able to exercise these powers in respect of their child, probably to a greater extent than if the child was not handicapped. The problem arises in relation to people who are no longer children; no one has the automatic right to take decisions on behalf of another adult. There are, however, adults affected by mental disability who will require supervision, guidance and, in some cases, control in the areas mentioned above, and in respect of whom a personal guardian may need to be appointed to do this.

At the moment there are two main types of personal guardians: mental health guardians and tutors-dative. One successful application has also been made for appointment as a tutor-at-law. There has been some criticism of the adequacy of the law in this area, and the Scottish Law Commission has proposed substantial reforms.[3]

## (4) Mental health guardians

As is noted above, this type of guardian can be appointed where the patient suffers from a mental disorder justifying reception into guardianship and it is in the patient's interest that this should happen. The whole process is overseen by the social work department, and in most cases it will be the guardian appointed. The powers of guardians are limited to deciding where the patient should live; making the patient attend for medical treatment, work, education or training; and ensuring that doctors and the MHO have access to the patient. Guardians, therefore, do not have a right of custody, that is, the power to ensure that the patient stays in a particular

1 See the discussion in G Ashton and A Ward *Mental Handicap and the Law* (1992), pp 136–141.
2 See ch 3, pt 1(3).
3 Scottish Law Commission *Report on Incapable Adults* Cm 2962 (1995). See also the discussion paper referred to above and A Ward *The Power to Act* (1990), chs 4–6.

place (though they can have the patient brought back if he/she goes away), nor can they consent to beneficial medical treatment on behalf of the patient.

## (5) Tutors-dative

A 'tutor-dative' is someone appointed by the Court of Session to act on behalf of a mentally handicapped person. This procedure was revived in 1986 as a way of providing some supervision to mentally handicapped adults, and small but significant numbers of appointments have been made since then. In strict law, the tutor is appointed for an indefinite period and has the power to act on behalf of the disabled person in all areas of his/her life. In practice, the recent appointments have been of tutors with specific powers, which have been detailed in the application for appointment and tailored to the needs of the disabled person, and have generally been limited to 5 years.[1] In one case it was suggested that the necessity for appointing a tutor-dative had to be established, and that in the absence of any immediate need for the sort of decisions a tutor might take, appointment was regarded as inappropriate.[2] Appointment of a tutor-dative has been made with power to consent to sterilisation of the ward.[3]

## (6) Tutor-at-law

Appointment of a tutor-at-law is based on an Act of 1585 and is restricted to the nearest, male relative of the ward. In the only recent reported case on such an appointment the view seemed to be taken that an application would be granted provided the medical evidence satisfied the court that the appointment was necessary.[4] The main difference between a tutor-dative and a tutor-at-law is that the latter has all the powers that a parent has in respect of a young child, while the former's powers are restricted to those specifically sought in the petition for appointment.

1 Mental Welfare Commission, Annual Report 1994-95, p 31.
2 *Chapman, Petitioners* 1993 SCLR 236.
3 *L, Petitioner* 1996 SCLR 538.
4 *Britton v Britton's Curator Bonis* 1992 SCLR 947.

## (7) Management of affairs

The next six sections are concerned with the management of the property and financial affairs of someone suffering from mental disability. The extent to which intervention in one of the forms noted below is necessary will depend on the amount and nature of the individual's property and on the degree of the disability. It will also depend on whether it is possible to manage these affairs through an essentially informal arrangement, such as a joint bank account or an account held by someone 'in trust for' the disabled person.

At this stage it is also worth noting that contracts entered into by people suffering from mental disorder may be void, with the exception of those involving the supply of necessaries. This is the case if the person was unable to understand the nature of the contract or its effects. Clearly, this will depend on the nature of the contract and the degree of disability of the individual concerned. The person wishing to challenge a contract entered into by someone with mental disability has the burden of proving that the individual with mental disability was incapable of understanding the contract, and until that is done the contract is presumed to be valid.

## (8) Curator bonis

A 'curator bonis' can be appointed to manage the affairs of a person who is incapable of coping with them him/herself. The application for appointment can be made at the sheriff court and must be supported by two medical certificates. Local authorities may come under an obligation to apply for the appointment of a curator bonis in respect of an individual where this appears to be necessary and no application has been made by anyone else.

This method of managing the affairs of persons who are disabled has been criticised. It is expensive and is only really worthwhile if the estate involved is substantial. The curator may have no expertise in the field of mental disability, and there have been complaints in the past that curators have not met their wards or their families, and have not been responsive to their needs or wishes. A more fundamental difficulty is that appointment of a curator transfers all powers of management to the curator. It therefore does not recognise the possibility that the disabled person may be able to take some decisions independently. Some of these problems can be overcome by sensitivity on the part of the curator, but proposals for reform in this area have been put forward by the Scottish Law Commission.

### (9) Management by hospital authorities

Under section 94 of the Mental Health (Scotland) Act 1984 hospital managers have the power to deal with property belonging to patients who are incapable of managing it themselves because of mental disorder. This incapacity is established by a certificate to that effect granted by the doctor in charge of the patient's treatment. These management powers apply automatically to property up to £5,000, but this limit can be increased in individual cases by the Mental Welfare Commission.

### (10) Department of Social Security appointees

Anyone over the age of 18 may be appointed to deal with Social Security benefits on behalf of someone who is unable to manage his/her own affairs. The appointee is able to apply for, receive and deal with benefits on behalf of the disabled person. The procedure for appointment is simply that the application is made to the DSS on the appropriate form.[1] The Scottish Law Commission notes that this procedure is widely used and that '[a]ppointees are generally relatives, home helps, or managers of residential or nursing homes in which the recipient lives'.[2]

### (11) Trusts

Trusts are legal entities which hold and administer property on behalf of someone else, with the administration being carried out by trustees appointed for that purpose. This type of arrangement is favoured by some organisations, such as ENABLE, as the best way of managing property which a disabled person cannot manage him/herself. The terms of the trust can be designed to meet the specific needs of the individual concerned, and the trustees are not

1 Social Security (Claims and Payments) Regulations 1987, SI 1987/1968, reg 33.
2 *Mentally Disabled Adults: Legal Arrangements for Managing their Welfare and Finances* (1991), para 4.15.

subject to the same detailed rules and supervision as curators. Setting up of a trust requires forward planning, as once property actually belongs to a disabled person who is unable to manage his/her affairs it cannot be transferred to a trust. The reason for this is that the only person who can transfer property to a trust is the owner of the property and the disabled person is unlikely to have the legal capacity to do this. If the disable person did have this capacity, the trust would probably be unnecessary.

### (12) *Negotiorum gestio*

This is a legal principle which allows someone to act on your behalf when you are incapable of acting for yourself, and where, were you able to, you would have authorised him/her to act on your behalf. The relevance here is that the inability may be due to mental disability and this principle may, for example, allow a friend or relative to act on behalf of someone who is unable to do so him/herself.

### (13) Power of attorney

This is a written authorisation allowing someone to act and take decisions on your behalf. In order to grant the authorisation you must be legally capable of doing so. A power of attorney could therefore not be granted by someone suffering a disability which deprived that individual of such capacity. On the other hand, once granted, the power of attorney does not terminate if the granter becomes legally incapable of acting. This might therefore be used when someone was aware that at some time in the future a disability would deprive that person of the ability to manage his/her own affairs.

### (14) Consent to medical treatment

In general terms, medical treatment can be given only with the consent of the patient; further, the consent must be based on an understanding of the treatment and its risks. There are, of course, cases where consent is not necessary; the main examples being emergency treatment, and treatment of patients compulsorily detained under the Mental Health (Scotland) Act 1984.

Difficulties can arise in the case of adults with mental disabilities who are unable to give the sort of consent mentioned above. Clearly, the extent to which a disability affects the ability to give consent will depend on the nature and extent of the disability and the type of treatment, but problems can arise. When they do, there is no one who can consent on behalf of the disabled person, unless a tutor-dative with that specific power has been appointed. Ward suggests that in such circumstances a tutor should be appointed to give consent or application made to court for consent in all cases other than emergencies.[1] This view is now supported by the views of the Court of Session that 'where the incapax is in need of treatment to preserve life or for the carrying out of surgical procedures which are in his or her best interests, the preferable course will be to appoint a tutor-dative with the powers necessary to enable these purposes to be carried out'.[2] In one case a tutor was appointed with power to consent to the sterilisation of an autistic young woman. The test for granting this power was expressed to be what is necessary and in the best interests of the ward.[3] The Scottish Law Commission has recommended changes in the law in this area. It suggests that doctors should have the power to treat patients who are incapable of consenting, provided that the treatment is reasonable in the circumstances to safeguard or promote the patient's health. Consultation with patient's relatives, but not court approval, would be necessary in most cases, but there would still be some treatments such as sterilisation and psychosurgery, which would need court approval.[4]

## (15) The Mental Welfare Commission

The Mental Welfare Commission is appointed by the Crown on the recommendation of the Secretary of State. There must be at least three women, three medical practitioners and a solicitor or advocate amongst its members.

The general role of the Mental Welfare Commission is to exercise a protective function in respect of those suffering from mental disorder, and it therefore has an interest in mentally disordered patients whether detained or voluntary patients and whether in hospital or in the community. It is empowered to look into cases of

1 A Ward *The Power to Act,* ch 8.
2 *Law Hospital NHS Trust v Lord Advocate* 1996 SC 301 at 315, per Lord President Hope.
3 *L, Petitioner* 1996 SCLR 538.
4 Scottish Law Commission *Report on Incapable Adults,* Cm 2962 (1995), Part 5.

ill-treatment, deficiency of care, improper detention and loss of, or damage to, patients' property.

The Mental Welfare Commission is also required to discharge patients if it thinks fit; advise the Secretary of State on the discharge of Secretary of State's patients; visit detained patients and those subject to guardianship orders; adjudicate on the withholding of mail; and consent to treatment where this is necessary as noted in part 5(8) above.

## 8. MENTAL ILLNESS AND DISABILITY: OTHER LOCAL AUTHORITY FUNCTIONS AND DUTIES

The provisions which have already been noted in parts 2 and 3 are clearly relevant here. In addition, the social work department has a number of specific responsibilities to those suffering or recovered from mental disorder. These include:

(a) provision of after-care services for persons who are or have been suffering from mental disorder;
(b) to act as parents as regards, for example, visits to any child in respect of whom a parental responsibilities order has been made transferring rights and responsibilities to the local authority, or to anyone for whom they are a guardian under the 1984 Act, who is admitted to hospital;
(c) provision of suitable training and occupation for people over the age of 16 who suffer from mental handicap (learning disabilities).

Increasingly these provisions are becoming more central as the emphasis shifts away from institutional care for persons with mental health problems and persons with learning difficulties. Local authority social workers who are not MHOs are encountering more and more situations in which such persons are finding themselves to be homeless, misplaced in prisons and within the community with few appropriate resources.

## 9. OLD AGE

### (1) Introduction

Persons who are elderly are a large and growing group within society. Currently about 15% of the population is over the age of 65 and the number involved will grow significantly by the beginning of the next century. On 1 April 1993 the legislation came into force which shifted responsibility for the long-term care of elderly persons from the National Health Service to social work departments. This in turn has necessitated massive changes in the internal structures of many social work departments, with community care becoming identified as a focus for more specialised work. Thus the profile of working with persons who are elderly has been considerably raised. There is very little specific legal provision for elderly persons in contrast, for example, with the volume of law relating to children.

Attention is drawn to all of the preceding sections in this chapter which refer to provisions which may be relevant to a person suffering disability because of his/her age. It should also be remembered that the definition of 'person in need' in the 1968 Act refers specifically to those in need of care and attention arising out of . . . age.[1] This provision must be juxtaposed with all the consequential problems of the increasing demand for services and facilities in an economic and social climate in which funding has not kept pace. The remainder of this section looks at some specific provisions which may be associated with old age, although, of course, they may be relevant in the context of other sources of disability.

### (2) Residential accommodation

Local authorities are empowered, and in terms of the 1968 Act, obliged, to provide residential accommodation in fulfilment of their statutory obligations, and this includes providing residential accommodation for persons who are elderly. Local authorities may not, however, provide residential accommodation with nursing. They can **arrange** for such accommodation, but it must be provided by someone other than the local authority.

In spite of advances in inter-disciplinary and multi-disciplinary work in hospitals and increasingly good channels of communication amongst professionals, there are still situations when people who are elderly are discharged from hospital while still in need of considerable nursing care. The law is unclear about whose responsibility it is to arrange suitable accommodation and there is a reliance on local agreements about the timing of discharges and the completion of assessments.

1 1968 Act, s 94(1).

Residential accommodation is increasingly provided by the private sector which has seen a major growth in the last 15 to 20 years. Private sector establishments may be purely residential, they may be nursing homes, or they may provide both personal care and nursing care. Residential homes must be registered with the local authority, which has powers of inspection and supervision. Nursing homes must be registered with the health board, which has powers of inspection and supervision. They differ from residential homes in that they provide nursing care. Finally, homes providing both types of care must register both with the local authority and with the health board.

All residential establishments are subject to local authority inspection. This process is likely to be extended from the present arms-length inspection of residential homes for persons who are elderly to the inspection of residential homes for children. Additionally, in April 1992, the Social Work Services Inspectorate was established within the Scottish Office with a remit which includes the right to inspect residential homes run by the local authority, and voluntary and private agencies. The inspectors may hear residents' complaints but they are not obliged to do so.

## (3) Compulsory treatment

Section 47 of the National Assistance Act 1948[1] provides that treatment or other necessary care and attention can be given compulsorily to certain categories of people. The conditions which must be fulfilled before compulsory treatment can be contemplated are that the person concerned is unable to take proper care of him/herself and is not being properly cared for by anyone else **and** that **either** the person is suffering from a grave chronic disease, **or** he/she is aged, infirm or physically incapacitated and living in insanitary conditions.

If these preconditions relating to inability to care for him/herself and disease/incapacity are fulfilled, proceedings can be started for the removal of the person concerned to hospital or some other suitable place (for example, a residential or nursing home). The procedure is as follows:

(a) A certificate is obtained from the designated medical officer (DMO, designated by the health board) to the effect that the

1 For the background to s 47 see A Norman *Rights and Risk* (1980), pp 29–37.

DMO is satisfied that the person should be removed from the place where he/she is staying for one of the following reasons:
(i) it is in the person's interest;
(ii) it is necessary to prevent injury to the health of others;
(iii) it is necessary for the prevention of a serious nuisance to other people.

(b) After the certificate is obtained the DMO or the local authority applies to the sheriff court for an order removing the person to a hospital or other suitable place. Normally, 7 days' notice of the intention to make an application must be given to the person concerned. However, the requirement for notice can be dispensed with in emergencies if the DMO and another doctor certify that it is necessary in the person's interests that he/she be removed without delay. The DMO and any other doctor involved must attend court to give evidence in support of their certificates.
(c) The court may then grant the order sought. Before doing so the sheriff must be satisfied both as to the allegations contained in the certificate(s) and as to the desirability of making the order.
(d) Once granted, the order remains in force for the period specified in it, which can be up to 3 months, and can be extended for further periods of up to 3 months. An emergency order lasts initially for 3 weeks and can also be renewed.
(e) An application can be made to revoke an order, other than an emergency order, 6 weeks after the granting of the order.

This rather draconian procedure is not often encountered in practice, although it is used from time to time.

### (4) Protection of property

Local authorities have a statutory duty[1] to take steps to protect the property of those who are admitted to hospital as patients; admitted to residential accommodation (whether provided by the authority or not); or subjected to compulsory treatment as described above. Where there is a danger of loss of or damage to the moveable property of such people and no other suitable arrangements have been made, the local authority must take reasonable steps to prevent or mitigate any loss or damage. In fulfill-

1 National Assistance Act 1948, s 48(2).

ing this duty the authority is empowered to enter the person's usual residence and it can also recover any reasonable expenses.

## (5) Guardianship

Guardianship has been considered more fully earlier (see part 6 above). The particular relevance of this to persons who are elderly is that dementia is a mental disorder which, if severe enough, could warrant the appointment of a guardian. The guardian has the power to decide where the patient should live and it has been pointed out that '... there has been a growing use of the procedure by social work departments to protect people suffering from dementia by ensuring their admission into residential care, which they are unwilling or unable to accept voluntarily'.[1] In most cases the guardian appointed is the social work department.

1 Blackie and Patrick *Mental Health: A Guide to the Law in Scotland* (1990), p 32.

# 7. Offenders

## 1. LAW AND CRIME

As we noted in chapter 1, one of the principal functions of law is the maintenance of order in society. In turn, one of the main ways in which this is done is through the criminal law and the police, prosecution, court and other associated organisations. This chapter will look in more detail at the sentences available to courts and the roles that social workers play in the criminal justice system concluding with a brief description of some of the more common crimes and offences. Before doing this, however, we want to provide a context for the rest of the chapter.

Traditionally, a link was made between crime and moral repugnance. Hume, for example, defined crime as 'a doleful or wilful offence against society in the matter of violence, dishonesty, falsehood, irreligion'. With the passing of time and the growth in the number of offences this link has become weaker. It is difficult to imagine that a substantial level of moral outrage is generated by the behaviour of someone who is drunk and incapable or of someone convicted of a minor breach of the peace. This is even clearer in the case of a large number of statutory offences. It is common, for example, for motoring offenders not to regard themselves as 'real' criminals.

In addition, it should be noted that the majority of criminal offences in Scotland are the product of the common law: that is, their scope is determined by judicial decision rather than being defined in statute. This has important consequences. First, aside from the limits set on the sentencing powers of particular courts, there is no limit on the sentence that can be imposed for common law crimes and offences. This is in contrast to statutory offences where, usually, the statute creating the offence will set a maximum penalty. Secondly, following from this, all common law crimes are potentially punishable by imprisonment. Thirdly, these crimes are subject to redefinition and refinement by the courts, with possible extension to cover novel circumstances. Examples of this include the extension of breach of the peace to cover a man dressed as a woman walking about in a red-light district and the view of the High Court that selling what were effectively glue-sniffing kits amounted to 'a modern example of conduct which our law has for long regarded as criminal ... [that is,] actions of any kind which cause or are a cause of real injury to the person.[1]

Furthermore, a distinction is sometimes drawn between crimes and offences (for example, in the presentation of criminal statistics) with the implication that crimes are more serious than offences. It is not clear that there is a sound legal basis for this.

Moreover, some indication should be given of the balance of crime. In terms of reports of crime, the largest proportion are offences involving dishonesty, particularly theft and motoring offences, which both account for about 30% of reports. Other significant contributors are miscellaneous offences, for example, drunkenness, minor assault or breach of the peace (accounting for about 15%) and wilful fire-raising and vandalism (10%). Violent crimes are less than 3% of the total. Looking at convictions, the largest contributor is motoring offences (around 40%), followed by miscellaneous offences (about 30%) and dishonesty (about 20%). Crimes of violence account for about 9% of cases.

Finally, issues relating to gender, class, age and race and the law are especially significant for social workers. Indeed, as some small indication of the increasing recognition of the relevance of such factors, the Criminal Justice (Scotland) Act 1995 imposes a duty on those involved in the administration of criminal justice to avoid discrimination on the grounds of race or sex or any other improper ground.[2] Clearly, the patterns of women's careers in the criminal justice system are very different from men's, with some research demonstrating that tariffs are normally higher and that custodial penalties are imposed sooner. Other research paints a much more complex picture reflecting 'combinations of leniency and harshness' dependent upon the person's age and the nature of offence.[3] Mary Eaton[4] asks: 'Is it inevitable that the assumptions, language

1 *Khaliq v HMA* 1984 SLT 137 at 142–143.
2 Criminal Justice (Scotland) Act 1995, s 306(1)(b).
3 See S Asquith (ed) *Children and Young People in Conflict with the Law* (1996) ch 6 by E Samuel and K Tisdall; and for a detailed account and analysis of recent research see 'Young Offenders and Gender: The Scottish Evidence' in S Asquith and E Samuel's *Criminal Justice and Related Services for Young Adult Offenders* (1994).
4 In Pat Carlen and Anne Worrall (eds) *Gender, Crime and Justice* (1987), p 100.

and practices of the courts and prisons reflect and reinforce the prevailing picture of women's "proper" and relatively powerless place in the social order?' Questions are being raised about the psychology of women[1] which may lead to a more lenient legal view of what constitutes provocation and the timescales which apply, particularly with reference to violence within the family and women killing their partners.

To date, there has been even less research published about the variables associated with the experience of working class people, of young people or of black people in the Scottish criminal justice system. One contribution to an understanding of influences associated with class arises from the discipline of criminology in the form of 'strain theory' which places great weight on the importance of economic factors.[2] Other contributions from research suggest that the peak age for criminal activity for both men and women is 18.[3] The evidence of research in England suggests that black people are more likely to be imprisoned than white people and that police and victims may discriminate on the basis of perceived race.[4] The presence of institutional racism as being 'built into the structure of society' is widely acknowledged[5] and as such will inevitably have implications for people's experience.

## 2. SOCIAL WORK FUNCTIONS

In Scotland, work specified by statute with offenders and ex-offenders is principally the responsibility of local authority social workers. Also unlike the current arrangements in England and Wales, these functions are mainly carried out by professionally qualified social workers. Most of the social work functions in the criminal justice process are covered by the *National Objectives and Standards for Social Work Services in the Criminal Justice System*

1 See M W Matlin in *The Psychology of Women* (3rd edn, 1996).
2 D Smith *Criminology for Social Work* (1995), p 46.
3 S Asquith and E Samuel *Criminal Justice and Related Services for Young Adult Offenders* (1994), p 109.
4 R Hood *Race and Sentencing* (1992); R Skellington *'Race' in Britain Today* (2nd edn, 1996), ch 8. Also see R Harris *Crime, Criminal Justice and the Probation Service* (1992), chs 5 and 6.
5 See, for example, A Bowes and D Sim in *Demands and Constraints – Ethnic Minorities and Social Services in Scotland* (1991).

(commonly referred to as *National Standards*) originally issued in 1991 and up-dated in May 1996 by the Scottish Office. These cover the provision of social enquiry reports and court based services, probation, throughcare, and community service. *National Standards* was associated with a change in the funding arrangements for financing social work services. Services in the areas covered are now 100% funded by central government. The up-dated version includes added services like supervised attendance orders and these arrangements have facilitated the promotion, in some settings, of an organisational culture in which initiatives and projects designed to meet the needs of offenders and ex-offenders have been enabled to flourish. The 11 objectives cited for social work practice begin with the working toward 'a reduction in the incidence of custody ... where it is used for lack of a suitable, available community-based social work disposal' and include the further development of such community-based social work disposals; the increase in the number of bail release schemes; the provision of services to offenders and their families both in prison and in the community; work with offenders to change their behaviour; the further development of schemes to divert appropriate alleged offenders from criminal prosecution and to social work services; work with victims of crime; and work to reduce and prevent crime. *National Standards* was also associated with a change in the organisation of social work provision. These services are now primarily to be provided by specialist staff, some of whom will work full-time in this area. In practice, working with offenders and ex-offenders has proved a relatively attractive prospect to social workers who welcome the opportunity to work in a fairly prescribed and planned manner. The use of social workers' legally defined powers is an especially prominent feature of the work.[1]

The social worker performing any of the functions noted above is accountable not only to the court but also to his/her own employer. The differing value bases, policies and procedures often produce tensions which can sometimes escalate into conflicting demands being made upon the social worker.[2] Involvement with the criminal justice system is likely to be stressful for everyone, but especially so for the accused, offender or ex-offender who may be at risk of losing liberty, money or other valued things. The structures and procedures of the criminal justice system are complex

1 See M Payne *What is Professional Social Work?* (1996), ch 6 for a detailed presentation about power, authority and social work.

2 For a fuller discussion of this see S Braye and M Preston-Shoot *Practising Social Work Law* (1992), pp 32–35.

and can be particularly difficult to navigate for a person who is possibly in a state of crisis. In this situation, the social worker may contribute toward the alleviation of excessive anxiety and unclarity on the part of the accused, offender, or ex-offender by taking on both a supportive and an educative role. As in many settings which are not primarily defined by social work values and knowledge, the social worker's most notable offering may be to help to broaden the perspective of all the players to include social factors.

## (1) Court-based social workers

There are social work staff permanently based in larger, busier courts, while in other courts the provision may be part-time. The main functions of these court-based social workers are dealing with requests for social enquiry reports and ensuring that they are timeously provided; monitoring the standard of reports; conducting stand-down interviews (in which the social worker interviews the offender during a brief court recess); and providing oral reports to the court; interviewing offenders immediately following a request for a report; interviewing offenders after custodial remand or sentence; interviewing offenders following sentences involving a social work contribution; and liaison with the others involved in the operation of the court.

Court-based social workers not only perform a range of services for the court but may also be able to provide assistance to the families of those on trial or who have been sentenced, particularly those who have been sentenced to custody, and to victims of crime and to witnesses. This duality of purpose once more provides the potential for social workers to experience conflicts in relation to the various demands being made and their professional orientation. The social worker may be in a position to support and provide clarification about what is happening for the families of those appearing in court. In court when the disposal is pronounced, the offender may well be anxious and suffering from situational deafness, and unable to hear and process what is heard. In many courts there is the added practical difficulty of physically hearing the disposal when there is no sound amplification or the crucial information is not clearly announced. Moreover, some of the non-custodial disposals are not very widely used or known and so it may be necessary and appropriate for social workers to assume an educative and interpretative role with the offender in clarifying what the meaning and implications of various disposals are likely to be. In addition, the court-based social worker may be providing an intake and referral service for those at the court who are in need.

### (2) Social enquiry reports

Most reports are prepared following a plea of guilty or a finding of guilt while the court adjourns the case (under section 201 of the Criminal Procedure (Scotland) Act 1995) and prior to the decision regarding sentence or disposal of the case. Section 27(1)(a) of the Social Work (Scotland) Act 1968 (the 1968 Act) imposes a duty on local authority social work departments to 'provide reports relating to persons appearing before the court which the court may require for the disposal of the case'.[1] Although the 1968 Act refers to social background reports, in the context of the criminal court system these reports are known as social enquiry reports (SER). A detailed discussion of the contents of such reports and the methodology for preparing them is beyond the scope of this text and detailed guidelines and standards can be found in *National Standards*. Particularly in reports written about active or known social work department service users, it is hoped that there will be a strong element of a shared understanding of the problem areas with a commitment to the empowerment of the service user.

Social enquiry reports **must** be obtained by courts before making a probation order;[2] in the case of children under 16 appearing before the court instead of being referred to the Reporter to the children's hearing; and in respect of someone under 18 who is subject to a supervision requirement from a children's hearing.[3] In addition, a court must obtain 'such information as it can about an offender's circumstances, character and physical and mental condition' before imposing the first sentence of imprisonment on an offender of 21 or over and before sentencing someone between 16 and 20 to detention. The normal mechanism for obtaining this information is the social enquiry report. Prior to the court making

1 The Crime and Punishment (Scotland) Act 1997 will add a duty to provide reports on people charged with an offence if requested by the Lord Advocate or procurator fiscal.

2 Strictly speaking, not all types of probation order require a report from the local authority, but all require a report on the 'circumstances and character of the offender' (Criminal Procedure (Scotland) Act 1995, s 228(1)(b)), and this will be provided by obtaining an SER. See also pt (5) below and SWSI *Helping the Court Decide* (1996), para 2.3.

3 Criminal Procedure (Scotland) Act 1995, s 42(8).

a community service order, a report by an officer of the local authority must be submitted which details information about the offender's circumstances as well as suitability for community service.[1] A report must be obtained before making a supervised release order. Finally, before sentencing someone who is already being supervised by the social work department and is convicted of a further offence, the court, other than the district court, must obtain a report on the character of the individual, including behaviour while under supervision.[2] Social workers have an opportunity to provide a concise but comprehensive systemic assessment which emphasises the social functioning equation for the court. It is crucial for the court to have access to information about the offender's normal coping capacities as well as the unusual environmental demands being made on the offender.

Normally, the period available for preparation of the report is 3 weeks when the offender has been remanded in custody; otherwise it is 4 weeks or 8 weeks on cause shown. These periods are reduced by the time taken to process the request and the need to complete the report in time to have it submitted to the clerk of court by midday on the day preceding the court hearing which will consider it. If the report has not been completed or further inquiries must be made, then, when the case is called, an explanation must be made to the court and the case can be continued for a further period equal to the original one. Where the offender is remanded on bail, it is a condition of the bail that the offender makes him/herself available for the purpose of preparation of any reports. Failure to co-operate should be reported to the court and is an offence.[3] What is not so clear is what happens when the offender is available to meet the social worker, but refuses to co-operate. Moore and Wood suggest that failure to cooperate may amount to contempt of court and while this may be a possibility, there is no legal authority on the issue.[4]

The report is the property of the court and a copy of it is made available to the offender or his/her solicitor by the clerk of court. It will also be seen by the prosecutor and the judge, and some com-

1 This requirement is contained in section 238(2)(c) of the Criminal Procedure (Scotland) Act 1995. It is referred to by G Moore and C Wood as a 'suitability assessment' in their book *Social Work and Criminal Law in Scotland* (2nd edn, 1992).

2 Criminal Procedure (Scotland) Act 1995, s 203.

3 See also ch 1, pt 8(6)(e).

4 G Moore and C Wood *Social Work and Criminal Law in Scotland* (2nd edn, 1992), pp 66–67.

ment may be made on its contents in open court. Because of this, problems about confidentiality may arise. Sensitive information may need to be noted as such in the report with a request that it is not disclosed, or it may be omitted from the report and brought to the attention of the judge in chambers in the presence of the offender and the defence agent.

The court may request that the writer is present at the hearing where the report will be presented in the court. Additionally, *National Standards* suggests that attendance is advisable where an unusual or complex recommendation is being made; where the writer's presence may tip the balance in favour of a non-custodial disposal; and where a report is being considered in connection with breach of a statutory order. In such cases the presence of the report writer may have a direct influence on the sentence passed. Where the writer is not present, a court-based social worker may be able to assist the court on behalf of the writer.

Finally, it is worth noting that one of the objectives of social enquiry reports is variously stated to be '[t]o provide information and advice which may make it possible to increase the use of community-based disposals where custody is likely', and 'assisting the court's consideration of community-based options'. Part of the social worker's considerations are about the potential risk of the offender to him/herself and others in prison or in the community. In Scotland, where there is an acceptance that a sizeable proportion of persons currently in prison are no such risk to themselves or others, it is a rare and priceless opportunity for social workers to provide information to influence the sentencers to ends which are more compatible with social work values.

A considerably smaller number of reports are ordered prior to the alleged offender going to trial. Examples of when a pre-trial report might be requested include when the person is under the age of 21 or is an adult who has not previously been in custody and has been committed to the High Court for trial. Here, the alleged offender is not required to co-operate in the preparation of the report. A recommendation to abandon pre-trial reports, except in cases where there was a plea of guilty in advance, was made by the Social Work Services Inspectorate in 1996.[1]

There has been considerable discussion about the appropriateness and/or advisability of social workers making recommendations highlighting preferred disposals in their reports. *National Standards* assumes that this is both appropriate and advisable, while Moore

1 *Helping the Court Decide*, para 9.10. At the time of writing this recommendation has not been implemented.

and Wood quote various statements from the bench and a government White Paper which forcefully express the view that recommendations are unwelcome and outwith the social work remit. *National Standards* includes amongst the objectives for social enquiry reports requirements to 'make recommendations which are consistent with the principle of minimum intervention'[1] and especially to comment upon recommendations which involve social work resources. In this circumstance, the prevailing local views should inform social work practice while not losing sight of opportunities other than recommendations as to disposal to present a social work perspective.

### (3) Supervision

Social work departments are expected to provide supervision in a variety of situations. The main examples are probation, community service, fine supervision orders, supervised attendance orders and supervision after release from custody. These are all considered more fully below. Social workers may also be involved in diversion schemes, where alleged offenders are diverted into some form of social work intervention rather than being prosecuted, and this is also considered below.

### (4) Appearing in court

Social workers are occasionally called as witnesses in civil or criminal proceedings where they may be seen as experts on social concerns. They may also be the applicant in situations where there has been a breach of an order. In each of these situations, social workers may be cross-examined and must take an oath or affirm. It is important that the social worker prepare thoroughly, bringing notes and copies of the relevant material to court. This last can be important, since witnesses are allowed to refer to contemporaneous notes, that is, notes made at the time of or shortly after the events to which they refer, while they are giving evidence.

Suggestions for social workers from Colin Fishwick in *Court Work*[2] include accommodating to the formal codes and norms of

1 *National Standards*, para 9.
2 C Fishwick *Court Work* (2nd edn, 1989).

the court situation; being prepared to have one's practice exposed; preparing 'authoritative statements rather than interpretative remarks'; direct and clear communication; and appropriate style of dress. As this list suggests, court proceedings generally take place in a very formal atmosphere subject to detailed rules as to procedure[1] and as to how evidence may be given, and indeed what counts as evidence.[2] This formality is reflected in the forms of address: magistrates are referred to as 'your honour', sheriffs and High Court judges as 'your lordship' or 'your ladyship'.

### (5) Court reports concerning children

When a child is charged with an offence which requires a court appearance,[3] there is a requirement for the local authority to be notified. The social work department must then provide the court with a pre-conviction report detailing the home background and social circumstances of the child to facilitate disposal of the case.[4] Useful research findings suggest that significant predictors of children's offending behaviour are more focused on the 'closeness of parental supervision and levels of parental expectation of behaviour regarding offending' than on 'social hardship'.[5]

## 3. SENTENCING: OBJECTIVES AND CRITERIA

The objectives of sentencing and punishment have produced a substantial literature. The main objectives canvassed in the past have included individual and general deterrence; rehabilitation or reform; retribution; denunciation; and containment or protection of the public. The extent to which the sentences available to the courts can meet any of these objectives is increasingly open to doubt. For example, it is debatable whether the element of calculation required for deterrence to operate is present in most crimes; the possibility of reforming someone and preparing him/her for a

1 See ch 1, pt 8(6).
2 See ch 1, pt 9.
3 See ch 5, pt 3(i).
4 Criminal Procedure (Scotland) Act 1995, s 42(7) and (8).
5 S Asquith (ed) *Children and Young People in Conflict with the Law* (1996), ch 3; 'Children's Hearings and Children in Trouble', p 63, by J McGhee, L Waterhouse and B Whyte.

life integrated in society by isolating them in prison is equally debatable. The only objectives that the system can be said to attain are retribution and denunciation with, in some cases, compensation for the victim of crime, and in other cases, the possibility of some reformation. This, indeed, was recognised in the White Paper *Crime, Justice and Protecting the Public*,[1] which also contained the novel suggestion that the objective of sentencing was ensuring that criminals received their just desserts.

On a more practical level there are factors which clearly have an influence on the sentence imposed in particular cases. These include the severity of the offence; the offender's previous record; the offender's attitude towards the offence; the offender's culpability; the existence of any provocation; and background information about the offender. In contrast to the position in England, however, there is no discount on sentence for a plea of guilty. On the other hand, if the accused pleads guilty the court can take into account when and in what circumstances it was indicated that a guilty plea would be made in fixing the sentence.[2] On the basis of these factors experienced practitioners, on both sides of the law, can often predict the likely outcome of a particular case. The High Court also has the power when hearing appeals against sentence to give its opinion on appropriate sentences in similar cases.[3]

Although these factors exist, and have to some extent been given judicial recognition, there is some evidence of disparities in sentencing between different courts and between different judges.[4]

In practice the vast majority of sentences are non-custodial. In 1995, for example, just over 10% of those sentenced were sentenced to custody. It should be noted, however, that the use of custody is increasing; in 1979 this figure was just over 4%.

## 4. NON-CUSTODIAL DISPOSALS

### (1) Absolute discharge

An absolute discharge is appropriate where in view of the circumstances, including the nature of the offence and the character of the

1 Cm 965 (1990).
2 Criminal Procedure (Scotland) Act 1995, s 196.
3 Ibid, ss 118(7), 190(7).
4 See N Hutton and C Tata *Patterns of Custodial Sentencing in the Sheriff Court* (1995).

offender, the court decides that it is inexpedient to inflict punishment and that a probation order is not appropriate. It is used very rarely and in 1995 was used in only 0.4% of cases. This disposal will count as a previous conviction if a further offence is committed subsequently.

### (2) Admonition

An offender may be admonished where it appears to meet the justice of the case. The court may simply announce that the offender is admonished and leave it at that, or the court may add some well chosen words of warning. This disposal counts as a conviction.[1]

### (3) Caution[2]

An offender may be required to 'find caution' for good behaviour. This involves lodging a sum of money in court. The period of good behaviour may be up to 6 months in the district court, 12 months in the sheriff summary court and for statutory offences tried on indictment; otherwise there is no maximum. The maximum amount of caution which can be required by a solemn court is unlimited; otherwise it is £5,000 in the sheriff court and £2,500 in the district court. If the offender is of good behaviour during this period, then the caution is returned with interest. If the offender is not of good behaviour during the period, in particular, if he/she commits a further offence, then the caution is forfeited.

### (4) Fines

This disposal takes the form of a financial penalty paid by the offender. Fines are by far the commonest form of disposal, though their use is declining.[3] It is, therefore, vital for social workers to

1 See accounts of the case of P Brady, admonished on 14 October 1996 for the culpable homicide of his brother who was suffering from an incurable illness: The Scotsman, 15 October 1996.
2 Pronounced 'kayshun'.
3 In 1984 they accounted for nearly 80% of disposals; by 1995 the figure was 70%.

appreciate how they are levied and collected. Social workers also play a central role in the preparation of means enquiry reports for the court.[1] Non-payment of a fine places the offender at risk of imprisonment or a supervised attendance order.[2]

### *(a) Levels of fine*

In fixing the level of fine for a particular offender the court must, amongst other considerations, take the means of the offender into account; there is clearly little point in levying a fine which the offender has no practical prospect of paying. If a fine is excessive in relation to the means of the offender this will be a ground for appealing against the fine imposed.[3] Here, the social worker who is asked to prepare a social enquiry report is ideally placed to help to minimise the prospect of an unpayable fine being levied by providing the sentencer with comprehensive and accurate information about the financial incomings and outgoings of the offender.

In the case of both common law and statutory offences tried on indictment, there is no maximum limit on the fine which can be imposed. In summary courts there are limits. For common law offences these are currently £5,000 in the sheriff court and for stipendiary magistrates, and £2,500 for lay magistrates in the district court. In the case of statutory offences the statute creating the offence will normally fix the maximum fine, and this will be done by reference to one of five levels, rather than by reference to an amount of money. The reason for this is simple; it is much easier to change the values attached to the levels than to amend the amounts stated in a large, and growing, number of Acts of Parliament. Currently the levels are as follows:

| | |
|---|---|
| Level 1 | £ 200 |
| Level 2 | £ 500 |
| Level 3 | £1,000 |
| Level 4 | £2,500 |
| Level 5 | £5,000 |

1 See pt 4(4)(e) below.

2 Research indicates a rise of 36% since 1990 in the number of people imprisoned for fine default in England and Wales, most of whom were originally convicted of an offence which did not, in itself, carry imprisonment as a possible penalty. See H Fletcher *'Fines, default and debtors' goal'* NAPO News, 61: 10–11 (1994) quoted in T May and A Vass (eds) *Working with Offenders* (1996).

3 *Hamilton v Scott* 1987 SCCR 188.

It should be noted that the maximum fine that can be levied by lay magistrates in the district court is stated to be level 4 and the money value will therefore change automatically when the levels change.

*(b) Time for payment*

The offender must be allowed at least 7 days to pay the fine, or if it is to be paid in instalments, the first instalment of the fine. The only exceptions to this, when the fine is payable immediately, are where the offender has no fixed abode; where the offender appears to have sufficient means to pay the fine forthwith; where the offender indicates that time to pay is not wanted; and where the court is satisfied that other special reasons exist for not allowing time to pay. If the court decides that no time will be allowed to pay the fine, then it must state the reasons for this decision. A summary court may order the offender to be searched and any money found to be applied to payment of the fine unless the court is satisfied that the money belongs to someone else or that the loss of the money would be more injurious.

The offender may, either when the fine is imposed or subsequently, apply for more time to pay or to be allowed to pay by instalments. Further time to pay must be allowed following an application unless it appears that the offender's failure to pay is wilful or that there is no reasonable prospect of paying the fine. Social workers may find that the role of advocate on behalf of service users in negotiating for a feasible instalment schedule would be appropriate, since offenders often experience difficulty in overcoming their inhibitions in the courtroom or with the clerk of the relevant court to make such arrangements.

*(c) Alternative of imprisonment*[1]

An alternative sentence of imprisonment may be imposed at the same time as the fine and will become operational without the need for a means enquiry court (see (e) below) in the event of default in payment. Such an alternative is not to be imposed unless the court considers it expedient having regard to the gravity of the offence, the character of the offender or other special circumstances. The offender must be present in this instance.

1 Criminal Procedure (Scotland) Act 1995, ss 214(4), 219(1)(b).

### *(d) Fine supervision*

In cases where an offender is given time to pay or payment is to be by instalments, the offender may be made subject to a fine supervision order and be placed under the supervision of a social worker or other social work department employee. The offender does not need to consent to such an order being made and the order remains in force until the fine is paid in full, the offender is imprisoned for fine default, another order is made concerning the fine, or the order is transferred to another court area. An offender under 21 cannot be detained in the event of non-payment unless placed on supervision or it was not reasonably practicable to do this. In the event of non-payment the supervising social worker should provide a report to the court hearing called to enquire as to the reasons for non-payment (the means enquiry court: see below). There have been arguments advanced over the years that supervising the payment of fines places social workers in an unacceptable position as debt collectors for the courts, but compulsory contact between the offender and the social worker does offer the potential opportunity for more substantive and negotiated work to be undertaken together.

### *(e) Enforcement: imprisonment on default*

Generally speaking, fines are enforced by the courts which imposed them. The exceptions to this are High Court fines, which are enforced by the appropriate sheriff court, and cases where the offender has moved. In the latter case the fine will normally be transferred to the appropriate court covering the offender's new place of residence.

If the offender fails to pay the fine he/she may, subject to the proviso below, be imprisoned or detained instead. Where time to pay has been allowed and no alternative imposed at the time of the fine, imprisonment can take place only after enquiry by the court as to the reasons for non-payment. The hearing at which this enquiry is made is usually referred to as a 'means enquiry court'. At this hearing the offender may be imprisoned or given further time to pay. There is statutory provision for the period of imprisonment in the event of non-payment. At the moment this ranges from 7 days for a fine of up to £200 to 10 years for a fine in excess of £1 million. The relevant amount for the purpose of calculating the period of imprisonment is the amount of the fine which remains outstanding. The same provisions apply, subject to the proviso noted above, for the imposition of an alternative of detention on a young offender.

Where no time to pay is allowed and immediate payment is not made, the offender may, subject to the exception noted below, be committed to prison or to a young offenders institution forthwith. The exception arises in the case of an offender who has not previously served a term of imprisonment or detention and who is not legally represented. Such an offender cannot be immediately imprisoned unless legal aid has been refused on financial grounds or, knowing of the possibility of applying for legal aid, the offender has chosen not to apply for it.

In these instances, a person can be imprisoned for an offence which did not originally carry imprisonment as a possible penalty and for an offence for which prison had not been envisioned as a possible penalty. In 1994 about 40% of sentenced prisoners received into prison were fine defaulters (around 25% of all receptions).

If the fine is paid while the offender is in prison or young offenders institution for fine default, then release can be secured.

The proviso referred to above is that where the amount of the fine which is outstanding is less than level 2, the court must, instead of imprisoning someone over 18, make a supervised attendance order.[1] This requirement applies only to courts prescribed by the Secretary of State.

### *(f) Supervised attendance orders*[2]

In an attempt to reduce the number of fine defaulters sent to prison or young offenders institution and as an alternative to imprisonment, the district or sheriff courts can (and in the circumstances explained above, must) impose a 'supervised attendance order'. These orders require the offender to attend at a specified place for between 10 and 100 hours and during that time to comply with the instructions of the supervising officer who is appointed or assigned by the local authority. The maximum number of hours depends on the amount of the fine which is outstanding. For fines not exceeding level 1 it is 50 hours; for fines above this it is 100 hours. Supervised attendance orders can be used only in respect of offenders over 18 in cases where the offender would otherwise have been imprisoned. The offender does not have to consent to such an

1 Criminal Procedure (Scotland) Act 1995, s 235(1) and (4).
2 Ibid, ss 235–237 and Sch 7.

order being made which may have serious repercussions for its implementation. The order can be made either at the time of the fine as an alternative in the same way as imprisonment, or at a later stage on default by the offender. Once a supervised attendance order is made, the fine it replaces is discharged.

Before the order is made the court must explain, in ordinary language:

(a) the purpose and effect of the order;
(b) the obligations of the offender, in particular to report to the supervising officer and advise the supervisor of any change of address or working hours, and to comply with the instructions of the supervising officer which, so far as practicable, should not conflict with the offender's religious beliefs, normal working hours, or attendance at school or other educational institution;
(c) the consequences of failure to comply: these are possible revocation of the order and imposition of imprisonment or a variation of the number of hours specified in the order, subject to the statutory maxima;
(d) the court's power to review the order on the application of the offender or a local authority officer.

The supervised attendance order remains in force, unless revoked, until the specified number of hours are completed, though these should normally be completed during a 12-month period.

Supervised attendance orders can also, in principle, be used by summary courts in respect of 16 and 17 year olds. Here it can be used as an alternative to a fine, rather than as an alternative to custody. If the court considers that the appropriate sentence is a fine it must decide how much the fine should be and then consider whether the offender is likely to pay any fine within 28 days. If it concludes that the offender is likely to pay, the fine is imposed and an order may be imposed in case of default. If the view is taken that the offender is not likely to pay within 28 days, then the order is made in place of the fine. At present there is, however, only one area which has a scheme for 16 and 17 year olds and where such an order can be made.

Failure by the offender to comply with the obligations imposed by the order will lead to breach of the order. Proceedings for breach will normally be initiated by the supervising officer. The court can cite the offender to appear in court or can issue an arrest warrant. If the court is satisfied that the offender has failed to comply with the order without reasonable cause, it may revoke the order and impose the alternative of imprisonment dictated by the outstanding amount of fine or it may vary the number of hours, provided the total does not exceed 100. The maximum custodial sentences which can be imposed are 60 days in the district court and 3 months in the sheriff court. Only one witness is necessary to provide evidence for breach proceedings.

The offender or supervisor may apply to court for the order to be extended beyond the normal 12 months; for the number of hours to be varied; for revocation; and for revocation and the imposition of imprisonment. The court should grant such an application if it appears to it that 'it would be in the interests of justice to do so having regard to circumstances which have arisen since the order was made'.[1]

There is also provision for transfer of orders where the offender moves and arrangements exist in the new area for supervised attendance. Because of the limited coverage of supervised attendance orders at the moment, problems may arise in respect of transfer of the order. If the offender moves such transfer is possible only if a scheme is available in the new area.

## (5) Probation

### *(a) Introduction*

Probation is a disposal that requires the offender to be under the supervision of a professionally qualified social worker who is appointed as supervisor for a period between 6 months and 3 years. The offender must comply with the instructions of the supervisor and with any conditions attached to the supervision order. A court may deal with an offender by way of probation if 'it is of the opinion ... having regard to the circumstances, including the nature of the offence and the character of the offender'[2] that it is expedient to do so. *National Standards* suggests that priority should be given in recommending probation to two groups: (i) offenders whose current offending places them at risk of custody, who have significant underlying problems and who seem likely to re-offend; and (ii) repeat offenders with significant underlying problems who are at risk of custody, even if the current offence is trivial. It also suggests

1 Criminal Procedure (Scotland) Act 1995, Sch 7, para 5(1).
2 Ibid, s 228(1).

some priority for offenders who may be likely to receive a custodial disposal if their offending behaviour continues unchecked.

Before a probation order is made the court must obtain a report on the 'circumstances and character' of the offender, which will usually be in the form of a social enquiry report.[1] In addition, if a requirement as to performance of unpaid work is to be made (see below) the court must consider a report from the local authority about the offender and his/her circumstances and suitability for such an order.[2] If the writer of the report is recommending probation, the report should also detail the action plan to be followed during the probation period and any special conditions which should be attached to the order. The offender must consent to the making of a probation order, and part of the social work function in preparing the report involves explaining the consequences of a probation order to the offender and obtaining the offender's consent to the order. The court must also explain the meaning and effect of the order and the consequences of breach of conditions of the order or commission of a further offence. Copies of the order must be supplied to the offender and to the supervising social worker.

### *(b) Social work contribution*

Once the order has been made, the supervising social worker should see the probationer within a week, giving him/her a copy of the order and having the signing of that order by the probationer witnessed. The signing is taken to be the evidence that the probationer understands the meaning and conditions of the order. In the event of subsequent breach proceedings, failure to complete this procedure might provide the probationer with grounds to contest the proceedings. Research findings[3] provide clear evidence that the central tenets of social work feature prominently in effective work with offenders. The core conditions of genuineness, non-possessive warmth and accurate empathy provide the basis for trusting relationships within which the probation order can be used to confront the offender with the consequences of his/her offending behaviour. Various restrictions on the probationer's activities can be made; as

1 Note that Moore and Wood's view of the law as stated on p 60 of the second edition of *Social Work and Criminal Law in Scotland* is **wrong**. A report must be obtained before **any** probation order is made: Criminal Procedure (Scotland) Act 1995, s 228(1)(b).

2 Criminal Procedure (Scotland) Act 1995, s 229(4)(a).

3 See G Boswell 'The Essential Skills of Probation Work' in T May and A Vass (eds) *Working with Offenders* (1996).

the basis for identifying and resolving some of the problems which led into offending behaviour; as a means of working with the offender towards a clearer and more acceptable understanding of his/her place in society; and as a credible alternative to the court in controlling and providing an opportunity for self-help. There is a staggering amount of research evidence[1] documenting the complex inter-relationships amongst offending behaviour, poverty, employment, housing and health. Each of these areas may become the basis for conditions attached to probation orders and each of them generates concerns which are well known to social work practitioners and may well form the basis for effective intervention.

It is also clear from a world-wide body of research that 'some things do work' with persistent offenders. In her review of this literature, Gill McIvor cites the following factors which augur well for successful social work involvement:[2]

(a) a focus on the offence and on problem solving;
(b) targeting high-risk offenders rather than net widening;
(c) using a range of interventions which are based on thorough assessments of the offender, the situation and the environment;
(d) the offering of appropriate, specific and concrete services.

Further to these factors, McIvor (in referring to the work of Petersilia, 1990) also cites a set of conditions which are prerequisites for effective probation project work:

(i) clear purpose;
(ii) organisational support and encouragement;
(iii) targeting relatively straightforward change;
(iv) stable and committed leadership;
(v) 'practitioner ownership'.[3]

The care/control dichotomy/dilemma is probably nowhere more evident than in the relationship between probationer and social worker. A detailed discussion of the contradictory demands made of supervisors of probation orders can be found elsewhere.[4] Detailed guidelines for the frequency and the content of contact

1 See M Drakeford and M Vanstone (eds) *Beyond Offending Behaviour* (1996).
2 G McIvor *Sanctions for Serious or Persistent Offenders: A Review of the Literature* (1990).
3 See P Raynor, D Smith and M Vanstone *Effective Probation Practice* (1994), pp 75–77.
4 See eg Tim May in *Probation: Politics, Policy and Practice* (1990) and John Rodger in *Family Life and Social Control* (1996).

through the initial, middle and final phases of the probation are available in *National Standards*.

### *(c) Conditions*

There are certain standard or core conditions which apply to all probation orders. These are that the offender is to be of good behaviour; is to comply with instructions given by the supervising officer; and must inform the supervisor at once of any change of address or employment. There are also specified requirements for the social worker to confront the offender with his/her responsibility to abide by the rule of law, to oversee the offender's compliance with the probation order and to provide the offender with advice, guidance and assistance.[1]

In addition to these core conditions there are others envisaged and provided for in the legislation. These are residence (the home surroundings of the offender must be considered before imposing such a condition); performance of unpaid work; requiring the payment of compensation to the victim of the offence; and requiring medical treatment for mental illness. Each of these will be considered in turn in the following paragraphs.

A requirement regarding residence can take two forms: it can require the offender to reside at a named place or in a named institution, or it can require that the offender's place of residence be approved by the supervisor. In the former case the requirement can last for up to 12 months from the making of the order.

The performance of unpaid work can be made a condition of a probation order where the offender has committed an offence punishable by imprisonment and is at serious risk of a custodial sentence. As we have already noted, the first of these requirements is not very restrictive as all common law crimes and offences are potentially punishable by imprisonment. The minimum period of work is 40 hours and the maximum 240 hours.

Although a compensation order (see below) cannot be made at the same time as a probation order, it is possible to make payment of compensation a condition of a probation order. The supervisor has responsibility for supervising the payment of compensation into court.

Treatment for mental disorder can be made a condition of a probation order where the court is satisfied that the offender suffers

1 Criminal Procedure (Scotland) Act 1995, s 228.

from a mental condition which requires and may be susceptible to treatment, but that the mental condition is not such as to justify the making of a hospital order (see below). The court can make this decision on the basis of the evidence of a registered medical practitioner. The probation condition may require treatment as an in-patient, as an out-patient, or by a named doctor or chartered psychologist for up to 12 months from the date of the order. It may be amended to allow for better or more convenient treatment and the court must be informed of the discontinuation of treatment. Where the requirement is for in-patient treatment the role of the supervisor may well be restricted.

Finally, as well as these conditions which the legislation specifically provides for, the social worker may recommend and the court may impose any other condition which it considers to be conducive to securing the good conduct of the offender and preventing re-offending. Examples of such conditions include refraining from association with known offenders or ex-offenders, refraining from specified behaviours like drinking, or participating in identified therapeutic or other programmes, such as motoring projects.

*(d) Amendment, discharge or transfer of order*

The order may be amended on the application of the offender or the supervisor. Any amendment cannot reduce the period of probation or extend it beyond the 3-year maximum and cannot extend the period of residence in a named place or of medical treatment beyond 12 months from the date the order was originally made.

If the offender moves, application may be made for transfer of the order to the new area either by the offender or by the supervisor. If the application is made by the supervisor the court must grant the application.

Either the probationer or the supervisor may apply for discharge of the order. *National Standards* suggests that the possibility of application for discharge should be considered half way through the order and at subsequent reviews.

*(e) Breach of order: failure to comply with conditions*

Where the offender breaches any of the requirements of the order, for example, by unsatisfactory performance of work or failure to comply with instructions of the supervisor, breach proceedings before the court may be initiated. In deciding whether or not to initiate proceedings the supervisor should consider the seriousness of the breach and the reasonableness of the explanation for it offered by the offender. *National Standards* suggests that less serious cases should be dealt with by way of a formal written warning, with the proviso that after two warnings the breach procedure should be initiated. Since there is some discretion in this process, it is imperative that social workers and their managers have considered and agreed criteria for the decisions taken. Clearly, these decisions are not taken lightly since the liberty of an individual is in jeopardy and so it is imperative that there be internal logic and consistency. This is unfortunately also necessary in view of a history of some social worker's therapeutic optimism and/or over-identification with the service user.

Breach proceedings are initiated by the supervisor applying to the court for a breach of probation. It is then up to the court to decide whether to take action against the offender. If it does, the breach need no longer be sworn to by the supervisor. The court may then issue a warrant for the arrest of the offender or cite him/her to attend court. As in the case of the breach of supervised attendance orders, the evidence of one witness is sufficient in these proceedings. The precise details as to how breach proceedings are initiated are the subject of local agreements.

If the breach is proved or admitted the court may impose a fine up to level 3 (currently £1,000); revoke the order and sentence the offender for the original offence; vary the conditions attached to the order, providing that this does not extend the order beyond 3 years; or continue the order and impose, in addition, a community service order (CSO). Before this last option can be used the preconditions for imposing a CSO must be fulfilled (see below).

#### *(f) Breach of order: commission of further offence*

When an offender on probation commits a further offence during the life of the order, breach proceedings should **always** be initiated. In this case the powers of the court are to continue the probation order or to impose sentence for the original offence.

### (6) Community service

#### *(a) Introduction*

A community service order requires the offender to perform between 80 and 300 hours (240 in a summary court) of unpaid work (the average number of hours is around 140). The sentence should normally be completed within 12 months, though the order remains in force until the number of hours specified has been worked. If the hours are not completed within 12 months, application to extend that period will need to be made.[1] The up-dated *National Standards* notes that periods of work need not be kept to less than 21 hours in any one week but that if the offender is receiving state benefit, the conditions for continued claims must not be compromised by the CSO work arrangements.

Before a CSO is used in a particular case, the court must have obtained a social enquiry report which includes an assessment of the offender's suitability for the community service scheme and of the suitability of the available work. In producing this report the community service scheme (that is, the body which administers community service, providing and supervising placements) must be consulted. The writer of the report should explain to the offender what a CSO involves so that he/she is in a position to consent to it.

Community service orders are seen by the relevant legislation explicitly as an alternative to imprisonment or detention;[2] in other words, they should be used only where the alternative is a custodial disposal and never as a net widener. It is available only to offenders over the age of 16 and counts as a conviction.

### *(b) The order*

In making the order the court must explain the purpose and effect of the order, the consequences of failure to comply with it, and the court's power to revoke and amend the order at the instance either of the offender or the supervisor. The consent of the offender to the order must be obtained and the order must specify the number of hours to be worked.

Following sentence the offender will be seen by a community service officer who will be employed by a social work department but may not be a qualified social worker. The community service officer will allocate a work placement and be responsible for supervision during the life of the order. There is a statutory requirement to avoid conflict as far as practicable with the offender's religious beliefs and employment or education. In addition, other factors are clearly relevant, for example any skills or impairment. Typically,

1 See *HMA v Hood* 1987 SCCR 63.
2 Criminal Procedure (Scotland) Act 1995, s 238(1).

the work will be in painting and decorating, gardening, cleaning and kitchen work or in sports and youth clubs and the beneficiaries will be people who are elderly or frail or community neighbourhood charities. Occasionally, the work will provide opportunities for the offender to learn new skills. Appropriate performance and behaviour standards will be set at the outset and work placements must be closely monitored to ensure that these are met. The offender must notify the supervisor at once of any chance of address or change in the times of work.

### (c) Breach

The procedures to be followed in the event of breach are considered in detail in *National Standards*. These envisage, in serious cases, a three-stage process of formal warning, final warning and breach proceedings. At the final stage an application is made to court to institute breach proceedings. The application must be accompanied by a report from the community service officer and then it is up to the court to decide on the institution of proceedings. As in the cases of breach of a probation order or a supervised attendance order, the evidence of one witness is sufficient. If the breach is admitted or established the court may continue the order with the possible addition of a fine up to level 3 (currently £1,000); vary the number of hours, provided that the total does not exceed 300 (240 for summary courts); or revoke the order and sentence the offender for the original offence. Since a CSO is to be used only in cases where otherwise a custodial disposal would be used, it will almost certainly be the case that the alternative sentence will be custodial.

### (d) Revocation, amendment and transfer

Either the supervisor or the offender may apply for revocation or amendment of the order, and the court must grant the application if it appears to be in the interests of justice to do so having regard to changes in circumstances since the order was made. Examples would include prolonged illness or change in the offender's employment situation. The amendment may be to alter the number of hours or to extend the 12-month period in which the work is to be completed. In the case of revocation the court may simply revoke the order, or may revoke the order and substitute another sentence.

Where the offender moves and there are facilities for community service in the new area, the offender or the supervisor may apply for a transfer of the order to the new area. If the application is made by the supervisor the court must grant the application.

### (7) Compensation order

Compensation orders were introduced by the Criminal Justice (Scotland) Act 1980. This disposal counts as a sentence when convictions are libelled. Courts have the power to grant compensation orders up to the amount of the maximum fine which they can levy. The compensation order is designed to compensate the victim for any personal injury, loss or damage caused to them by the offender. In making a compensation order the court must take into account the means of the offender and so here again it is vital that any social enquiry report include accurate and comprehensive information about the offender's income and expenses. Where the offender's means are not sufficient to pay both a fine and a compensation order the latter should be preferred. The compensation order may be imposed in addition to as well as instead of other penalties. A compensation order cannot be imposed together with an absolute discharge, probation order or a deferred sentence, though the court could defer sentence and make payment of compensation a condition of the deferral, so that upon the expiry of the deferred sentence, if the payment had been made, the expectation would be that the subsequent disposal would be more lenient.

The provisions for review, remission and enforcement of compensation orders are similar to those considered above for fines, though, in addition, review may be sought where the victim's loss turns out to be less than it appeared at the time of the order. Payment of the sum ordered is made to the clerk of the court who passes it on to the victim. Payments made by the offender will be counted towards a compensation order before any fine made at the same time.

The making of a compensation order will not affect the victim's ability to raise a civil action for damages against the offender or to claim under the criminal injuries compensation scheme (see below). In either case, however, the amount of a compensation order will be deducted from any award made to the victim.

### (8) Deferred sentence

This is not strictly a disposal, but amounts to the court deferring sentence for a period of time. Adjournments to obtain reports are not deferments of sentence and the deferred sentence provisions cannot be used to avoid the time limits on such adjournments. Sentence is usually deferred for a longer period of 3, 6 or 12 months. A court may defer sentence, for example, for the offender to be of good behaviour during the period of deferment or to allow the offender to make reparation to the victim. In such cases the expectation is that if the condition attached to the deferment is fulfilled a lesser sentence will be imposed than otherwise. Where sentence is deferred in a case where a social enquiry report has been prepared, the court will often ask for a supplementary report to be prepared for the deferred hearing.

If the offender commits another offence during the period of deferment he/she may be brought before the court for sentence without waiting for the deferred date.

The time of deferral can be used constructively by the social worker and offender to identify and explore problem areas and evaluate the potential effectiveness of various disposals. Although sentence can be deferred, there is no provision such as exists in England and Wales for sentences to be suspended. Unlike a deferred sentence a suspended sentence involves the imposition of a sentence of detention, the effect of which is suspended for a fixed period and will be served only if the offender commits a further offence punishable by imprisonment during that period.

## 5. DIVERSION FROM PROSECUTION

### (1) Conditional offers of fixed penalties

#### *(a) Criminal Procedure (Scotland) Act 1995, sections 302 and 303*

These provisions allow a procurator fiscal to make a conditional offer of a fixed penalty in the case of any offence which could be prosecuted in the district court, subject to the general exclusion of motoring offences. If the offer is accepted no proceedings will be taken against the alleged offender and no conviction will be recorded. In the event that the offer is accepted and the alleged offender then defaults, recovery of the remainder of the penalty is by way of civil diligence. Apart from that, many of the provisions applicable to fine recovery apply, so that enforcement must be preceded by a means enquiry court and the individual could be placed on supervision until the penalty is paid. The amount of the penalty will be either £25, £50, £75 or £100.

These provisions have been used quite extensively, mostly for breach of the peace. About 80% of offers have been accepted, with most of the remainder prosecuted.[1] These measures do, however, raise a number of questions about rights of individuals to have their guilt or innocence established.

*(b) Road Traffic Offenders Act 1988*

This legislation allows the procurator fiscal or the police to make a conditional offer of a fixed penalty in respect of a number of motoring offences. The procedure is similar to that outlined above. Most offers are made by the police.

### (2) Social work diversion

There are a number of diversion schemes operating in Scotland which involve social work input. They generally involve diversion before prosecution. In other words, the person involved accepts some appropriate form of social work intervention, for example, to tackle an alcohol problem, as an alternative to prosecution. In some schemes the acceptance of social work intervention means that no prosecution will take place, while in others the decision not to prosecute is taken after assessing the outcome of the diversion. There has also been at least one experiment with mediation.[2] Questions abound concerning the difficulty of getting informed consent by the person either threatened with prosecution or having already begun the process of being prosecuted.

Individuals will normally be assessed by the social work department before being accepted for diversion. The role of the social worker is complex and contradictory with respect to this task, in that the worker is responsible for data collection and analysis under what are probably very stressful circumstances; for explaining the procedure to the service user; and for offering other appropriate social work services in supporting the service user and the family through what may well be a crisis. The existence of these schemes raises a number of important issues including concerns about net widening. In other words, there is the possibility that the existence of the scheme leads to intervention where previously there would have been

1 Scottish Office Statistical Bulletin *Criminal Proceedings in Scottish Courts 1990*, CRJ 1992/3, p 22.

2 See R Mackay 'ADR and Scottish Criminal Justice' in Moody and Mackay (eds) *Green's Guide to Alternative Dispute Resolution in Scotland* (1995).

no prosecution, or a warning letter would have been sent; and there are concerns about the types of case where diversion is appropriate, the most contentious being violent assault in the family.

## 6. COMPENSATION FOR CRIMINAL INJURIES

People who suffer personal injury as a result of violent crimes and are considered to be 'blameless' victims are entitled to claim compensation under the criminal injuries compensation scheme, which is administered by the Criminal Injuries Compensation Authority (CICA). The crime which forms the basis for the claim need not have been established in a criminal court by a prior conviction. Awards are made on the basis of a tariff which sets a value against particular types of injury. Claims which would result in an award of less than £1,000 will not be entertained. Claims must normally be made within 3 years.

One area of recent interest is the possibility of claiming compensation for child abuse. In some cases, where the child concerned is being looked after by the local authority, the social work department may be directly involved in assisting a child to make a claim under the scheme or may in fact be the object of the claim if the child was abused while being looked after by the local authority. In child abuse cases an award will be made only if certain requirements are fulfilled. First, in cases where the victim and person responsible for the injury were living in the same household, there must have been a prosecution of the person responsible or good reasons for no prosecution. Secondly, the guilty party must not benefit from the award (as might happen if victim and perpetrator were once again in the same household). Thirdly, making an award must not be against the child's interests. Substantial awards made to children will generally be managed by the CICA until the child is 18, except where the child is being looked after in which case the expectation is that the award will be administered by the social work department.

## 7. CUSTODIAL DISPOSALS

### (1) Imprisonment

Imprisonment is a disposal available only for those aged 21 or over. Where an offender has not previously been sentenced to imprisonment or detention the court cannot impose a sentence of imprisonment (except the mandatory life sentence for murder) without first considering information regarding the offender's character, circumstances and physical and mental condition (usually provided in a social enquiry report). In addition, the court must consider that no other disposal is appropriate and, if it is a summary court, must state and record the reason for this opinion. Someone who has not previously been imprisoned must have had legal representation, unless legal aid was refused on financial grounds or, having been informed of the right to legal aid, the offender has not applied for it.

The maximum length of sentence may be restricted in the case of a statutory offence by the statute creating it. In other cases the limit will be the maximum sentence the court can impose. In the case of lay magistrates this is 60 days. For stipendiary magistrates and the sheriff summary court the limit is 3 months, except where the conviction is for a crime of violence or dishonesty and there is a previous conviction for a cognate offence (for example, if the offender is found guilty of theft for the second time); here the maximum is 6 months. The sheriff solemn court can imprison for up to 3 years, and has the power, rarely used, to remit a case to the High Court for sentence where its powers are inadequate. There is no limit on the period of imprisonment that can be imposed by the High Court.

Where an offender is convicted of two or more offences, sentences of imprisonment may be imposed which are concurrent or consecutive; if the latter, the terms of imprisonment follow on from each other. Courts' powers to impose consecutive sentences may be limited by their maximum sentencing powers: for example, a sheriff sitting in a summary court could not normally impose consecutive sentences which, when added together, exceeded 3 months. This limitation will **not** apply where the convictions are on separate complaints or indictments and arise from distinct incidents. When imposing a sentence of imprisonment or detention, the court must take into account any period of time which the offender has already spent in custody or on remand awaiting trial or sentence.

It is generally agreed that it is hard to justify the present extent of the use of custodial measures in Scotland. As argued earlier, it is mainly ineffective and it is very expensive compared to any other alternative. Social workers have a special opportunity, particularly in the current climate, to develop credible alternatives and to publicise these options to sentencers; indeed, as we have seen, this is the perspective adopted by *National Standards*.

The law relating to release is dealt with in part 8 below.

### (2) Detention of young offenders

Offenders between 16 and 20 may be sentenced to detention in a young offenders institution. Previously, offenders in this age group could be sentenced to borstal training or to detention in a detention centre but these options are no longer available. Young offenders are incarcerated in separate institutions from adult offenders and there is a greater emphasis, where possible, on high standards of discipline and training. Reconviction rates and recidivism remain very high. Before sentencing an offender to detention the court must consider the same information as is appropriate in the case of an offender of 21 and over who is sentenced to a first term of imprisonment. The court must also be of the opinion, based on this information, that no other way of dealing with the offender is appropriate and, except for the High Court, must record the reason for this opinion. Offenders aged between 18 and 21 who are convicted of murder will be sentenced to detention for life rather than a period of imprisonment and will be transferred from a young offenders institution to a prison at some time between their 21st and 23rd birthdays. Other young offenders will also be transferred in the same way. Release is subject to the same rules as release from prison.

### (3) Detention of children[1]

A child under the age of 18 who is convicted of murder is to be detained without limit of time in a place and on conditions specified by the Secretary of State with transfer to prison at the age of 21. Children under 16 convicted in a solemn court may be sentenced to detention, again in a place and on conditions determined by the Secretary of State.[2] The sheriff summary court may impose sentences of detention in residential care for up to 12 months on offenders under 16 and in this case the care is provided by the relevant local authority, and it is up to it, not the court, to select the appropriate accommodation.[3] The numbers of children sentenced to detention are small: in 1994 only 28 were dealt with in this way.[4]

1 See also ch 5, pt 5.
2 Criminal Procedure (Scotland) Act 1995, s 208.
3 Ibid, s 44; *B, Petitioner* 1992 SCCR 596.
4 See B Kelly *Children Inside – Rhetoric and Practice in a Locked Institution for Children* (1992) for a research study highlighting the conditions and issues in Scotland.

The children's hearing will normally have had some involvement in such cases in providing consultation and advice. Social workers must ask if the child in question is a danger to him/herself or others and must attempt to present this and other relevant information to the sentencers.

## (4) Social work in prison

There are local authority social workers based in the prisons in Scotland with the general remit of providing a social work service to prisoners in need. The overwhelming fact of life for this work is that security is the primary objective of the host institution and all other considerations are subject to directives arising out of that factor. This manifests itself in practical problems, including arranging to interview prisoners; arranging for 'welfare visits' for prisoners with their families; communicating information to prisoners and receiving information from prisoners; and prison regimes restricting the time, timing and place for interviews. Other problems include working with the possibly very different value base, attitudes and assumptions of prison staff; working within an extremely hierarchically organised institution; working within the restrictions imposed by the Official Secrets Act; and, possibly, working with one member of a family system which has been broken apart. Social workers should be familiar with the rules contained in the Prisons and Young Offenders Institutions (Scotland) Rules 1994.[1] These include rules about the reception of prisoners, health and welfare, communications and visits, work, education, recreation, discipline, requests and complaints, female prisoners, discharge and temporary release. Prisoners are classified in accordance with their age, sex, offence, sentence and previous record of offences as one of four security categories:

(a) national security risk, highly dangerous (kept in maximum security);
(b) likely to be a danger to the public (secure conditions to prevent escape);
(c) unlikely to be a danger to the public (minimum restrictions); and
(d) not a danger to the public (open conditions). These ratings will also determine the prison in which male offenders serve their sentences.

1 SI 1994/1931.

There are extraordinary opportunities potentially available to social workers in prison, as anyone who has worked with people in crisis and with a high level of motivation will know. At the time of entry and just before release from prison it is likely that the prisoner will demonstrate a drive to solve problems caused by imprisonment, resolve difficulties which led to offending behaviour, and lay the groundwork for returning to live in the community.

In recent years, social workers in prisons have initiated the development of a whole range of innovatory services and programmes including working with those who have sexually abused children, who have acknowledged problems with substance abuse, who have been homeless, and who have mental health problems. As other long-stay institutions decrease in size and close, it is clear that more people who previously had been in such institutions are finding their way into the prisons, and social workers in prison will be increasingly called upon to provide a wider range of services to meet these people's needs.[1]

## 8. RELEASE FROM PRISON AND DETENTION

The Prisoners and Criminal Proceedings (Scotland) Act 1993 introduced new provisions for release of prisoners, applying both to adult prisoners and to young offenders. These, in general, apply only to prisoners convicted after 1 October 1993. Prisoners convicted prior to then will be subject to the previous regime of remission and parole and so it is important for social workers to have a working knowledge of both schemes. Under the new scheme, treatment depends on whether the prisoner is a short-term prisoner (serving between 5 days and 4 years), a long-term prisoner (serving 4 years or more), a life prisoner, or a discretionary life prisoner.

### (1) Short-term prisoners

Short-term prisoners sentenced after 1 October 1993 are to be released automatically on serving half of their sentence. There are conditions which apply if the ex-offender is subject to any supervised release order or is involved in the commission of a further

1 See B Williams *Work with Prisoners* (1991).

offence. If the offender appears before a court which has at least the same level of sentencing power as the one which levied the original sentence and is convicted of an offence which is punishable by imprisonment, then the court can order the balance of the sentence still outstanding to be served, in addition to whatever other sentence is imposed. Under the scheme by which short-term prisoners are released having served half the sentence, the ex-offender may request that the local authority provide supervision and the local authority has a duty to do this. In practice, this supervision would be provided by a social worker.

### (2) Long-term prisoners

These prisoners are to be released on licence after completion of two-thirds of their sentence. Once half of the sentence has been served the prisoner is eligible to be considered for parole. It is up to the prisoner whether he/she wishes to be considered and around 10% of those eligible decline the opportunity. The prisoner will be interviewed and a dossier is then prepared, including a 'home circumstances report' prepared by a social worker in the area where the prisoner intends to live on release.

The ideal model for the compiling of these reports would be if the field social worker who wrote the original social enquiry report for the court, if one was required, or who has been working with the family of the prisoner and has maintained a through-care contact with the prisoner is the person who now completes the home circumstances report. The prison social worker who has been working with the prisoner in resolving some of the problems associated with imprisonment would ideally be the one to compile the dossier. Difficulties typically arise when there has been a break in the contact between the prisoner and the person(s) with whom the prisoner proposes to live and/or misunderstandings have arisen between these parties. After all, families have learned to live without the prisoner and may appreciate the contribution of a social worker in helping them to clarify their thoughts and feelings about the prisoner's impending return to the community.

All the information in the dossier is disclosed to the prisoner who may comment on it. The dossier then goes to the Parole Board which makes a recommendation to the Secretary of State as to whether the prisoner should be released on parole. A prisoner serving less than 10 years must be released by the Secretary of State if the Board recommends this. In other cases it is up to the Secretary of State to decide whether to accept a recommendation for release. A prisoner released on parole is subject to a licence lasting until the end of the sentence.

Social work with a prisoner released on licence should always be based on a comprehensive systemic assessment of the individual and situation. There are, however, several special areas which must be considered. These include helping the individual to make sense of the new living environment which may have altered considerably in the absence of the prisoner. Practical problems usually take centre stage initially, such as arranging for the payment of income maintenance from the Benefits Agency and finding accommodation. Relationships with others may have been strained beyond reparation while others may require much effort and understanding to rejuvenate. Finding work may be especially difficult. Former prisoners are generally very vulnerable to the problems associated with mass unemployment and deprivation and unless some of the problems which resulted in offending behaviour have been outgrown or resolved, they are likely to resurface relatively quickly. Here the support and guidance of a social worker can be invaluable.

### (3) Mandatory life prisoners

The cases of mandatory life prisoners (that is, those convicted of crimes the mandatory penalty for which is life imprisonment) are reviewed 4 years into their sentence to recommend a date for first consideration of the prisoner for release on licence. The procedure for release of life prisoners is more complicated. It starts with a reference of the case by the Secretary of State to the Parole Board. The Parole Board then considers the case and makes a recommendation. If the recommendation is for release, the Secretary of State can order release on licence only after consultation with the Lord Justice General (or Lord Justice Clerk if he is not available) and, if available, the trial judge.

### (4) Discretionary life prisoners

These are life prisoners who:

(a) have committed an offence for which the penalty is not fixed by law; and

(b) in respect of whom the judge has fixed a period before which no consideration can be given for release.

If no order specifying a period is made, the judge must give reasons for this and it then appears that the prisoner is to be treated in the same way as a prisoner serving a mandatory life sentence. Once the specified period has been served, the prisoner is eligible for release on licence and may require the Secretary of State to refer the case to the Parole Board. If the Parole Board considers that continued detention is not necessary for the protection of the public it can direct the Secretary of State to release the prisoner. The Secretary of State must act on that direction. If release is refused, the prisoner is entitled to have the case considered again at two-yearly intervals, while the Secretary of State may refer to the Board at any time. For these purposes, the Parole Board is considered to sit as a court and legal aid is available to prisoners.

### (5) Compassionate release[1]

This provision is as it sounds and allows the Secretary of State to release all prisoners – prior to and since 1 October 1993 – on 'compassionate' grounds. These grounds are not defined in the Prisoners and Criminal Proceedings (Scotland) Act 1993. For long-term prisoners and those serving life sentences, the Parole Board must be consulted. This release is also on licence with conditions and subject to recall. Children are also entitled to be considered for compassionate release as a result of an amendment made in the Criminal Justice Act 1993.

### (6) Release on licence

Where a prisoner is released on licence, the licence lasts until the expiry of the sentence imposed by the court (for life prisoners, until death). The licence may contain any conditions considered appropriate by the Secretary of State, and must include a condition requiring supervision by a local authority officer and a requirement to comply with the instructions of the officer. In the

1 Prisoners and Criminal Proceedings (Scotland) Act 1993, s 3.

case of life prisoners, this requirement for supervision can be removed 10 years after their release. The standard conditions also include a requirement to be of good behaviour and to keep the peace and a requirement to obtain the supervising officer's permission before leaving Great Britain. Licence conditions can be varied, inserted or cancelled at any time by the Secretary of State. Conditions in licences for discretionary life prisoners can be inserted or varied only on the recommendation of the Parole Board; in the case of other life prisoners, and long-term prisoners the Board must be consulted about the conditions included in the licence. The licence can be revoked by the Secretary of State, either on the recommendation of the Parole Board or, if it is not practicable to await such a recommendation, on the Secretary of State's own initiative where revocation and recall are expedient in the public interest.

In practice, revocation of the licence and recall to prison is initiated by the supervisor, who has some discretion in deciding whether or not to initiate this process. A report from the supervisor will be considered by the Parole Board which makes a recommendation to the Secretary of State. In some cases the case will be dealt with by way of a warning letter, but in others the parolee will be recalled to custody. On recall the parolee has a statutory right to make representations to the Parole Board, which may order re-release. In practice, recalls are referred to the Parole Board whether or not the parolee makes representations. Again, *National Standards* outlines detailed guidance on the criteria for social workers making decisions regarding the initiation of proceedings. A recalled prisoner has the right to make representations about the recall which will be considered by the Parole Board who can recommend release on licence.

### (7) Commission of a further offence by released prisoner

A prisoner who commits a further offence before the date on which the sentence, if served in full, would have expired may be returned to detention for a period not exceeding the length of time between the date of commission of the offence and the date on which the sentence would have been served in full. Note that this applies whether or not the released prisoner is on licence. Thus, a released short-term prisoner could be returned to serve the rest of the sentence under this provision.

### (8) Supervised release orders

This is available to courts in respect of prisoners who are sentenced to between 12 months and 4 years imprisonment. In other words, it provides supervision on release of such prisoners who, as short-term prisoners, would normally be released unconditionally. Before an order can be made the court must be satisfied that it is necessary to protect the public from serious harm from the offender on release, a report must be obtained from the local authority, and the effect and consequences of the order must be explained to the offender by the court. The order requires local authority supervision and compliance with the requirements set out in the order and those reasonably specified by the supervising officer. The object of these requirements is to secure the good conduct of the offender or to prevent or lessen the possibility of further offending. The order can be for up to 12 months, provided that it cannot extend beyond the expiry of the period of imprisonment fixed by the court. The conditions in the order can be varied by the court on application by the offender or by the supervising officer.

On breach of a supervised release order, the court can order return to prison for a period equal to the period between the date of the breach and the end of the order or vary the order. The initiative for starting breach proceedings comes from the supervising officer and the evidence of one witness is sufficient to prove the breach.

### (9) Pre-1993 sentences

Prisoners sentenced before 1 October 1993 will in general be subject to the old rules for release. Briefly, these provided for remission of one-third of the sentence (which means that the offender is simply released) and release on parole (in which case the released offender will be released on licence), with the licence operating in much the same way as that outlined above. A prisoner is eligible for parole after serving one-third of the sentence. The prisoner is notified of this and asked if he/she wishes to apply. If so, a dossier will be compiled on the prisoner which will include a home circumstances report prepared by a social worker. The dossier will go to the Parole Board, which will then make a recommendation to the Secretary of State. A prisoner serving less than 10 years must be released by the Secretary of State if the Board recommends this. If parole is not granted the case will normally be reviewed in 12 months. The licence remains in force until the two-thirds point in the original sentence. Certain types of offender are more restricted in the availability of parole: for example, terrorists will not be paroled and offenders imprisoned for more than 5 years for violent offences will not normally be paroled until a few months before the end of their sentence. There are special provisions for supervision of young offenders.

Finally, discretionary life prisoners in prison on 1 October 1993 have to have their cases considered to decide whether, if they had been sentenced after that date, the court would have specified a period to be served before the prisoner could be considered for release.

## (10) Early release of children

### *(a) Children detained after sentence on indictment*

Such children can be released on licence at any time by the Secretary of State on the recommendation of the Parole Board. A child sentenced to less than 4 years detention must be released on licence after serving half of the sentence; those serving 4 years or more must be released on licence after serving two-thirds of the sentence. A child who has been released on licence may be returned to detention on the commission of a further offence or have the licence revoked for breach of the licence conditions. Children sentenced to be detained without limit of time can be released by the Secretary of State at any time on the recommendation of the Parole Board. The number of children involved is small.

### *(b) Children detained after sentence on complaint*[1]

Such children are kept at a place determined by the local authority. The local authority has the same powers and duties in respect of the child as it does towards a child subject to a supervision requirement. The child may be released, either conditionally or unconditionally, at any time provided that a review has been carried out and after having regard to the best interests of the child and the need to protect members of the public. In any event, the child is entitled to be released after serving half of the period of

1 Criminal Procedure (Scotland) Act 1995, s 44.

detention, but the local authority may require the child to submit to supervision for the outstanding period of the sentence. Once released, the child may be returned to detention if a further offence is committed before the end of the originally imposed period of detention. As stressful as the arrangements for release are likely to be for adults and young adults, that pressure is likely to be considerably worse for the child and family going through similar processes. Social workers will already be involved in most of these situations and so can hopefully build upon established relationships to use this period constructively. Here again, the developmental stage and tasks and the particular influence of the child's peer group are liable to be relevant in the social worker's involvement as well as the re-establishment of viable familial relationships.

## (11) Crime and Punishment (Scotland) Act 1997

This legislation was passed shortly before the change of government in May 1997. It appears that some of its provisions are not going to be brought into effect, notably changes to release of prisoners and mandatory life sentences for certain offenders. At the time of writing, it appears that the provision in the Act for a mandatory period of imprisonment on a third conviction for certain drug trafficking offences,[1] the provisions allowing for changes in the system of criminal legal aid[2] and restriction of liberty orders[3] will be brought into effect in October 1997. The restriction of liberty order would require the person on whom it was imposed to be at a specified place at specified times. Offenders subject to such orders will be monitored by electronic tagging.

A number of provisions, for example increasing penalties for certain sexual offences, extending special procedures for children giving evidence to 'vulnerable' adults, and increasing the prosecutor's right of appeal were brought into effect in August 1997.

The government is still considering whether to introduce other provisions, for example increasing the sentencing powers of sheriff courts.

1 Crime and Punishment (Scotland) Act 1997, s 2.
2 1997 Act, Pt V.
3 1997 Act, s 5.

# 9. MENTAL HEALTH AND CRIMINAL LAW

## (1) Remand before trial

Courts can remand an individual awaiting trial to hospital if they are satisfied, on the basis of evidence from a single doctor, that the individual is suffering from a mental disorder. Before making the order the court must be satisfied that a suitable hospital place is available. Once in hospital he/she will be examined by the responsible medical officer (RMO) and can be kept in hospital only if suffering from a mental disorder justifying compulsory admission under the Mental Health (Scotland) Act 1984.

## (2) Interim hospital order

After conviction, where the sheriff in a summary case is satisfied as to guilt, or where the case has been remitted to the sheriff by a district court,[1] an interim hospital order can be made. Before making it the court must be satisfied, on the evidence of two doctors, that the offender is suffering from a mental disorder and that the offender may appropriately be dealt with by way of a hospital order. The order lasts for up to 12 weeks, but can be renewed for further 28-day periods up to a maximum of 6 months.[2] The hospital must be specified in the order and a place must be available at that hospital.

## (3) Remand for medical examination

Where a court requires further information regarding the physical or mental health of an offender, it has the power to order a remand for up to 3 weeks for medical examination. A condition of a remand for inquiry into the offender's mental condition will be that the offender must be examined by two doctors. If the remand is not in custody a condition as to residence may be imposed.

1 The district court has the power to remit a case to the sheriff court if a person charged with a crime punishable by imprisonment appears to be suffering from a mental disorder: Criminal Procedure (Scotland) Act 1995, s 58(10).

2 This will be increased to 12 months under the Crime and Punishment (Scotland) Act 1997, s 11.

## (4) Hospital and guardianship orders

These orders can be made in respect of offenders found guilty of an offence punishable by imprisonment. This qualification, in fact, covers a wide area, as all common law offences, including breach of the peace and other minor offences, are punishable by imprisonment. The orders can be made only by the High Court and the sheriff court. Appropriate cases arising in the district court must be referred to the sheriff court.

Before making a hospital order the court must be satisfied that the grounds for compulsory admission set out in the Mental Health (Scotland) Act 1984 apply to the offender;[1] that a hospital order is the most suitable method of dealing with the case; and that the hospital named in the order will be able to admit the offender within 28 days. If the named hospital is the state hospital the court must be satisfied that the patient, on account of the patient's dangerous, violent or criminal propensities, requires treatment in conditions of special security and cannot be suitably cared for in any other hospital.

Before making a guardianship order the court must be satisfied that the grounds for reception into guardianship specified in the Mental Health (Scotland) Act 1984 apply to the offender,[2] and that a guardianship order is the most suitable way of disposing of the case. The effect of hospital and guardianship orders are, respectively, similar to compulsory detention and guardianship under the Mental Health (Scotland) Act 1984.[3] The main difference is that discharge cannot be ordered by the nearest relative.

## (5) Restriction order

The court may attach a restriction order to a hospital order, which will be for a fixed period. A restriction order may be imposed if the court is of the opinion that, having regard to the nature of the offence, the offender's antecedents and the risk of re-offending, it is necessary for the protection of the public from serious harm. As long as the order is in force the offender must be treated as a state patient.

1 See ch 6, pt 5(2).
2 See ch 6, pt 6(1).
3 See ch 6, pts 5 and 6.

## (6) Insanity in bar of trial or as a ground for acquittal

If a court is satisfied that a person appearing before it charged with a crime or offence is insane so that the trial of that person cannot proceed or continue, then it must make a finding that this is the case; order an 'examination of facts'; and remand the accused to appear at that examination. The remand may be to a hospital (by way of a temporary hospital order) if the accused is suffering from a disorder that would justify compulsory admission under the Mental Health (Scotland) Act 1984. Evidence both of the insanity and the degree of disorder must be provided by two doctors.

The 'examination of facts' is a further court hearing, which can take the form of a continuation of the trial diet if that is the stage at which the order for it to take place is made. At this hearing the court has to decide two things. First, it must decide if it is satisfied, beyond a reasonable doubt, that the accused committed the offence. Secondly it must be satisfied, on the balance of probabilities, that there are no grounds for acquitting the accused. If the court decides that it is satisfied on both of these then it must make a finding to that effect. If it is not so satisfied the accused is to be acquitted.

Where a finding is made in these terms or where the accused is acquitted by reason of insanity at the time of the offence, the court has four options for disposal: an order for detention in hospital with or without a restriction order;[1] an order equivalent to a guardianship order; or a supervision and treatment order.

## (7) Supervision and treatment order

This places the individual under social work supervision for a period of up to 3 years and requires the individual to comply with the instructions of the supervisor and to submit to treatment for the improvement of his/her mental condition. Before an order can be made the court must be satisfied that it is the most suitable way of dealing with the individual; that the person's mental condition is treatable and not such as to warrant the equivalent of a hospital or guardianship order; that the supervisor is willing to supervise; and that arrangements have been made for the treatment specified in

1 Where the offence is murder a hospital order accompanied by a restriction order must be made.

the order. Before the order is made the effect of the order and the powers of the courts to review the order must be explained to the individual in ordinary language. There are provisions for amending and revoking the order, but no specific provision for alternative action in the case of breach of its terms.

### (8) Transfer of those awaiting trial or sentence

Individuals remanded in custody awaiting trial or sentence may be transferred to hospital. The transfer is made on a transfer order granted by a sheriff on the application of the Secretary of State. A transfer order has the effect of a hospital order with an unlimited restriction order.

### (9) Transfer of sentenced prisoners

The Secretary of State may make an order transferring prisoners to hospital. Before doing so he/she must be satisfied, on the evidence of two doctors, that the prisoner suffers from a mental disorder. A transfer direction has the same effect as a hospital order and may have added to it a restriction direction having the same effect as a restriction order, though the restriction is limited in time to the unexpired period of sentence.

### (10) State patients and the state hospital

A state patient is a patient who cannot be discharged, given leave of absence or transferred without the consent of the Secretary of State, and the authority for whose detention continues indefinitely. There is, however, a right of appeal to the sheriff once every 12 months. The state hospital is situated at Carstairs and is designed to provide treatment in conditions of special security to patients who have dangerous, violent or criminal propensities.

### (11) Hospital direction

Under the Crime and Punishment (Scotland) Act 1997, it will be possible to impose a hospital direction authorising detention of a prisoner in hospital at the same time as passing a sentence of imprisonment.[1]

## 10. REHABILITATION OF OFFENDERS

All ex-offenders including parolees are subject to the stipulations of the Rehabilitation of Offenders Act 1974 which is a legislative attempt to enable ex-offenders to put their histories behind them. The main exceptions to the law are life imprisonment and sentences of more than 30 months. Once the period of rehabilitation is over, and this involves complex calculations for various sentences but is generally a period of 5, 7 or 10 years which is halved if the offender was under 17 at the time of the offence, then the person is to be treated as if the offence had not been committed . 'Spent' convictions need not be disclosed in applying for jobs, making agreements for credit or insurance, or giving evidence in civil proceedings. There are certain exceptions to this which include the disclosure of an offence relating to children or of violence when applying to work for a social work department; when a fine for the conviction is outstanding; when a prohibition or disqualification (as in driving) is in effect for a period longer than the period during which the conviction is spent; and in circumstances where there has been royal intervention.

## 11. CRIMES AND OFFENCES

What follows is a brief description of some of the crimes and offences most commonly committed and encountered by social work practitioners. These are all crimes which are created and defined by common law.

### (1) Assault

An assault involves an attack on someone which either causes physical injury to the victim or causes fear of physical injury. This

1 Crime and Punishment (Scotland) Act 1997, s 6, inserting a new s 59A into the Criminal Procedure (Scotland) Act 1995, and s 7 inserting a new s 62A into the Mental Health (Scotland) Act 1984.

means that as well as the stereotypical assault which causes actual injury, it is just as much assault if the offender acts in such a way as to make the victim afraid that he or she is going to suffer injury. Examples of this latter sort of assault would be cases where someone is threatened with a knife or other weapon, or where a fist is shaken menacingly in the face of the victim. In cases where actual injury is caused, the resulting harm need not be great. If great harm is caused this might lead to a charge of one of the aggravated assaults, for example, assault to severe injury or assault to permanent disfigurement. The intention of the assailant may also give rise to a charge of aggravated assault, for example, assault with intent to rob.

In some cases, the use of reasonable force will not amount to assault. One example of this is the use of reasonable force by police officers in the execution of their duty. Another, more controversial, example is the use of force on children which is regarded as reasonable chastisement.[1]

Assaults are usually direct, that is carried out by the assailant, but they can be indirect. One example of this is setting dogs on the victim, as in the case of *Quinn v Lees*[2] in which a purported defence that it was done as a joke was rejected. Finally, it should be noted that assaults on police officers are usually charged as a statutory offence.[3]

## (2) Breach of the peace

This covers a variety of circumstances in which someone behaves in a way that causes or is likely to cause annoyance, upset, embarrassment, outrage or some similar emotion in members of the public, even if there are no members of the public available to give evidence of being annoyed etc. This is reflected in the definition of the offence which is most often cited:

> 'It is usual to charge this offence as breach of the peace, because it is a species of disorderly conduct; where something is done in breach of public order or decorum which might reasonably be expected to lead to the lieges being alarmed or upset or tempted to make reprisals at their own hand, the circumstances are such as to amount to breach of the peace.'[4]

1 See, for example, *B v Harris* 1990 SLT 208 and *Byrd v Wither* 1991 SLT 206.
2 1994 SCCR 159.
3 Police (Scotland) Act 1967, s 41.
4 *Raffaeli v Heatly* 1949 JC 101 at 104.

The offence commonly arises from an incident involving shouting and swearing in public. Often the only witnesses will be the two police officers effecting the arrest, but the ambit of the crime has been extended to cover new instances and to cover cases where there is no one actually present whose peace is breached. Examples include:

(a) playing football in the street where the participants were shouting and bawling. Cars and pedestrians had to take evasive action and it was reasonable to expect this might lead to members of the public being upset or being tempted to take reprisals;[1]
(b) a man peering through a hole in the wall of a cubicle in a swimming baths and looking at women using sunbeds in the solarium. The view was taken that he could easily be discovered and that if he was, members of the public might reasonably be expected to be upset, alarmed or disgusted;[2]
(c) a man dressed as a woman walking about in the red light district of Aberdeen. A man approaching him expecting a female prostitute might get a shock and in response might become violent;[3]
(d) a deputy headmaster of a private school making an indecent suggestion to a pupil in the privacy of the former's study;[4]
(e) two individuals accosting people, offering to shake hands with them, patting them on the shoulder and asking for money. The conduct was such that it might reasonably be expected to lead to members of the public being alarmed, upset or annoyed.[5]

The motive or intention leading to the breach of the peace is irrelevant. In one case a group of men saw a friend of theirs being taken away by two men. Unaware that the two men were plain clothes police officers effecting an arrest, the group surrounded them and shouted abuse at them. The group of men were convicted of breach of the peace.[6]

1 *Cameron v Normand* 1992 SCCR 866.
2 *MacDougall v Dochree* 1992 SCCR 531.
3 *Stewart v Lockhart* 1991 SLT 835.
4 *Young v Heatly* 1959 JC 66.
5 *Wyness v Lockhart* 1992 SCCR 808.
6 *Woods v Normand* 1992 SCCR 805.

### (3) Fraud

Fraud simply involves getting someone to take some form of action on the basis of a false pretence. The important elements are that some false statement is made; that the recipient believes it to be true; and that he or she, relying on the statement, then undertakes some action which they would not have undertaken. In most cases the object of the fraud will be to acquire goods or money. An example of the latter is use of a stolen cheque book.

### (4) Malicious mischief

This involves causing damage to property either intentionally or recklessly. It is closely linked to the statutory crime of vandalism.

### (5) Murder and culpable homicide

Murder involves a killing of another human being where either the assailant intended to murder the victim or attacked the victim violently without caring whether the victim was killed. Culpable homicide involves killing which does not amount to murder.

The types of case where killing amounts to culpable homicide rather than murder have been categorised as follows:

(a) cases where death results from an assault but was not a foreseeable consequence of the assault;
(b) cases where another crime is committed which might be expected to result in physical injury, such as wilful fireraising, but which results instead in death;
(c) cases where some activity which is lawful in itself is carried out in a reckless fashion and causes death, such as demolition of a building;
(d) cases where the assailant was provoked into the action which led to death;
(e) cases where the assailant successfully establishes diminished responsibility. This is a reduction in capacity or capability which is less than suffering from mental illness;
(f) cases which are dealt with by the prosecuting authorities as culpable homicide rather than murder, such as suicide pacts and euthanasia.

## (6) Rape

In Scotland, rape involves sexual intercourse between a man and a woman by force or threat of force and against her will. It is now clearly established that rape can take place within marriage, even where the couple are still living together.[1]

## (7) Reset

This involves being in possession of goods which have been dishonestly acquired, knowing that they are dishonestly acquired and with the intention of keeping the goods from their true owner. In this context dishonest acquisition covers theft, fraud and embezzlement. For someone to be guilty of reset, it is not necessary that the goods were acquired from their owner. All that is necessary is knowledge that the goods have been dishonestly acquired. Indeed, it is not necessary for the resetter to know the identity of the owner of the goods.

## (8) Robbery

This describes a theft achieved by force or violence. The force or violence need not amount to assault, but it is common to find this charged as assault and robbery where the force does amount to assault.

## (9) Theft

This simply involves the appropriation of property belonging to another, with the intention of depriving him/her of it permanently or of depriving him/her of it temporarily for a nefarious purpose. There are two common aggravations of theft. 'Theft by housebreaking' involves breaking into premises which are closed against entry and in which forcible entry is normally involved, but housebreaking can be committed with a stolen key or a skeleton key.

1 *Stallard v HMA* 1989 SCCR 248. Note that 'a male person cannot be raped': G H Gordon *Criminal Law* (2nd edn, 1978), para 33-03.

'Theft by opening a lockfast place' describes breaking into anything which is locked other than premises. For example, it includes breaking into a car and breaking into a locked room in a house which has been entered by housebreaking. Other possible charges are attempts at theft in these ways and housebreaking or opening a lockfast place with intent to steal where nothing is in fact stolen.

# 8. Professional responsibility and accountability

## 1. INTRODUCTION

There is a recognition that social workers are unique in the extent to which they are expected to be legally, organisationally and ethically responsible and accountable. These expectations do not sit neatly together, are often confusing or vague and may even be contradictory. Social workers also have a special set of responsibilities arising from the nature of the work undertaken and by virtue of the vulnerability of many service users. Legal responsibilities are generally concerned with minimum acceptable standards and will be dealt with below. Organisational responsibilities are context-dependent but often relate to the managerial requirements of large bureaucratic structures which are reliant upon conformity to policy and regulations. Ethical responsibilities complicate this picture further. Social workers have a commitment to service user empowerment and all that entails and yet remain accountable to both service user and employer while continuing to fulfil legal responsibilities.

The arguments about whether social workers meet the criteria to be considered professionals are outwith the scope of this text, but suffice it to say that the extent and level of responsibilities of social workers are such that to expect anyone other than a professional to undertake them would be unreasonable. Nearly every day reports appear in the press about the activities of social workers and upon closer reading, it is clear that the term social worker is being used interchangeably with anyone working in the welfare and caring fields. This is confusing and reflects poorly on qualified social workers. The United Kingdom has not followed worldwide trends in either increasing the length of educational preparation or in providing a general council empowered to accredit and register qualified workers as well as impose sanctions for unacceptable practice. Most social workers are employed by local authorities which are bureaucratic hierarchies with command structures which are less than amenable to the requirements of relatively autonomous professional workers. Thus, the infrastructure for professional responsibility and accountability requires considerable development and at present leaves social workers in an environment which lends itself indifferently to the support of best practice in this area.

Most social workers would agree that financial gain was certainly not amongst their motivations for embarking upon a career in social work. In fact, most would argue that social work salaries are no reflection of the level of responsibility inherent in the work and the disparity is even more striking in residential social work. In spite of all of these factors, it has been suggested that social workers are unique in accepting a professional responsibility which is more in tune with their sense of moral responsibility than with the responsibility imposed on them by the law. We look below at the legal position regarding accountability and liability.

## 2. THE LEGAL FRAMEWORK

People who are unhappy about social work decisions or actions may seek either to claim compensation for any harm they claim to have suffered as a result[1] or to change the decision or course of action. If they are seeking compensation, the normal way of doing this is by claiming breach of a legal duty. If they are seeking to challenge the decision, there are a variety of avenues open to them: the complaints procedure; a complaint to the local government ombudsman; or judicial review.

### (a) Breach of duty

The breach claimed may be breach of a statutory duty by an authority.[2] Success in such a claim is difficult. The claimant has to establish that the statute was designed to protect a limited group of people of which the claimant is a member and, more importantly, that the terms of the Act in question indicate a clear intention to create a right to claim compensation for breach of a duty. The existence of other forms of redress and the wide discretion usually conferred on authorities make proving this second element difficult. In the context of child care there is an especial reluctance to interfere with the performance of authorities' statutory duties.

1 The harm may involve physical harm, damage to property or psychological harm.
2 See ch 1, pt 5 for a discussion of legal duty.

Breach of a common law duty of care may also be claimed. It may be argued that the authority itself owes a duty of care to the affected individual or it may be argued that the individual worker owes the duty. Where the worker owes a duty and is doing what he/she is employed to do, the doctrine of vicarious liability makes the employer liable for any damage caused by an employee's breach of duty.

In general terms, you will owe a common law duty of care if:

(i) loss to the injured person is a foreseeable consequence of your actions (this may include inaction or giving advice);
(ii) the relationship between you and the person suffering the loss is close enough to give rise to a duty of care; and
(iii) it is just and reasonable to impose a duty of care in all the circumstances of the case.[1]

Once the existence of a duty of care is established, it is fulfilled by taking reasonable care in the circumstances and liability is restricted to those harmful consequences which are foreseeable if this standard is not achieved. For professionals, the standard will be the standard of a reasonably competent member of the profession. Following common practice will usually be enough to meet the standard of care required, but it should not be assumed that it will automatically do so, nor should it be assumed that departing from common practice will, in itself, amount to negligence. Departures will be acceptable where they are reasonable in the circumstances. Breach of this sort of common law duty has formed the basis of a number of cases that we will look at below.[2]

A final point is that there is virtually no Scottish case law in this area; all of the cases referred to are therefore English. It is likely that Scottish courts would reach similar conclusions.

## (b) Judicial review[3]

As we have already seen, judicial review offers a means of challenging decisions made by local authorities. Sometimes the consequence of a successful application for review will be that a local

1 *Caparo Industries plc v Dickman* [1990] 1 All ER 568.
2 There is a considerable US literature on social work liability: see eg F Reamer *Social Work Malpractice and Liability* (1994); D Besharov *The Vulnerable Social Worker* (1985).
3 See ch 1, pt 13.

authority is directed to act in a particular way. On other occasions the decision of the authority will be set aside and will have to be taken again, often with a strong hint from the court about what the new decision should be. It is not, in general, possible to claim compensation in judicial review proceedings and applications may be refused where there are other remedies available, most notably, in this context, the complaints and representations procedure.[1]

An applicant for judicial review must argue that there has been a defect in the decision-making process rather than simply arguing that the decision is wrong, and the grounds for such arguments are relatively restricted. They can be categorised in a variety of ways. One common approach sets out three categories:

(i) The authority has acted *ultra vires*; it has, in other words, done something which it has no power to do. This may involve exercising a power which it is not entitled to or reaching a decision in a way in which it is not entitled to.
(ii) There has been a breach of the requirements of natural justice. Briefly, these require decision-makers to be impartial and to give people likely to be affected by a decision the right to put their point of view before the decision is taken.
(iii) The authority has acted unreasonably. Examples of this might include taking into account things which were irrelevant to the decision or failing to take into account something which they were required by law or by guidance to take account of.

### (c) Other remedies

Aside from court action, there are two other remedies which can be used by people unhappy with social work services. One is the complaints procedure which each local authority is required to have and which deals with complaints about all types of social work services.[2] The other is the Commissioner for Local Administration in Scotland, otherwise known as the Local Government Ombudsman. Complaints about a local authority can be made direct to the Ombudsman, though in general complaints cannot be investigated if the person complaining has some right of recourse through an appeals procedure. Once a complaint is accepted, it will

1 See *R v Birmingham City Council, ex parte A* (10 February 1997, unreported) QB.
2 See ch 1, pt 15(5).

be investigated. Initially this may take the form of an informal approach to the local authority and many complaints are resolved at this stage. If there is no resolution an investigation will be carried out and a report produced. This may recommend action on the part of the authority and may recommend the payment of compensation to someone who has suffered as a result of what the authority did. Councils are not bound to follow the recommendation of the Ombudsman, though in practice most do, and the Ombudsman has no power to force them to comply.

## 3. LIABILITY IN CHILD CARE AND CHILD PROTECTION[1]

It is clear that local authorities have certain statutory duties in respect of child protection and certain duties towards children who are being looked after by them. If they fail in these duties, what remedy does the injured party have?

In the context of child protection there are two possible types of failure. The authority may have failed to intervene appropriately with the result that a child was harmed, or the authority may have intervened inappropriately, also causing harm to a child. Both of these possibilities came before the House of Lords when they dealt at the same time with the cases of *X (minors) v Bedfordshire County Council* and *M (a minor) v Newham London Borough Council* (the X and M cases).[2] In these cases, children who claimed to have been harmed respectively by under and over intervention sought to claim damages from the authorities responsible. They set out three grounds for their claim.

First, they argued that there had been a breach of the duties imposed by statute on the authorities. This argument was rejected on the grounds that the statute involved did not confer a clear right on children to claim damages if duties were not complied with. All of the statutory provisions concerned were in general terms and conferred considerable discretion on local authorities.

Secondly, they claimed that the local authority owed them a common law duty of care. Although it was accepted that the first

1 See T Guthrie *Legal Liability and Accountability for Child Care Decisions* to be published in the British Journal of Social Work.
2 [1995] 2 AC 633. See P Cane 'Suing Public Authorities in Tort' (1996) 112 LQR 13, for a discussion of the general issues raised by this decision.

two requirements for such a duty which were noted above applied, the claimed duty was rejected on the grounds that it was not just and reasonable to impose a duty on the authority. A variety of policy reasons were put forward for this, most of them, it must be said, highly contentious and speculative. Amongst these were the arguments that allowing liability would give rise to defensive practice; that resources would be diverted from child care to fighting compensation claims; that the decisions involved were very difficult and delicate (since they involved interfering between parent and child) and the courts should not intrude; that there were other remedies available by way of judicial review and the complaints process; and that imposing liability only on the local authority would be unfair because of the multidisciplinary approach taken to children at risk.

Finally, it was argued that the authorities were vicariously liable for the actions of their employees. For this to be the case it would have to be established that the workers owed the children a duty of care. It was held that they did not; the children were not clients of the workers; and that the workers' job was to provide a report for the local authority. The position of the worker was likened to that of a doctor who carries out an examination to provide a report for an insurance company. Such a doctor owes a duty of care to the company, but not to the person examined.

The outcome of this case is quite clear: social workers and local authorities cannot be liable for decisions they take in child protection; they cannot be liable because they owe children no legal duty of care. It might be thought that this exclusion of liability would extend only to decisions about children who were not already in care, and that a duty would be owed to children who were being looked after by the local authority. This is not the view that has been taken in the English courts, at least as far as a child on a foster placement is concerned.[1] A child who had been in care over many years claimed that he had been harmed by the activities of a foster parent and that despite complaints to the authority it had not investigated properly or taken action. It was held that no claim could be allowed because no duty of care was owed. The duty was ruled out by the same policy considerations as applied in the X case. It is doubtful if this reasoning stands up. Two reasons might be offered for saying this. In the first place, the duties imposed on local authorities as far as children being looked after are concerned are far more specific than those owed to children at large.

1 *H v Norfolk County Council* (10 May 1996, unreported) CA. See also *Barrett v Enfield London Borough Council* [1997] 3 All ER 171.

Secondly, by taking a child away from home and placing that child with foster parents the authority is surely assuming some responsibility for the safety of the child. An analogy might be drawn with the case discussed later where a social worker who gave advice to a parent was held to owe the parent a duty of care because he assumed responsibility for the accuracy of the advice.

The reluctance of the courts to apportion blame in these cases is strikingly at odds with the position taken in many inquiries into the treatment of children and with the approach of the press.

## 4. LIABILITY IN OTHER CASES

Outwith the area of child protection, there is no reason why individual social workers and social work departments should not owe a duty of care to service users and to members of the public. In the M case, for example, the point was made in the Court of Appeal 'that the social worker owes some duty to the person in his care; for example, he should not advise or encourage a child to engage in some activity which has a hidden danger, such as taking drugs or running across the road'.[1] Equally, a social worker having the care or supervision of a child, or indeed anyone else, will be under a duty to take reasonable care for their safety, for example, by ensuring adequate supervision or ensuring that they are not avoidably placed in a position where they risk coming to harm. In this respect the social worker is in the same position as everyone else.[2]

It is clear, however, that the duty may extend beyond this to cases where those under a social worker's charge cause damage to the property of another person. The best known instance of this is a case where the Home Office was held liable for inadequate supervision of a group of borstal trainees which resulted in damage to property.[3] There are illustrations of this in the context of social work. A court social worker did not inform those responsible for placing a child remanded into the care of a social services department of the child's suspected involvement in arson. He was placed in a community home under light supervision, left the home, and

1 *M (a minor) v Newham London Borough Council* [1994] 4 All ER 602 at 629i, per Staughton LJ.

2 See *Clunis v Camden and Islington Health Authority* (1996) Times, 27 December and *Kirkham v Chief Constable of the Greater Manchester Police* [1990] 3 All ER 246 for examples of duties owed by hospital authorities and the police to people in their care suffering from mental illness.

3 *Dorset Yacht Co Ltd v Home Office* [1970] AC 1004.

set a fire in a church causing considerable damage. It was held that the authority was in breach of its duty of supervision of the child, though this case also involved negligence by the court social worker in failing to pass on all the relevant information.[1] That the duty of supervision involves only a requirement to take **reasonable** care is illustrated by another example where a person under supervision set a fire. There had been an earlier fire, but it was not clear that it had been started by the person setting the second fire. Therefore there was no obligation to exercise close supervision over her, since there were no reasonable grounds for suspecting that she would do what she did.[2] In that case the point was made that 'a balance has to be struck between the risk of damage to others and the risk of impairing the treatment being given' through excessively rigorous control and supervision.

Liability can arise not only for damage caused by an action on the part of a social worker, or indeed inaction on his/her part, but also for negligent advice. Where advice is offered in the knowledge that the person receiving the advice is likely to rely on it in deciding what to do the person giving the advice will usually, provided the advice is given in a professional capacity, be regarded as undertaking a duty of care towards the person advised. Most reported cases of this concern other professions, but there is one case illustrating this in the context of social work. A mother wanted to place her son, T, with a child minder. She identified one possibility and phoned the social worker who co-ordinated child minding for the local authority to check on her suitability. The advice given was that there was no reason why the child should not be placed with the particular child minder. This advice was given despite the fact that the worker giving it knew that a child had previously suffered a non-accidental injury while in the care of the child minder and that the minder had voluntarily agreed not to accept any young children into her care. T suffered a non-accidental injury while in the care of the minder and sued the authority. He was successful in a claim based on negligent advice given by the worker. The worker had undertaken to give advice to T's mother and in doing so had undertaken a duty not to give negligent advice.[3] Potential liability for negligent advice could cover a wide range of advice given by social workers, but it should be stressed again that the worker's duty, in law, is to take **reasonable** care, not to guarantee the accuracy of the advice.

1 *Vicar of Writtle v Essex County Council* (1979) 77 LGR 656.
2 *Swift v Westham Central Mission* (6 June 1984, unreported) QB.
3 *T (a minor) v Surrey County Council* [1994] 4 All ER 577.

Another example of potential liability is a case where a child is placed for adoption but is then discovered to have a serious medical condition. This question arose in *M and M v Glasgow Corporation*[1] where a child placed with the pursuers was later diagnosed as being severely mentally subnormal to the extent that she would always be dependent on them. They sued arguing that the local authority (acting as adoption agency) had a duty of care to ensure that a child medically unfit in this way was not placed for adoption. They were unsuccessful as the adoption agency did not have, and could not be expected to have, the medical skill needed to foresee the problems that arose in this case. The sheriff did, however, canvass the possibility of action if the agency had failed to carry through the correct procedures, for example, by failing to obtain a medical report and concluded that:

'If a local authority negligently ignored some medical warning in the statutory medical report that a child was medically unsuitable for placing for adoption they might well be required to answer for it . . . '[2]

Social workers and their employers may be liable for failing to give adequate information to foster carers about a child placed in their care.[3]

## 5. JUDICIAL REVIEW: EXAMPLES

### (a) Fostering cases

Under this broad heading are cases dealing with decisions to remove a child from a foster placement; decisions to remove a person from a list of approved foster carers; and decisions to inform other foster carers of allegations of sexual abuse against a foster parent.

In the last category is *R v Lewisham London Borough Council, ex parte P*.[4] The applicant had been a foster carer. Allegations of sexual abuse had been made against him by one former foster child and the authority decided, following its policy, to advise people having care of children who had previously been fostered by P of the allegations of abuse and the identity of the alleged abuser. P

1 1976 SLT (Sh Ct) 45. See also *P v Tayside Regional Council* 1989 SCLR 165.
2 *M and M v Glasgow Corporation* 1976 SLT (Sh Ct) 45 at 49.
3 *W v Essex County Council* (1997) Times, 16 July.
4 [1991] 3 All ER 529.

successfully challenged the decision to identify him. The court took the view that the authority had simply carried out its policy without properly weighing up all the relevant factors in the case, for example, the reliability of the accusations, and had therefore acted unreasonably.

Where removal from the list of foster carers takes place, the prospects of success in an action for judicial review will depend on the reasons behind the removal. If they relate to the character or temperament of the foster carer they will not be reviewable. On the other hand, if they arise from allegations about the conduct of the foster carer that individual has a right to be informed of the allegations and to be heard in reply. Where a foster carer was not told the substance of the case against her and given the chance to make a case to challenge them, her removal from the list was quashed on review.[1] The ground for this decision was that the requirements of natural justice had not been complied with. This case also makes the point that the decisions that have to be made about reputation, character, etc in approving a foster carer are not open to challenge.

If foster carers are closely involved in the decision as to placement of a child, especially when the placement is to be a long-term one, they have a legitimate expectation that they will be consulted before the child is taken out of their care. Failure to consult and to allow them to make representations will be a breach of natural justice.[2] This requirement to consult would not arise in cases where serious allegations were made about the foster carers which required urgent action on the part of the local authority to protect the interests of a child. In such cases the local authority would have a statutory obligation to take action,[3] though, as we have seen, it might not be subject to a common law duty of care owed to the child.[4]

1 *R v London Borough of Wandsworth, ex parte P* [1989] 1 FLR 387. Contrast *R v Avon County Council, ex parte Crabtree* (22 March 1994, unreported) QB, where a foster carer was given the opportunity to be heard and his removal from the list was not challengeable by judicial review.

2 *R v Hereford and Worcester County Council, ex parte D* [1992] 1 FLR 448.

3 See eg the Arrangements to Look After Children (Scotland) Regulations 1996, SI 1996/3262, reg 19(1).

4 In contrast to the United States: see, for example, *S v County of San Diego* (1993) 16 Cal App 4th 887, concerning an adoption placement.

### (b) Child protection cases

In *R v Harrow London Borough Council, ex parte D*[1] the applicant for judicial review was a woman whose children had been placed on the child protection register after a case conference which the applicant was not allowed to attend, though she was allowed to make written submissions. The decision of the authority was not regarded as unreasonable. There was medical and other evidence suggesting that the applicant was responsible for injuries to the children and there was no breach of the requirements of natural justice because she had been given the opportunity to put her version of events before the case conference.

One notable point to come out of the *Harrow* case is that it will be very difficult in cases involving child protection to succeed in a case based on judicial review. The view was expressed by the Court of Appeal that review would succeed only in an exceptional case raising an important point of principle and that the decision of the local authority would have to be utterly unreasonable.[2] The reason for this is that in the child protection system the interests of the adults involved come second to those of the children. The point was made as follows by Butler-Sloss LJ:

> 'In balancing adequate protection for the child and fairness to the adult, the interests of an adult may have to be placed second to the needs of a child. All concerned in this difficult and delicate area should be allowed to perform their task without looking over their shoulder all the time for possible intervention of the court. The important power of the court to intervene should be kept very much in reserve, perhaps confined to the exceptional case which involves a point of principle which needs to be resolved, not only for the individual case but in general, so as to establish that registration is not being conducted in an unsatisfactory manner . . . In this area unbridled resort to judicial review could frustrate the ability of those involved in their effort to protect the victim of abuse.'[3]

### (c) Removal from parents while on home placement

Social work departments have a statutory duty to seek to have the care of a child who is being looked after by them taken over by that

1 [1990] 3 All ER 12.

2 A successful application for review was made in *R v Norfolk County Council, ex parte M* [1989] 2 All ER 359.

3 *R v Harrow London Borough Council, ex parte D* [1990] 3 All ER 12 at 17b–e. This point is reflected in one of the policy reasons given in the X and M cases for refusing to recognise the existence of a duty of care.

child's parent(s). What happens when additionally the authority has parental rights or responsibilities and placement with the parents is not working? Can the parents seek review of a decision to remove the children from their care, and in what circumstances is such a review likely to succeed? The only reported cases on this issue suggest that a parent will succeed in an application for review only if the reason for removal was an unsubstantiated allegation and the parent was not given an opportunity to respond to it before the decision to remove was made.[1] On the other hand, where a decision is based on a number of factors, such as the knowledge of social workers, assessments of the parent(s), reports from school and the views of doctors, the decision will not be challengeable. Such a decision is well within the scope of parental discretion allowed to an authority which has parental rights or responsibilities.[2]

What all of these cases indicate is that, as suggested in *Harrow*, the courts will be prepared to intervene only where a decision is based on an allegation which the complainer has not had the opportunity to challenge: in other words, where there has been a failure to comply with the requirements of natural justice. In the absence of a case based on natural justice, the courts are reluctant to overturn a local authority decision on the grounds that it is unreasonable. Courts often refer to the words of Lord Diplock in defining what criteria have to be met before a decision can be regarded as unreasonable. He said of unreasonableness that:

> 'It applies to a decision which is so outrageous in its defiance of logic or of accepted moral standards that no sensible person who had applied his mind to the question to be decided could have arrived at it.'[3]

This standard is so exacting that it is very difficult to meet.

### (d) Other cases

Although judicial review may be difficult to use in the context of child protection, there is no reason why it should not be used successfully in other areas of social work provision. For example, in *R v London Borough of Ealing, ex parte Leaman*[4] Mr Leaman applied

1 *R v Bedfordshire County Council, ex parte C* [1987] 1 FLR 239.
2 *R v Hertfordshire County Council, ex parte B* [1987] 1 FLR 239.
3 *Council of Civil Service Unions v Minister for the Civil Service* [1985] AC 374 at 410D.
4 (1984) Times, 10 February.

for assistance towards the cost of a holiday under the Chronically Sick and Disabled Persons Act 1970. The council, without considering the merits of the application, responded that because of financial constraints no grants were available for private holidays. It was held that they had acted improperly in declining to consider the application and simply applying a blanket policy without consideration of the merits of the application.

In *R v Avon County Council, ex parte M*[1] the placement of M, an adult with Down's Syndrome, was the subject of a dispute between the local authority and M's parents. It was agreed that M's needs would be assessed by the review panel set up under the council's complaints procedure. This panel heard evidence and reported, recommending a placement at an establishment called Milton Heights. The recommendation went to the social services committee who overturned it and substituted an alternative placement. That decision was overturned on application to the court, partly because the committee had failed to take M's psychological needs into account as required by the relevant legislation, and partly because the committee had failed to give proper weight to the panel's recommendation.

## 6. CONFIDENTIALITY AND DISCLOSURE

The law will protect what it describes as 'confidential information'. Broadly speaking, this is information which is not publicly known and which is disclosed by one person (the confider) to another (the confidant) in circumstances where it is clear that it is being disclosed in confidence. The fact that disclosure is in confidence may be clear from the relationship between the confider and the confidant, such as doctor/patient, or because the confider makes it clear that the information is to go no further. If the information is about to be disclosed, the law will allow the confider to prevent disclosure. If it has been disclosed and become public, the confider will be able to claim damages. It should be noted that this duty not to disclose confidences extends not only to the confidant, but also to anyone the information is passed on to, provided that it is clear that the information is confidential. In *Stephens v Avery*[2] a woman told her friend that she had had a lesbian affair with the wife of a well-

1 [1994] 2 FCR 259.
2 [1988] 2 All ER 477.

known criminal. Her friend passed the information on to a newspaper which published it. As far as the original confider was concerned, the paper was a third party; despite this, she was held to be entitled to seek compensation from them for distress caused by the publication.

The relevance of this for social workers is that information disclosed to them by service users (unless otherwise publicly available) is confidential. This applies whether they are regarded as clients in law or in social work practice. Disclosure of such information to a third party is therefore in breach of confidence. There are, of course, exceptions to this which cover disclosure in the proper performance of their duties (for example, in a case conference) or where they are providing a report which they are legally obliged to complete (such as a social enquiry report or a social background report). Aside from these exceptions (and a possible exception discussed below) any disclosure of information would entitle the service user to seek a remedy under breach of confidence.[1]

It is, of course, true that a person who is the subject of information is entitled to prevent its disclosure only if that person is the source of that information. If information comes from a third party or from observation, the subject of the information cannot prevent its publication since there is no law of privacy in the UK. Publication could be restricted in law only if there was another relationship of confidence to be protected or if the information was defamatory.[2] There are, of course, other professional and ethical obligations which should prevent disclosure of such information.

## 7. DUTIES TO WARN

In *Tarasoff v Regents of the University of California*[3] the family of a young woman sought compensation from a psychologist, Moore, who had failed to warn their daughter, Tatiana, of the potential danger posed to her by one of his patients. The patient, Poddar, had confided in Moore his intention of killing a young woman who could easily have been identified as Tatiana. Moore notified the

1 See the Code on Confidentiality of Social Work Records (1989), issued with SWSG Circular 1/89.

2 By 'publication' is meant communication to others, not necessarily by publishing in a newspaper etc.

3 (1976) 17 Cal 3d 425.

campus police and Poddar was briefly detained. A few weeks later, Poddar murdered Tatiana. One basis of the claim by the family was the existence of a duty to warn potential victims whose life or safety was at risk.[1] The Supreme Court of California concluded that:

'[O]nce a therapist does in fact determine, or under applicable professional standards reasonably should have determined, that a patient poses a serious danger of violence to others, he bears a duty to exercise reasonable care to protect the foreseeable victim of the danger.'[2]

The *Tarasoff* decision has had a varied subsequent career in the US and does not yet seem to have been applied to social workers.[3] One suggested difficulty which might arise in extending the rationale to social workers is establishing their diagnostic competence to decide when someone poses a serious threat to another person.

Whether a duty to warn exists in the UK is also open to doubt. On the face of it, it is plausible that a duty could arise when the three requirements set out above for the existence of a duty of care exist: that is, where loss is foreseeable; there is sufficient proximity between the parties; and there are no countervailing considerations. In the *Tarasoff* type of case where the victim is clearly identifiable it might be thought that at least the first two of these requirements are met. Difficulty might arise over the last. The objection here might be that disclosure was inconsistent with the obligation of confidence which a social worker owed to the service user. This is a point made by Parker and Spencer in the context of medical confidentiality.[4] The public interest in maintaining confidentiality was considered in *Tarasoff*, but was considered to be outweighed by the public interest in safety from violent assault.

It is almost certainly the case that a court in the UK would not accept a legally enforceable duty to the public at large, as suggested by Parker and Spencer.[5] What is more uncertain is whether the

1 The other basis was a failure in a duty to control or to commit Poddar.

2 (1976) 17 Cal 3d 425 at 439.

3 See James C Beck 'Current Status of the Duty to Protect' in James C Beck (ed) *Confidentiality Versus the Duty to Protect: Foreseeable Harm in the Practice of Psychiatry* (1990); M Weil and E Sanchez 'The Impact of the *Tarasoff* Decision on Clinical Social Work Practice' (1983) 57 Social Service Review 112; S Kopels and J D Kagle 'Do Social Workers Have a Duty to Warn?' (1993) 67 Social Service Review 101; J D Kagle and S Kopels 'Confidentiality after *Tarasoff*' (1994) Health and Social Work, Vol 19, No 3, 217.

4 See G Parker and M Spencer 'Confidentiality – Medical Records' in M Powers and N Harris (eds) *Medical Negligence* (2nd edn, 1994) at paras 7.36 to 7.38.

5 Such a general duty has, of course, been rejected in American cases. For example, one case against clinical social workers in the field of mental health was unsuccessful because no duty was held to be owed to the public at large to restrain a potentially dangerous patient: *Matt v Burrell Inc* (1995) 892 SW 2d 796.

existence of an obligation of confidence would be enough to override a duty arising where the other two requirements for setting up the duty are established. Parker and Spencer appear to base their overall rejection of a *Tarasoff* type duty on the narrow scope given to the public interest exception in UK courts and they refer to the case of *X v Y.*[1] Perhaps of more use in this situation is *W v Egdell*[2] which concerned the disclosure of a report on a psychiatric patient to hospital authorities and to the Home Office. The patient, W, was seeking a review of his case by a mental health review tribunal, with a view to discharge or transfer to a regional secure unit from the secure hospital where he was detained. There were two reports favourable to the transfer which had in the past been refused by the Home Office. The prisoner's solicitors sought a third report from Dr Egdell, who concluded that, for reasons not explored in the other reports, W was still highly dangerous. In light of this report the application to the review tribunal was withdrawn. Some time later, Dr Egdell spoke to the assistant medical director of the secure hospital who had not seen the report but indicated that he would welcome sight of it. W's solicitors refused permission for a copy to be forwarded, but Dr Egdell sent on a copy anyway and on his insistence a copy was sent to the Home Office. W raised a breach of confidence action.

The Court of Appeal took the view that there were two public interests to be balanced: the public interest in confidentiality and the public interest in disclosure of the information to the relevant authorities. In this case the latter won.

'The suppression of the material contained in his [Dr Egdell's] report would have deprived both the hospital and the Secretary of State of vital information, directly relevant to questions of public safety.'[3]

'There is one consideration which in my judgment ... weighs the balance of public interest decisively in favour of disclosure. It may be shortly put. Where a man has committed multiple killings under the disability of serious mental illness, decisions which may lead directly or indirectly to his release from hospital should not be made unless a responsible authority is properly able to make an informed judgment that the risk of repetition is so small as to be acceptable. A consultant psychiatrist who becomes aware, even in the course of a confidential relationship, of information which leads him ... to fear that such decisions may be made on the basis of inadequate information and with a real risk of consequent danger to the public

1 [1988] 2 All ER 648.
2 [1990] 1 All ER 835.
3 At 846f, per Sir Stephen Brown P.

is entitled to take such steps as are reasonable in all the circumstances to communicate the grounds of his concern to the responsible authorities.'[1]

Both judgments given in the Court of Appeal quote an extract from the judgment of Scott J at first instance where he said:

'In my view, a doctor called on, as Dr Egdell was, to examine a patient such as W owes a duty not only to his patient but also a duty to the public. His duty to the public would require him, in my opinion, to place before the proper authorities the result of his examination if, in his opinion, the public interest so required. This would be so, in my opinion, whether or not the patient instructed him not to do so'.[2]

The only disapproval of this was to the extent that the discretion of the doctor should be determinative of the public interest.[3] Of course, the statement about the extension of the duty is an *obiter dictum*,[4] since the matter did not have to be decided in *W v Egdell*, concerned as it was with a defence to a breach of confidence action. Nevertheless, it suggests that in appropriate circumstances a positive duty might be incumbent on a doctor (or indeed any other professional) to disclose information to the relevant authority.[5] This duty is, of course, different from that found to exist in *Tarasoff* since it is stated to be owed to the public, but it is surely not too much to suggest that given the appropriate factual situation, the duty could not be owed to a specific individual who is at risk.

Another instance of a public duty being held to exist involved a man against whom allegations of child sexual abuse had been made. Although he was not prosecuted, members of a social services department warned people with whom he subsequently lived of the allegations of child abuse and of the possibility that their children would be placed on the child protection register if he continued living with them. An attempt by the man to stop this course of conduct was unsuccessful:

1 [1990] 1 All ER 835 at 852j–853b, per Bingham LJ. Note that the public interest sanctions disclosure to the **responsible** authorities. Where the public interest justifies disclosure it will also usually limit the scope of disclosure. If a service user were to express a real threat to harm a third party confidence could be breached to the extent of informing the police, not ringing the *Daily Record*.

2 *W v Egdell* [1989] 1 All ER 1089 at 1104.

3 See *W v Egdell* [1990] 1 All ER 835 at 851b, per Bingham LJ.

4 As such, it is not binding on any other court.

5 In the context of suspected child abuse such a duty of disclosure seems to be presumed in official guidance. For example, *Effective Intervention: Child Abuse* published by the Scottish Office suggests, para 3.10, that: 'The starting point of the child protection system in Scotland is that any person who has knowledge or a reasonable suspicion that a child is being abused or at risk of abuse should communicate their concern [to an investigating agency].'

'In my judgment, social workers, in the discharge of the local authority's statutory obligation to protect the welfare of children, in this case, were under a duty to inform the two mothers and the one grandmother in this case that they believed that the applicant was an abuser, if they honestly believed on reasonable grounds that he was an abuser.'[1]

Leaving aside any **legal** duty to disclose, it is clear that in some circumstances social workers will have a professional duty to disclose. The British Association of Social Workers' *Code of Ethics* notes that social workers will divulge confidential information 'only with the consent of the client (or informant) except where there is clear evidence of serious danger to the client, worker, other persons or community or in other circumstances, judged exceptional, on the basis of professional consideration and consultation'.[2]

It has also been suggested that:

'Some information social workers receive in confidence they must pass on, whether the client concerned wishes them to or not, in the client's own interests or for the protection of others.'[3]

Therefore, even though there may be no duty to warn which can be enforced by the individual(s) potentially affected, there is a professional duty to pass on confidential information where this is for the protection of individuals or the community in general. This is perhaps the type of public duty which was alluded to in *W v Egdell.* Such a professional 'duty to warn' is clearly wider than the legal duty recognised in cases such as *Tarasoff* where there has to be an identifiable victim to whom a warning can be given. Fulfilment of the professional duty will generally be legally justified: the public interest in disclosure will override the service user's right to confidentiality. This issue has been raised recently in the context of whether neighbours and schools should be notified of the release of convicted paedophiles. Space does not permit discussion of the complex issues raised.

There is one area, however, where the duty to disclose confidential information is less clear. This is the situation where the service user confesses to a criminal act. If the confession is made in the course of preparation of a court report or a report for a children's hearing concerning that crime, then it would have to be disclosed

1 *R v Devon County Council, ex parte L* [1991] 2 FLR 541.
2 *Code of Ethics*, para 10.xi.
3 National Institute for Social Work *Social Workers: Their Role and Tasks* (1982), pp 146-147. '[F]ailure on the part of a social worker to act to protect or warn a potential victim of an assault threatened by a client constitutes a potentially criminal act and social negligence': Weil and Sanchez 'The Impact of the *Tarasoff* Decision on Clinical Social Work Practice' (1983), p 115.

to the court or hearing. Such disclosure is dictated by the social worker's responsibilities to the court or hearing in the preparation of the report. But what if the confession were made in the course of other work?

It is clear that a social worker would have to answer if questioned in court about any confession made to him/her. Confidential information does not, except for communication between lawyer and client, enjoy a privilege against disclosure in court. On the other hand, it is clear that there is no **legal** duty to volunteer information about criminal activities to the relevant authorities. In *Rice v Connolly* the law was expressed in these terms:[1]

> 'It seems to me quite clear that though every citizen has a moral duty or, if you like, a social duty to assist the police, there is no legal duty to that effect, and indeed the whole basis of the common law is the right of the individual to refuse to answer questions put to him by persons in authority...'

There are, of course, certain exceptions to this created by statute where there is a duty to answer questions and provide information required by the police, and individuals must not act in such a way as to obstruct the police.[2]

The legal position may be clear, but what about the ethical position? Disclosure in such circumstances is not directly addressed in the BASW code, but it might be argued that the information is such that it ought to be disclosed in the interests of the broader community. On the other hand, the social worker has obligations to the service user, and the public and community also have an interest in effective social work dependent on the maintenance of a working relationship with the service user. Perhaps it is not possible to offer any more definitive guidance than that offered by the British Medical Association:

> 'Occasions may arise which persuade the doctor that confidential information obtained in the course of his professional work should be disclosed. In such cases, the doctor should wherever possible seek to persuade the patient to disclose the information himself, or to consent to the doctor's disclosing it. Failing this, it will be for the doctor to decide the next course of action in accordance with his conscience, bearing in mind that he may be called to justify what he does.'[3]

1 [1966] 2 QB 414 at 419F.
2 Though it is not obstruction simply to not answer questions.
3 British Medical Association *Philosophy and Practice of Medical Ethics* (1988), p 23.

## 8. EMPLOYERS' LIABILITY FOR AND TO SOCIAL WORKERS

The contracts of employment which affect most social workers imply the acceptance of some degree of liability by the employer for the social worker. There are obligations for the social worker to be accountable to the employer and abide by the employer's policies and procedures and in turn the employer agrees to accept responsibility for the actions of the social worker undertaken on its behalf. Most of the major employers are covered by insurance for these areas and with respect to their employees suffering accidental injury or death, though most employers require social workers to take out their own insurance coverage for personal effects and for using their cars for business purposes. In practice, when there is public scrutiny of the actions of a social worker and the implication that malpractice may have occurred, the moral panic which ensues occasionally results in the employers jettisoning responsibility for the social worker and the direct line manager either in the short term or the long term. In light of the frequency of this experience, the major professional association, the British Association of Social Workers, has established an advice and representation service and additional insurance coverage for members who find themselves in this situation.

The nature of social work is such that sometimes it requires close contact by isolated workers with very vulnerable and needy people in situations which can be extremely stressful. An almost inevitable consequence is that occasionally a service user will resort to the use of violence directed at the social worker. Whether a social worker uses self-defence or retreats will depend on the particular circumstances and what is reasonably necessary to stop the violence, but a social worker choosing the former is as liable as any other individual to prosecution if the worker's actions are considered unreasonable by the procurator fiscal.

Anecdotal and research evidence[1] suggests that assaults on social workers are relatively frequent and reported to senior managers usually when there is no alternative. Many social workers hold the ill-founded belief that being assaulted reflects badly on their professional competence and many are confirmed in this belief by management practices. It is very important to report any assault to senior managers and many organisations have instituted policies

1 S Balloch 'Working in the social services: How staff cope with violence and stress' *Research Policy and Planning* (1996) 14(1), pp 74-76.

which require the reporting of any incident which is beneficial in relieving the possibly traumatised worker from the decision.

Like any other employer, the employer of a social worker owes employees certain duties of care. Some of these will be under the Health and Safety at Work etc Act 1974, but the employer also owes common law duties to the employee. One of these is the duty to provide a safe system of work. Breach of this obligation was the basis for a successful action by a social worker who claimed that stress at work had caused him a nervous breakdown.[1] The social worker had suffered one nervous breakdown, for which the authority was not liable because it was not reasonably foreseeable. He then returned to work. He raised concerns about his workload with his employers and they knew of his previous breakdown. In the circumstances it was foreseeable that he might suffer another breakdown if overworked. The employers' failure to take steps to reduce his workload was held to be in breach of their duty to provide a safe system of work. The duty they owed him was formulated as follows:

> 'It is clear law that the employer has a duty to provide his employee with a reasonably safe system of work and to take reasonable steps to protect him from risks which are reasonably foreseeable. Whereas the law on the extent of this duty has developed almost exclusively in cases involving physical injury to the employee as distinct from injury to his mental health, there is no logical reason why risk of psychiatric damage should be excluded from the scope of an employer's duty of care ...'[2]

The broad scope of this duty should be noted. It is arguable that it extends to circumstances where a social worker is being sent into a situation that is known to be dangerous, for example, to interview someone who is known to be violent, has a history of attacking workers or has a history of sexual assault. In such cases it would appear likely that the employer owes the worker a duty to guard against such risks and that an injured worker could sue the employer.

## 9. CONCLUSION

This survey indicates that there are a number of areas where social workers and their employers will clearly be legally liable for what is

1 *Walker v Northumberland County Council* [1995] 1 All ER 737.
2 At 749c-e, per Colman J.

done in the course of their work. Examples are breach of confidence, breaches of the requirements of natural justice in decision-making, and injury or loss arising from negligent advice where responsibility has been taken for the accuracy of the advice.

In other areas the law is less clear, for example, on the extent of the duty to warn and the extent of liability to children in care.[1] As regards the first of these it can be suggested that there is no duty owed to individuals who can sue for its breach,[2] but there is a public duty. Such a public duty will not be enforceable by any individual but rather provides a defence for disclosure of information which would otherwise be confidential.

Finally, there is the issue of taking or not taking children into care. The clear policy view at the moment[3] is that no action is available in such cases, though as can be seen from the views of the Master of the Rolls in the Court of Appeal,[4] that is not a unanimous view. There are, as the objections canvassed in the House of Lords indicate, good reasons for resisting the imposition of liability; but there are also good reasons for allowing effective remedies to children and parents who suffer because of negligent decision-making in this area. It is clear that simply having guidance and procedures does not stop errors. The debate should be about whether existing remedies are satisfactory and, if not, how they can be made effective.

1 See J Butler and G Wood '*Newham* and *Bedfordshire*: negligence in residential care' (1995) 145 NLJ 1826.

2 But see the duty of disclosure to foster carers noted in *W v Essex County Council* (1997) Times, 16 July.

3 It is noted on p viii of the annex to the preface of W V H Rogers *Winfield and Jolowicz on Tort* (14th edn, 1994) that: 'All the judgments … go directly to the issues of policy and are refreshingly free of the incantation of legal mantras and copious quotations which have marred so many recent negligence cases.'

4 See *M (a minor) v Newham London Borough Council; X (minors) v Bedfordshire County Council* [1994] 4 All ER 602 at 616ff, per Sir Thomas Bingham MR.

# Index

**Absconding**, 139, 169
**Absolute discharge**, 237, 238, 252
**Accelerated diets**, 24
**Access to information**, 70–76, 81, 163
  adoption records, 101
  children's records 131, 132
  credit references, 75
  data protection, 70, 71
  health records, 73, 75, 76
  medical records, 75
  personal information, 71–75
  reporters to children's panel, 73
  school records, 76, 163
  social work files, 71–75, 163
**Accommodation**
  children, provision for, 115–122, 125, 126, 145
    rights to object, 119–122
    social work role, 119
  rented –
    eviction, 44–46
    provision by local authority, 109, 115, 116, 123
    repairs, 42–44
    security of tenure, 44
    transfer of tenancy, 105, 107
  *See also* HOUSING; OCCUPANCY RIGHTS; EXCLUSION ORDER
**Administrative tribunals**, 33
**Admissible evidence**, 25–27
**Admission to hospital**, 165
  compulsory, 224, 225
**Admission to mental hospital**,
  compulsory, 202–212, 215
  community care orders, 210–211
**Admission to mental hospital** – *contd*
  consent to treatment, 207–208, 211
  detention, duration of, 206–207, 208
  grounds for, 203
  procedure, 203–205
  voluntary patients, 202, 208
  *See also* MENTAL HEALTH
**Admonition**, 238
**Adoption**, 13, 15, 35, 84, 92–102, 132, 136, 149, 171, 175, 285
  access to adoption records, 101
  adopted children's register, 100, 101
  adoption agencies, 92–99, 101
  adoption allowances, 101
  adoption panel, 92–94, 98
  alternatives to adoption, 93
  consent to, 95, 96
  curator ad litem, 99, 100
  definition, 92
  freeing for, 84, 92, 96–98, 144, 149, 171, 175
  homosexual relationship, 94
  post-placement support, 102
  procedure, 98–100
  related adoptions, 92, 93, 99
  report by local authority, 98, 99
  reporting officer, 99
  rights of parents, 95, 96
  who can adopt, 93–95
  who can be adopted, 95
**Advocate**, 8, 9
**Advocate Depute**, 9
**Aliment**, 58, 81, 90

**Appeals**, 280
children's hearings, from, 151, 172–174
civil, 13, 14
criminal, 17, 24
education, 77, 200
housing, 52
immigration, 63
mental health, 207, 213, 271
sentence, against, 24, 237
**Appearing in court**, 231, 235, 236
**Arrestment**, 58
**Assault**, 272
**Assessments**, 215
children, 126, 127, 200, 201
community care, 191–198
disabled children, 113, 193
disabled persons, 193, 194, 198
financial, 195
future needs, 201
guidance, 194, 195
process, 111, 112
provision of services, 115–117, 196, 198
resources, 197, 198
right to request, 113
statutory provisions, 192, 193
**Assistance in cash or kind**. *See* CASH ASSISTANCE

**Bail**, 18, 22–24, 230
**Benefits**, 41, 219
**Breach of the peace**, 228, 254, 268, 273, 274
**British Association of Social Workers**, 296
**British Medical Association**, 295
**Burden of proof**, 31
**Business meetings**, 162, 163

**Care plan**, 115, 120, 124–128, 131, 145, 190, 194–196
**Carers**, 193
**Case law**, 5, 6, 227
**Cash assistance**, 37, 59, 145, 200
**Caution**, 238
**Child assessment order**, 123, 128, 138, 140, 149, 151–153
**Child care**, 108, 113, 118, 278
local authority duties, 281–283
new laws, 39, 40, 108, 119, 147, 148
policy, 298
review, 265, 288
**Child Care Law Review**, 148
**Child protection**
local authority duty of care, 281–284, 287
**Child protection order**, 8, 121, 123, 128, 140, 148, 149, 176–183
discharge, 179–182
effect, 178, 179
emergency protection, 182, 183
grounds for application, 176–178
implementation, 179
**Child Support Agency**, 90
**Children**
after-care, 145
after-school services, 117
age of majority, 78
arrangements for on divorce, 89, 90
at risk, 108, 109
capacity/powers, 78–81
care plans, 124–127, 145
cash assistance, 122, 123
challenging decisions, 145, 146
chastisement. *See* DISCIPLINE
compassionate release, 262
compensation award/child abuse, 255
consent to medical treatment, 79, 80, 128, 134
court appearance, 236
day care, 117
definition of, 109
detention of, 141, 257, 258
development, 111
disabled, 110–114, 193
emergency protection, 147, 176–183

**Children** – *contd*
exclusion orders, 183–184
giving evidence, 27, 29, 31, 32
health care, 110, 127, 128
information, provision of, 163
in need, 108–123
local authority services to, 108–146
looked after by local authority, 109, 123–132, 170, 171, 175, 176, 185
parental contact, 83
parental responsibilities and rights. *See* PARENTAL RESPONSIBILITIES; PARENTAL RIGHTS
placement –
review of, 130, 265, 288
termination of, 130
protection of, 281–283
records, 131, 132
release from detention, 265, 266
residential establishment, 169
respite care, 128, 129
rights, 78, 81
school records, 76, 163
secure accommodation, 138–140, 170, 172
special educational needs, 200, 201
supervision of, 283–285
transactions entered into, 79, 80
visits, 129, 130, 137, 170
welfare. *See* WELFARE OF THE CHILD
**Children's hearings**, 33, 40, 73, 147, 151, 154, 160, 258
age of child, 78
appeals, 14, 15, 172–174
attendance at, 83, 160–162
business meetings, 162, 163
cases not referred, 159, 160
foster placements, 136, 168–169
grounds of referral, 148, 163–165, 167, 168, 173, 174
lack of parental care, 80
non-offence, 86
review of, 172–174
**Children's hearings** – *contd*
parental right to attend, 83
principles governing children's cases, 148–150
procedure, 164–166
proof hearing, 11, 15, 22, 28, 164–168
referrals from court, 174, 175
reporter to. *See* REPORTER TO CHILDREN'S HEARING
reviews, 171
secure accommodation, 140
social work department duties, 154
supervision requirement, 138, 142, 232
warrants for detention, 123, 149, 160, 166, 172
who can attend, 83, 160–162
**Children's panel**, 160
**Civil court system**, 13–15
**Civil legal aid**, 35, 36
**Civil procedure**, 14, 15
**Clyde Report**, 148
**Cohabitation**, 86–87, 90, 102, 107
**Commission for Racial Equality**, 62
**Commissioner for Local Administration**, 146, 280
**Common law duty of care**, 279, 281, 282
**Common law marriage**, 86
**Community care**, 38, 145, 189–198
orders, 210, 211
payment for services, 196
**Community service orders**, 230, 233, 235, 249, 249–252
breach, 251
revocation, amendment and transfer, 251
**Compensation order**, 247, 252
**Competent witnesses**, 27
**Complaints procedure**, 39, 280
**Compulsory measures of supervision**, 150–174
appeal, 172–174

**Compulsory measures of supervision** – *contd*
conditions, 154–159
duration and review, 171
duties of social work department, 151–154, 283–285
grounds for, 154–159
hearing by panel, 160
local authority accommodation, 175, 176
referrals from court, 174, 175
requirements, 168–170
**Computers**, 71
**Confessions**, 30, 294
**Confidentiality**, 74, 98, 234, 289–295, 298
**Contact**, 115, 123–126, 129, 135, 144, 152, 166, 168, 170, 179
order, 85, 89, 144, 185
**Corroboration**, 30, 31
**Court-based social work**, 231, 232, 235, 236
**Court of Session**, 9, 11, 13–15, 17, 34, 84, 86, 88, 173, 174, 213, 217
**Crime**, 167, 227–229, 272–276
**Criminal Injuries Compensation Scheme**, 252, 255
**Criminal justice**
children and, 145
**Criminal legal aid**, 36
**Criminal courts**,
district court, 16. *See also* DISTRICT COURT
High Court of Justiciary, 17. *See also* HIGH COURT OF JUSTICIARY
sheriff court, 17. *See also* SHERIFF; SHERIFF COURT
**Criminal procedure**,
accelerated diet, 24
appeals, 17, 24
bail, 18, 22–24, 230
custody, 18–19. *See also* CUSTODY
evidence. *See* EVIDENCE
pre-trial –
solemn, 18–20
**Criminal procedure** – *contd*
pre-trial – *contd*
summary, 17–18
time limits, 19
standard of proof, 22
trial, 20–22
**Crown Office**, 10
**Culpable homicide**, 274, 275
**Cultural background**, 93, 111, 115, 124
**Curator ad litem**, 99, 143
**Curator bonis**, 218, 219
**Custody**.
pending trial/sentence, 18, 175, 176
*See also* YOUNG OFFENDERS INSTITUTION; IMPRISONMENT

**Day care**, 117
**Debt recovery**, 55–59
arrestment, 58
court action, 55–57
decree for payment, 57
poinding and sale, 57, 58
social work contribution, 58, 59
**Deferred sentence**, 18, 19, 22, 252, 253
**Delegated legislation**, 5
**Diligence**, 57
**Diploma in Social Work**, 2
**Disability**
assessment of needs, 113, 114, 191, 194, 198
carer, 193
children, 112–114
disability, definition of, 65, 199
discrimination, 65–70, 199
education, 68, 69, 200, 201
employment, 66, 199
enforcement of rights, 69
National Disability Council, 69
premises, provision of, 68
services, provision of, 67, 193, 200
public transport, 69
social work contribution, 69, 70
*See also* MENTAL DISABILITY
**Discipline**, 77, 156, 157

**Disclosure**, 289, 290, 292, 294
**Discrimination**, 59–70, 199, 228
children in need, 62
criminal justice, 228
definition, 59, 60
direct and indirect, 60, 61
disability, 65–70, 199
exempted areas, 61
immigration, 62, 63
local authority duties, 60
remedies, 62
sectarianism, 64
social work contribution, 63, 64
**District court**, 11, 12, 16, 141, 233, 239, 242, 244, 267, 268
**Diversion**, 11, 230, 235, 253–255
**Divorce**, 13, 15, 87–90, 175
children, arrangements for, 89, 90
cohabitation, 90
financial provisions, 88, 89
grounds for, 87, 88
matrimonial proceedings report, 89
mediation, arrangements for, 91
procedure, 88
social work roles, 91
**Domestic violence**, 35, 48, 50, 102, 104, 106, 255

**Education**, 76–78, 82, 145, 200, 201, 213, 250
**80–day rule**, 19
**Emergency order**, 122
**Emergency protection of children**, 147
**Equal Opportunities Commission**, 62
**European Court of Human Rights**, 6, 32
**European Court of Justice**, 6, 32
**Eviction**, 12–14, 44–46, 115, 117
notice to quit, 44
tenant's rights, 45
**Evidence**
children, of, 27, 28–29, 31–32
confessions, 30
**Evidence** – *contd*
corroboration, 30–31
hearsay, 28–30
improper, 25, 26
opinion, 27
previous inconsistent statement, 30
privileged, 26
relevant, 25
*res gestae*, 30
video link, 31–32
**Exclusion order**
child protection, 148, 149, 183–185
legal aid for, 35
matrimonial, 103–105, 106
**Expert witnesses**, 27

**Family mediation**, 91
**Fines**, 238–244
alternative to imprisonment, 240
default, 241, 242, 253
enforcement, 241, 242
fine supervision, 234, 241
levels of, 239, 240
supervised attendance orders, 235, 242–244
time for payment, 240
**Fixed penalties**, 253, 254
**Fostering**, 74, 121, 122, 127, 132–138, 142, 168, 169
approval of foster carers, 133, 134
children looked after by local authority, 132–136
emergency placement, 135
fostering panel, 92, 133
immediate placement, 135
local authority duty of care, 285, 286
payment, 134
placement by children's hearing, 136
placement by local authority, 134–139, 144
private, 132, 136–138
responsibilities of local authority, 282, 283

**Fostering** – *contd*
short-term refuges, 185, 186
supervision of placements, 136, 168, 169
who can foster, 137
**Fraud**, 274
**Freeing for adoption**, 84, 92, 96–98, 144, 149, 171, 175
**Functions of law**, 3, 4, 227

**Griffiths Report**, 189
**Guardianship**
children, of, 79, 84
elderly, of, 266
mental health, 202, 212–214, 216, 217, 222, 226, 268–270
personal, 216

**Hearsay evidence**, 28–30
**High Court of Justiciary**, 9, 11, 17, 158, 234, 236–238, 241, 256, 257, 268
**Home circumstances report**, 260
**Home helps (domiciliary services)**, 38, 192, 200, 219
**Homelessness**, 46–55, 145
children, 115–117
code of guidance, 46, 47, 53, 54
definition, 47–48
flow diagram, 54, 55
housing authority obligations, 51
intentional homelessness, 49, 50, 115
local connection, 50, 51
priority need, 50, 115
review of decisions, 34, 52
social work role, 52, 53
threatened homelessness, 47, 48
**Hospital order**, 248, 269, 270
**House of Lords**, 14, 117, 197, 198, 281, 285, 298
**Housing**, 42–55
eviction. *See* EVICTION
homelessness. *See* HOMELESSNESS
repairs –
council's powers, 44

**Housing** – *contd*
repairs – *contd*
landlord's obligations, 42–44
tenant's remedies, 43, 44
social worker, role of, 44, 52–53
**Housing associations**, 42

**Immigration**, 62, 63
**Immigration Appeal Tribunal**, 63
**Imprisonment**, 175, 232, 255, 256
alternative to fine, 240
consecutive/concurrent sentences, 256
first imprisonment, 232, 256
on fine default, 241, 242
parole, 259, 265
remission, 264
transfer to mental hospital, 270
*See also* PRISONERS
**Improper evidence**, 25, 26
**Initial inquiry report**, 53
**Insanity in bar of trial**, 269
**Interdict**, 102, 105–107
**Interim hospital order**, 267
**Irregular marriage**, 86

**Judicial review**, 34, 52, 63, 146, 173, 279, 280, 285–289
**Justice of the peace**, 137, 182

**Kilbrandon report**, 36, 150, 151

**Learning disabilities**. *See* MENTAL DISABILITY
**Legal advice and assistance**, 35, 41, 46
**Legal aid**, 14, 35, 36, 55, 172, 242, 256, 262
**Legal framework**, 3, 4
**Legal personnel**, 8–12
**Legal rights**, 8
**Linguistic background**, 93, 111, 115, 124, 125

**Local authority**
children, supervision of, 79, 100, 123, 125, 129, 136, 138, 139, 150–174
duty of care, 281–285
duty to provide safe system of work, 297
judicial review of decisions, 278, 280, 285–289
liability in child care and protection, 281–283, 287
mental illness and disability, 222
offenders, supervision of, 38, 235
parental responsibilities, 141–144
patients subject to guardianship, supervision of, 213
services to children, 108–146
statutory duties towards children, 124
vicarious liability for employees, 282, 296, 297
**Local Government Ombudsman**, 146, 280, 281
**Lord Advocate**, 9, 158

**Magistrates**, 11
**Malicious mischief**, 274
**Mandatory life sentences**, 266
**Marriage**, 86–87
**Matrimonial homes**
cohabiting couples, 107
exclusion order, 103–104
occupancy rights, 102–103
tenancy, transfer of, 105
**Matrimonial interdicts**, 105–107
**Means enquiry**
court, 240, 241, 253
report, 239
**Mediation**,
family, 91
prosecution, as alternative to, 254
**Medical records**
access to, 75
**Medical treatment, consent to**,
children, 79, 80, 84, 122, 131, 153
mentally disabled, 220, 221
mental health, 207, 208, 213, 216
**Mental disability**, 214–222
after-care services, 209
consent to medical treatment, 220, 221
definitions, 214, 215
legal capacity, 214
management of affairs, 218, 219, 225
curator bonis, 218
*negotiorum gestio*, 220
power of attorney, 220
trusts, 219, 220
local authority duties, 218, 222, 225, 226
personal guardianship, 216
**Mental health**
after-care services, 209, 210
compulsory admission to hospital, 202–212, 215, 267–269
appeals, 207
application to sheriff, 203–205
consent to treatment, 207, 208
discharge, 209
duration of detention, 206, 207
emergency admission, 203, 205–207
grounds, 203
leave of absence, 210
procedure, 203–205
criminal law and –
guardianship orders, 268
hospital direction, 271
hospital orders, 267, 268
insanity in bar of trial, 269
remand, 267, 269
restriction order, 269
state patient/state hospital, 268, 270
transfer, 270

**Mental health** – *contd*
detention by nursing staff, 208
detention by police constable, 211, 212
detention in hospital, 269
emergency admission, 203, 205–207
guardianship, 212–217, 222, 226, 268
appeal, 213
discharge, 214
duration, 213
grounds, 212
personal, 216
procedure, 213
mental disorder, 192, 200, 202, 212, 221, 267
mental handicap, 192, 200, 202–214
mental illness, 202–214, 222
nearest relative, 203–205, 209, 212, 214, 268
treatment as condition of probation order, 247, 248
voluntary patients, 202, 208
**Mental health officer**, 202–207, 212–214, 216, 222
**Mental Health Review Tribunal**, 292
**Mental Welfare Commission**, 205, 207–211, 214, 221, 222
**Messengers-at-arms**, 12
**Misuse of alcohol or drugs**, 159
**Moral danger**, 155
**Murder**, 257, 269, 274

**National Disability Council**, 69
**National Objectives and Standards for Social Work**, 229, 230, 232, 234, 235, 244, 248, 250, 251, 256, 263
**Nationality**, 125
**Neglect**, 156
***Negotiorum gestio***, 220
**NHS trust**, 114
**Non-entitled partner**, 107
**Non-entitled spouse**, 103–105
**Nursing homes**, 224

**Occupancy rights**, 90, 102, 103, 107
**Offenders**
custodial disposals, 225–259
diversion, 253–255
local authority supervision, 38, 235
mental health and, 267–271
non-custodial disposals, 231, 234, 237–253
rehabilitation, 236, 271
release, 259–267
sentencing, 229, 236, 237, 239, 240, 244
social work functions, 229–236
**Old age**
compulsory treatment, 224, 225
guardianship, 226
protection of property, 225, 226
residential accommodation, 223, 224
**110–day rule**, 19
**Opinion evidence**, 27
**Ordinary procedure**, 15
**Orkney**, 148

**Parental care, lack of**, 155
**Parental duties**, 82
**Parental responsibilities**, 39, 40, 81, 82, 84–86, 89, 96, 109, 118, 119, 121, 127, 132, 134, 147, 154, 155, 170, 175, 185
order, 123, 125, 139, 141–144, 149, 159, 222
duration, 144
effect, 143, 144
grounds for application, 142, 143
procedure, 143
review of local authority decision, 288
who has, 83, 84
*See also* PARENTAL RIGHTS
**Parental rights**, 78–87, 89, 92, 119, 141, 154, 155, 170, 171, 175, 181, 201, 216
access, 85, 89

**Parental rights** – *contd*
acquisition by father, 84
adoption, 92, 93, 95–97, 100
application to court for, 84–86, 120
assumption of, 84
contact, 83, 129
custody, 85
exercise of, 82, 170, 179
review of local authority decision, 288
residence, 85
who has, 83–84
**Parental rights resolution**, 84, 141, 142
**Parole**, 259, 265
**Parole Board**, 260–265
**Periodical allowance**, 58, 89
**Persons in need**, 37, 38, 200, 215, 223
**Place of safety**, 165, 176, 179, 180, 182, 211
**Place of safety order**
children, 137, 138, 140, 148
mental health, 212
**Place of safety warrant**, 138, 140, 166
**Poinding and sale**, 57, 58
**Police**, 106, 122, 151, 159, 182, 186, 211, 212, 227, 272, 295
**Power of attorney**, 220
**Previous inconsistent statements**, 30
**Prison social work**, 258, 259
**Prisoners**
classification of, 258
commission of further offence, 259, 263, 264, 267
compassionate release, 262, 267
discretionary life, 261, 262, 265
long-term, 260, 261, 266
mandatory life, 261
release of, 259
release on licence, 38, 260–264
short-term, 259, 260, 266
*See also* IMPRISONMENT
**Private prosecutions**, 11
**Private sector**, 1, 196, 224
**Privileged evidence**, 26
**Probation**, 38, 230, 232, 235, 238, 244–249, 252
amendment of order, 248
breach proceedings, 248, 249, 251
conditions, 247, 248
contact, 246
discharge, 248
duration of, 244
need for consent, 245
priority groups, 244
social work and, 1, 245–247
**Procurators fiscal**, 9–11, 106, 151, 158, 253, 296

**Racial discrimination**, 59–62, 228
**Racial harassment**, 50
**Racial origin**, 93, 111, 115, 124, 125
**Rape**, 275
**Refuge, short-term**, 185, 186
**Rehabilitation of offenders**, 236, 271
**Relevant evidence**, 25
**Relevant person**, 109, 154, 155, 161–166, 168, 173, 181
**Religion**, 62, 81, 93, 111, 115, 124–126, 135, 250
**Remand**, 175, 176, 268
**Reporter to children's panel**, 165
access to information, 73
arranging a hearing, 171, 180
business meetings, 162, 163
discharge of CPO, 180
investigation by, 159, 160
principal reporter, 147
reference to, 77, 86, 89, 96, 121, 128, 142, 151, 232
requirement to inform, 139, 140, 152, 182
**Reporting officer**, 99, 143
***Res gestae***, 30
**Reset**, 275
**Residence order**, 85, 86, 142
**Residential establishments**, 37, 39, 126, 163, 192

**Residential establishments** – *contd*
children in need, 118, 169
children looked after by local authority, 126
detention of children in, 141, 257
elderly, 223, 224
secure accommodation, 139
registration, 224
short-term refuges, 185, 186
**Resources, availability of**, 197, 198
**Respite care**, 128–129, 200
**Responsible medical officer**, 205, 206, 209, 210, 267
**Restriction of liberty orders**, 266
**Robbery**, 275, 276

**Safeguarders**, 151, 162–164, 166
**Schedule 1 offences**, 137, 156, 157, 160, 167, 168, 175, 186–188
**School attendance**, 76, 158
**Scottish Child Law Centre**, 9
**Scottish Children's Reporter Administration**, 148
**Scottish Criminal Cases Review Commission**, 24
**Screening**, 169, 170
**Secretary of State**, 3, 6, 38, 47, 63, 92, 195, 221, 222
detention of children, 141, 257
directions, 109
guidance on discretion, 3
persons in need, 38
power to make regulations, 6
release of children, 265
release of prisoners, 260–264
state patients, 270, 271
transfer of individuals to hospital, 270
transfer of prisoners to hospital, 270
**Secure accommodation**, 138–141, 169–171
**Secure Placement Review Panel**, 141
**Sentencing**
appeal against, 24
breach of bail conditions, 24
deferred, 22, 252, 253
imprisonment, 240
objectives, 236, 237
policy, 64
powers, 227
suspended, 253
**Separation**, 87
**Sexual offences**, 158, 187
**Sheriff**, 11, 18, 29, 40, 45, 46, 106, 140, 142, 144, 152, 153, 156, 164, 166–168, 172–174, 176, 178, 180–182, 184, 203, 205, 206, 209, 211, 214, 236, 267, 271
**Sheriff clerk**, 12, 56, 88, 207, 233, 240, 252
**Sheriff court**
actions for debt recovery, 55–57
actions for discrimination, 62
actions for eviction, 45, 46
actions for judicial separation, 87
adoption orders, 99
application for compulsory admission to hospital, 203–206
appointment of curator bonis, 218
child assessment order, 152, 153
constitution of, 13
divorce procedure in, 88
enforcement of fines, 241, 244
hospital orders, 268
order for compulsory treatment, 225
parental responsibilities order, 142, 144
personnel, 11
place of safety order, 137
principles governing children's cases, 148–150
proof hearings, 164–168
prosecution in, 11, 158
reference to children's hearing, 174, 175

**Sheriff court** – *contd*
social enquiry reports, 232
solemn court, 17, 256, 257
summary court, 16, 123, 141, 175, 238–240, 243, 256, 257, 267
supervised attendance order, 242, 243
warrant for detention, 123, 150, 168
**Sheriff officers**, 12, 56
**Significant harm**, 177
**Small claims procedure**, 14, 55, 56
**Social background report**, 154, 159, 162, 163, 290
**Social circumstances report**, 205, 206
**Social enquiry report**, 12, 22, 23, 38, 230–235, 239, 245, 250, 253, 256, 260, 290
**Social Security Appeals Tribunal**, 33
**Social Work Services Group**, 3, 6, 109, 148, 177, 192, 209
**Social Work Services Inspectorate**, 224, 234
**Social worker**
accountability of, 230, 277–298
assessment of needs, 111, 112, 191–198
breach of duties, 278, 279
care management, role in, 189–191, 196
child protection, role in, 147, 176, 178
children's hearings, role in, 165, 166
confidentiality of information, 289–295, 298
debt, role in, 58, 59
demographic changes and, 91
discrimination, role in, 63, 64
diversion schemes, 254, 255
duty of care, 283–285
children, to, 281–283, 298
duty to warn, 290–295, 298
employment of, 277, 296
**Social worker** – *contd*
ethical responsibilities, 277, 294, 295
fines and, 239
housing, role in, 44, 52, 53
legal responsibilities, 277
negligent advice, 284, 298
offenders and, 229–236
organisational responsibilities, 277
powers and duties, 1, 7, 8, 37, 41, 44, 278, 279
prisoners and, 258, 259
probation, 244–247
professional responsibility, 277–298
social welfare, promotion of, 3, 4, 6, 7, 37, 44, 59, 200
supervision of offenders, 235, 270
violence and, 296
**Solemn procedure**, 10, 15, 18–22, 36, 238
**Solicitor**, 2, 8, 9, 14, 35, 56, 233
**Solicitor-advocate**, 9
**Solicitor General**, 9
**Sources of law**, 5, 6
**Special educational needs**, 200, 201, 215
record of needs, 74, 200, 201
**Specific issue order**, 85
**Standard of proof**, 15, 22
**State patients/state hospitals**, 270, 271
**Statute law**, 5, 6
**Summary cause procedure**, 14, 55, 56
**Summary procedure**, 10, 15, 17–19, 36, 238
**Supervised attendance orders**, 230, 235, 239, 242–244, 251
**Supervised release orders**, 259, 264, 266, 267
**Supervision orders/requirements**, 149, 168–170, 232, 265
appeal against, 172–174
child for adoption, 96, 97
conditions, 168

**Supervision orders/ requirements** – *contd*
duration and review, 171
treatment, and, 269, 270

**Tenant's remedies**, 43, 44
**Theft**, 256, 276
**Through-care**, 230, 260
**Transfer of tenancy**, 105, 107
**Trial, procedure at**, 20–22
**Trusts**, 219, 220
**Tutor-at-law**, 217
**Tutor-dative**, 213, 217, 221

**United Nations Convention on the Rights of the Child**, 81
**Unruly certificate**, 175

**Victim compensation**, 247, 253, 255
**Video evidence**, 32
**Views of the child**
age of child, 150
consideration of, 165
duty to have regard to, 82, 85, 93, 95, 115, 118, 124, 130, 135, 142, 149, 153, 186
obtaining, 161, 163
**Violence**. *See* DOMESTIC VIOLENCE
**Voluntary sector**, 1, 71, 72, 159, 196
**Voluntary supervision**, 159

**Warrant sale**, 12, 56, 57, 59
**Warrant to keep child**, 166, 172
**Welfare of the child**, 76, 85, 93, 99, 100, 108–110, 120, 128, 137, 138, 142, 143, 149, 161, 163–165, 179, 180, 183, 255, 265
promotion of, 109, 110, 113, 115, 121, 124, 125, 143

**Young offenders institution**
detention in, 232, 257, 258
alternative to fine, as, 241
default on fine, for, 242
parole, 259, 265